RECOVERY FROM
ANGER
ADDICTION

RECOVERY FROM
ANGER
ADDICTION

How I Recovered from Rage by
Resolving My Lifetime of Losses and Pain

VERRYL V. FOSNIGHT

ARCHWAY
PUBLISHING

Archway Publishing books may be ordered through booksellers or by contacting:

Archway Publishing
1663 Liberty Drive
Bloomington, IN 47403
www.archwaypublishing.com
1 (888) 242-5904

Because of the dynamic nature of the Internet, any web addresses or links contained in this book may have changed since publication and may no longer be valid. The views expressed in this work are solely those of the author and do not necessarily reflect the views of the publisher, and the publisher hereby disclaims any responsibility for them.

The information, ideas, and suggestions in this book are not intended as a substitute for professional medical advice. Before following any suggestions contained in this book, you should consult your personal physician, therapist, or counselor. Neither the author nor the publisher shall be liable or responsible for any loss or damage allegedly arising as a consequence of your use or application of any information or suggestions in this book.

Any people depicted in stock imagery provided by Thinkstock are models, and such images are being used for illustrative purposes only. Certain stock imagery © Thinkstock.

Scripture taken from the King James Version of the Bible.

ISBN: 978-1-4808-2756-1 (sc)
ISBN: 978-1-4808-2757-8 (hc)
ISBN: 978-1-4808-2758-5 (e)

Library of Congress Control Number: 2016904261

Print information available on the last page.

Archway Publishing rev. date: 3/29/2016

To my parents,
for the innumerable gifts they gave me
that taught me how to achieve;
those gifts have served me so well in life.
Most of all, despite their shortcomings,
which, along with my own,
have caused me so much grief in life,
I thank them for
the fortitude and the will to persevere,
which they gave me from their limitless supply.

It's a great life, if you don't weaken.
—*Kula Anita Swanner Fosnight (1917–2010)*

We live in a wonderful world that is full of beauty, charm and adventure. There is no end to the adventures that we can have if only we seek them with our eyes open.
—Jawaharlal Nehru

CONTENTS

Preface

I used to be angry all the time. I did not like being quick tempered or flying off into a rage often. I knew it damaged my marriages and my relationship with my parents. I was most angry at women, especially if they tended to be pushy or controlling—you know, bossy in an unreasonable or meddling way. I realized many years ago that they were much like my mother. I could really go off on women who were like that.

I was sharp tongued and critical with men also, but the anger tended more to sarcasm and other digs at them. I was a master at walking right up to the edge and pushing until just before physical retaliation started.

For many years my only physical fight was when someone crashed into me from behind after a city league basketball game as I was stepping off the court. I whirled and threw one punch, and that was the end of it—except I was banned from the league. It was the last game of the season, so it was not a big deal, except for the shame and embarrassment. I tried to defend my action, but of course I was denied. I was wrong; I did throw the punch.

Things changed in late 2007. I was physical with my wife. I grabbed her and held her and screamed at her. Two days later, I was arrested for spousal abuse and taken to jail. Again I was absolutely wrong. I did not argue with the police or try to defend my actions to anyone in the community cell or to the judge. I was plainly wrong.

You would think—I would think—this would have been a wakeup call for me, that it would have made me want to swing into action and take sincere and drastic steps to heal, get past my issues, or do whatever it took to stop my anger. I could have been tried and sent to jail or prison for a long time. But this event did not motivate me to act.

While I was in jail for thirty-two hours, my wife packed and left. The marriage had been on the rocks for four years, and it had been shaky for all seven of its years before that. I am sure that my anger, often erupting in threatening rages, was the prime cause of the bad marriage. My anger was bad for me, but for my wife, like all my wives and girlfriends, it must have been horrid and dreadful.

Immediately after I got out of jail on bail, I signed up for a one-week workshop at a noted recovery center on relationship addiction. My primary problem in my mind was my addiction to being in love. I thought that any relationship, no matter how bad, was better than none. I was clearly aware, as I had been for years that anger was the problem in all my romantic relationships, but my need for the validation of being in a loving and committed relationship was so strong that I ignored my rage as a problem. It had been that way for years, and to top that off, I never wondered or marveled at that badly misplaced attitude.

At the end of the week of the workshop the leader looked at me and made a simple observation that changed, and probably allowed me to reclaim, my life. Slowly and earnestly, in a somber voice, he described me as having "a lifetime of losses and pain." I immediately broke down and bawled, crying for some time in front of him and all the rest of the workshop. It was the beginning of my recovery from anger.

Months later I was led to address that pain by a new therapist. I cried a lot more in the next few weeks, and that grieving lightened my soul and changed my outlook. I became lighter and more patient, more easygoing and forgiving. Over the course of a very few weeks without that burden of pain I was able to think through anger-triggering events and keep myself from blowing up. I still got angry, just not as often and not as drastically or forcefully. I was learning to let things go rather easily.

I decided to write this book to present certain errors I made in my self-development through the years which culminated with my recovering from anger or rage. I wanted to share my journey just in case it would help someone else.

Everything in this book is based on my personal experiences, and I make no guarantees or assurances that what helped me will work that way for you. This book is in the spirit of twelve-step fellowships like AA and CoDA, where beginners are admonished not to give direct advice. If someone shares an issue in a meeting or privately, cross talk around the table is forbidden, but someone may say in his or her sharing, "Well, when that happened to me, here's what I did ..." Advice is avoided and reduced to a sharing of common experience. That is my purpose in this book.

I was abused as a child. The toxic shame of that led me to be codependent, as I discovered thanks to authors John Bradshaw and Pia Mellody. I made this discovery in my third year of sobriety in Alcoholics Anonymous. So I went to Codependents Anonymous (CoDA) to heal my toxic shame. Since toxic shame was the big offending emotion that led to low self-esteem, control characteristics, poor boundaries with others, and dysfunctional relationship, my goal was to heal my toxic shame and thereby heal my relationships. I did heal all of that and largely banished my toxic shame. But I remained just as angry as ever. My hope and belief was if I healed the shame, I would heal the anger. Nope.

That is first message of this book: for me, a drastic lessening of toxic shame had no effect on my anger. I extol Bradshaw and Mellody and other authors who helped me recognize toxic shame as the culprit for my codependence and its symptoms. These authors did not claim that healing shame would help anger, even though they occasionally listed anger as a possible byproduct of shame; that error was mine. So in case others make the same assumption I did, I want to emphasize that, for me, anger was not healed by healing shame.

The second message of the book is that I found my anger changed my moods; it made me feel good. I would get angry whenever my old losses seemed to recur, because a childlike feeling of helplessness and immature fear and pain would overcome me. Anger gave me a feeling of apparent power and control, and that overcoming of helplessness felt good.

My third message is that my recovery from anger took so many years after my recovery from alcoholism, codependence, and relationship addiction because of the mood-altering nature of my anger. I was in denial about just how bad my anger really was. I knew my behavior was bad, even horrendous, but it was too valuable to me to ease the helpless feelings, and so I was loathe to give it up.

My fourth message is that given the denial and mood-altering nature of my anger, my anger clung to me like a disease, and it had life-damaging consequences—I'll be darned! I finally realized that my *anger was an addiction, a disease, and therefore I could recover from it.* Formerly, like nearly everyone else, I considered my anger and rage to be bad behavior, and the implication was that bad people have bad behavior. A disease, another addiction, seemed much more amenable to healing, because that sort of healing would be recovery from definable causes, as opposed to a change of personality, which seemed vague and difficult.

My fifth message is that because of denial, I did not look for the true causes of my rages. Consequently, it took a long time for me to eventually find that other events and emotions caused originally by events early in my life were the true causes of my anger. These emotions were linked to toxic shame, but they were not solely toxic shame. Later in life, other events occurred that seemed to me to be a repetition of those early events, and these apparent repetitions amplified my rage. All of these early and later events were intimately related to shame, but toxic shame was not my direct emotional offender.

My final message is that for me the causative offenders were emotional and not rational. It was not a case of bad behavior by a bad person, that is, bad thinking leading to bad behavior. I found that I could *not* fix the offenders by rational thinking. It took deep emotional work to resolve the offending emotions in my emotional mind. Fortunately I found that such resolution was a fairly easy and quick process. After a good beginning of that emotional resolution, I found I could apply rational "right thinking" to alleviate and assuage the effects of my anger on me and on others. My anger thus has become less and less of a problem as I continue on this new path. As in true recovery from any addiction, I am today a sick person getting healthier and healthier. I have given up the non-productive persona of being a bad person trying to be better, which in a very true sense would involve changing into being a different person.

Verryl Fosnight
August 15, 2015

Acknowledgments

My anger recovery started with Alcoholics Anonymous, the fellowship of twelve-step meetings, and *Alcoholics Anonymous*, the Big Book. I am grateful to both for the love and kindness and wisdom of many, too numerous thank. Because of them I was spared an early death.

I got sober, and my life got better, but yet I was angry. I discovered dysfunction in families and I thought that should yield relief from anger while helping with my troubled marriage. For that help I thank many authors. The first was John Bradshaw. After seeing his Public Television series *Bradshaw on: the Family* and reading his book he published *Bradshaw on: the Family, A Revolutionary Way of Self-Discovery*, the door was open to the recovery from dysfunction; it was a truly groundbreaking book for me.

With Bradshaw's explanation of family systems and his introduction to shame, my living problems seemed explained, and I had hope for healing those problems. Bradshaw's other books were a godsend also, particularly *Healing the Shame that Binds You* and *Homecoming*. In the former he extends and clarifies many details about shame, thus helping me see how my life had turned out and why. In the latter I got confirmation that anger and childhood abuse were connected; that "deep emotional work," to use his term, was necessary for healing; and that healing could be rapid.

I am also greatly indebted to Pia Mellody, Andrea Wills Miller and J. Keith Miller for defining my living problems as *codependence*. In their book *Facing Codependence* they defined the symptoms of codependence, and explained where the symptoms came from. I learned how they arose in the family by describing the nature of a healthy child and how he or she is damaged by a dysfunctional family with the five types of child abuse that are the roots of codependence. And most importantly the book described the cure which I hoped would help with my anger. *Facing Codependence* is a landmark book, unequaled to me as a reference book on codependence and all its results. Armed with this additional information about codependence and toxic shame, I was sure my anger would recede as I healed my codependence. But it did not, but I was headed in the right direction.

I have read almost all of Alice Miller's thirteen books published in English. Each examines child abuse from a slightly different perspective. They were all were valuable to me in preparing this book. But my anger was not diminished. This was a puzzle, but I did not dwell on it. It eventually turned out I was on the right path to help with my anger by exploring child abuse.

I came to understand that an extreme effect of codependence for me was relationship addiction—*any relationship, no matter how bad, is better than none.* It seemed to me that working to relieve relationship addiction would help with my anger, because most of my anger was in relationships. Stephanie Covington and Liana Beckett helped me tremendously in my understandings of relationship addiction with their book *Leaving the Enchanted Forest.* But my anger remained. Still it felt like I was going the right way; everything but anger was improving.

Joseph Campbell taught me about the universality of the human condition and how we all are connected by the commonality of our life struggles as expressed down through the ages and in all peoples worldwide in myths, as related in *Joseph Campbell and the Power of Myth with Bill Moyers* and *The Hero With A Thousand Faces.* I am grateful for the comfort in knowing I was not alone in having living problems, and that others had struggled down through the ages with similar problems. It did not help me directly with my anger, but otherwise the mythology insights seemed useful to improve my general living problems.

Pia Mellody with Andrea Wills Miller and J. Keith Miller in *Facing Love Addiction* clarified and edified me on the machinations of relationship addiction and by such classification helped me recover from it. However, I got no relief of my anger, as I hoped I would.

All of the above authors led me to understand my dysfunctional family, the toxic shame from that family, how it harmed me, and led me as I recovered from shame which I always hoped would alleviate my anger. But recovering from toxic shame had no effect on my anger as I had hoped. I now know that it was necessary to heal my toxic shame and relationship addiction before I could have success against anger. But I misjudged what the connections were between my anger and toxic shame and relationship addiction.

Stephen Levine with *Unattended Sorrow: Recovering from Loss and Reviving the Heart* promised that if I could grieve my losses and pain, that I would be better for it. He outlined methods for dealing with trauma, and I tried my own similar method, and I immediately felt the relief of softening my hardened core by addressing brushed-off and hidden-away painful emotions. I was getting closer to a solution for my anger.

Putting my losses into perspective by comparing normal or accidental losses to chronic losses was of great help in clarifying my thinking about loss, pain, and my history. I have Claudia Black and her fine book *Changing Course: Healing from Loss, Abandonment, and Fear* and Judith Viorst and her book *Necessary Losses* to thank for this personal growth.

An anonymous friend in AA and I read all of Mellody's *Facing Codependence* out loud to each other. It was the second time through the book for me. It took us weeks because after nearly every paragraph, a memory would be triggered in one of us, and we would stop to recall and discuss it in depth. This process gave us a real-time, intimate understanding of the principles of codependence: "what it is, where it comes from, how it sabotaged our lives," as the book's subtitle puts it.

Another friend I met well into sobriety was dear to me for his constant support as I went through my last divorce and started the process that finally led to my anger recovery. We spent many hours talking about our relationships, the travails of breaking up, and my budding recovery from anger. I could always count on him to give me good counsel.

Finally, there is the love of my life, Sharon Cook, who has read the manuscript several times and always supported me no matter how many hours I ignored her while I wrote. She has also given me wise counsel on ways to express my thoughts.

Verryl Fosnight

INTRODUCTION

To live is the rarest thing in the world. Most people exist, that is all.
—Oscar Wilde

This book relates my personal odyssey of recovery from the addiction to anger. My recovery took over thirty-two years, but it did not have to take nearly that long. My recovery was slowed because I did not realize I was an anger addict, or that there was even such a thing as being addicted to anger. I thought my anger was just bad behavior.

My toxic anger, or rage, made me feel better in certain painful and fearful situations. It changed my feelings from pain and despair to power and control, and its usefulness in manipulating people made it my best friend, a friend that I could always depend on to make me feel better, even as it caused me to act bad. Compulsively and persistently using a substance or activity to alter one's mood is the hallmark of an addiction. As John Bradshaw put it, "When we are raging, we feel unified within—no longer split. We feel powerful. Everyone cowers in our presence. We no longer feel inadequate and defective. *As long as we can get away with it,* our rage becomes our mood alterer of choice. We become rage addicts."[1]

Anger became a way of life for me, just like alcohol had thirty-two years earlier. Unable to cope with life's problems without alcohol (or anger) I became an alcoholic (a rageaholic). My inability to cope was due to growing up without the proper skills to cope. Instead I relied on my drugs of choice, alcohol, anger, and other people to moderate my painful emotions.

I was an angry person from at least my early teen years. I had adopted characteristics that made anger a way to cope with my problems. Later I used alcohol and other people, especially girls and then women, as mood-altering agents to salve my needs. All these needs and problems were due to the emotion of toxic shame. I was not born full of toxic shame; I learned it. And the learned shame led to learned anger—I was not born angry either.

I learned about toxic shame and how it had affected my life after my first two years of recovery from alcohol in Alcoholics Anonymous by delving into other self-help programs. My toxic shame had led to extremely low self-esteem and compensating arrogance and had caused me to believe I needed the love of a woman to make me whole. This belief was the root of my relationship addiction. So while drinking and after getting sober, I was addicted to alcohol, to other people through toxic shame, and to my wife as a relationship or love addict. As I began to endeavor to recover from these other addictions as well as from alcohol, I assumed all along that curing my toxic shame would lead to relieving my anger.

This was a double mistake. First, I did not realize that my anger was an addiction like that to alcohol or to relationships. Second, I assumed that if I could change my beliefs about myself that were caused by the toxic shame, the anger would melt away. I eventually realized that toxic shame alone was not the emotion to be healed in conquering my anger addiction, because as I slowly got past toxic shame, I was still just as angry.

My anger was eventually dissipated only by healing the result of my toxic shame. My toxic shame had caused losses, and those losses had led to pain, and the pain had led to anger. To get over the anger I had to heal the shame to reveal the losses and then the pain, and then healing the pain led to recovery from the addiction of anger.

Therefore, I was correct when I first learned about toxic shame as being a root cause to all my problems but wrong that healing it would decrease my anger without other work.

It seems simple now as I describe it, but it was not easy to do. All of those addictions were the result of personality problems that a typical shame-based, dysfunctional person might have. They required my recovery from them one by one, so I cannot skip relating those other recoveries and skip right to anger.

First I had to get sober and stay sober. With my head clear and with the examples of others in meetings, I gained the hope of complete recovery, not only of drunkenness but also of the problems in living that I had had all through life. My toxic shame was the reason I drank. While high, I could avoid those debilitating feelings of low self-esteem.

Second, when I got sober, I realized that I was codependent—that is, dependent on other people for good feelings about myself. My toxic shame was also the reason I had such low self-esteem and required other-esteem to feel good, "other" being both things and people. I achieved some recovery from codependence, becoming much less dependent on others or things for my self-esteem. But I remained a "love addict." I still needed to be in a relationship to feel good about myself.

Love addiction, or relationship addiction, is an extreme type of codependence. These two addictions are sometimes properly classified as different addictions. For some relationship addicts, love is not required, just a relationship. I required both a relationship and needed it to be an intimate relationship that featured love. "Any relationship, no matter how bad, is better than none" was my unspoken mantra. Personally, if I would substitute *love* for *relationship* in the above mantra it would make perfect sense to me.

My relationship addiction was also shame based like my alcoholism. In a loving relationship, I felt better about myself; my wives and girlfriends were the mood-altering activity of that addiction just like booze was my mood altering substance in my alcoholism. I felt better because their love was apparent evidence that I was acceptable, not flawed or inadequate. My low self-esteem from my toxic shame was salved by them loving me.

Through it all, as I recovered from toxic shame, my anger remained unabated. My hope was that shame recovery would relieve my anger, but it did not. Although shame was the basis of my anger, there were missing pieces. The third important thing for me to relate is how I finally identified and healed those missing pieces of my anger is.

My anger recovery makes sense only as part of my whole recovery. I could never have recovered from anger without maturing and learning about myself through my successful recovery from alcohol and codependence. To do that, I needed to work at the feelings level of my being and do all the work that preceded my anger work. For that reason I need to tell the whole story of all my recoveries from my addictions to alcohol, people, and love. Finally, after I was in recovery from all the others, I was able to find a way to recover from anger addiction.

Sadly, the many different anger-management programs I participated in were ineffective for me. This may have been largely because of my reluctance to give anger up, in a word denial such as occurs in any addiction. But perhaps luckily, deep down inside I knew that I did not need to *manage* my anger but to *recover* from it, to be healed of it and be done with it. I found that this could only be done at the feelings level, and not at the rational thinking level where anger management operated.

"First things first" applied well to my anger recovery. I had to first get down to the core of it, and to do so I had to go through all the other recoveries and do so in the order I did. Otherwise I would have been blocked from any progress by my own shortcomings, which were based on toxic shame. Recovery from all the other addictions, diseases, maladies, or whatever you want to call them, gave me the tools to get along without my anger, which was manipulative. When I no longer needed anger to manipulate or control, it fell away in the cure, but only after I healed or resolved the one emotion that was at the core of my anger.

This is the story of how I found those missing pieces between toxic shame and anger and then healed them to recover from anger.

[1]   John Bradshaw, *Healing the Shame that Binds You* (Deerfield Beach, FL: Health Communications, 1988), 103 (emphasis added).

PART I:
WHAT I USED TO BE LIKE

Lying in the gutter, looking down at the world.

—Anonymous saying in Alcoholics Anonymous

1

LOOKING BACK

It seemed as if I was born angry. A type A personality, I had great ambition and energy. I was intelligent, well educated, successful, and eventually wealthy—and angry. My rage would explode, surprising everyone, even me. I tried until I was about sixty-seven years old to get over my fits of anger. At that age, I finally had a calamitous outburst of violence caused by my anger.

In a way, I *was* born angry, not in terms of my physical birth but in terms of my psychological birth. Psychological birth usually occurs around age six to eight, when a child emerges from symbiotic fusion with the mother toward affirmation of his or her own psychological separation. I spent many years shackled by anger and emoting to others. Those who loved me suffered my temper tantrums and diatribes, and their anguish was probably much greater than mine.

What was the cost of anger to me? This is a partial list:

- one eighteen-month living-together relationship, followed by a breakup
- one whirlwind engagement ending in an awkward breakup four days before the wedding, resulting in embarrassment, canceled invitations, canceled church, canceled reception, all of which caused unnecessary expenses and inconvenience for all
- quadruple bypass surgery, even though I had no history of heart disease in my family and did not have high blood pressure, high cholesterol, or other physical risk factors

- one arrest
- police record for spousal abuse
- court-mandated anger-management training
- a total of three marriages of nine and one-half, eighteen, and eleven years, followed by emotionally and financially draining divorces

They say there is always a silver lining:

- Discovering the root causes of my anger has been exciting. I've gotten to know myself, and it has been a wonderful journey. I cannot overstate the joy and rewards of learning about myself. As I came to understand myself better, I met the most fascinating person imaginable, at least to me, and that was me. And I got hooked on learning about what makes me tick and about life in general.
- I would not change a thing. I do not believe in predestination, but my life has been a heck of a ride, and I don't regret a minute of it—now that I have made my amends, that is.

The golden lining?

- The love of my life—my second wife, who divorced me after eighteen years of marriage—and I have now been back together for five years after eighteen years of total separation. Together again, I can say this is the way it should have always been. But neither of us was capable of being together until we recovered separately—apart and on our own
- Neither of us regrets a thing. We are both in recovery and realize it could not have been different. With the wisdom of understanding how my recovery unfolded and why has come peace and a desire to enjoy the present without regretting or forgetting the past. We now see what we each had to do to get to where we are today. Life is truly about the journey.

2

TWELVE-STEP PROGRAMS AND ME

My recovery from anger was not achieved by a twelve-step program, but the twelve-step programs I was in opened me to be receptive and to find the recovery for anger. Thus, I will describe what twelve-step programs gave to me as a model of what I think is required to recover from anger addiction.

About twenty years ago, I read that there were about fifty-four twelve-step recovery programs based on the twelve steps of Alcoholics Anonymous (AA). Those other programs simply changed the terminology of *alcohol* and *alcoholic* to describe their targeted drug or addiction. Wikipedia claims that "over 200 self-help organizations—often known as fellowships—with a worldwide membership of millions—now employ twelve-step principles for recovery."[1]

Another time I read an opinion piece that said when the history of the twentieth century is written, Alcoholics Anonymous and the twelve-step movement will be the outstanding medical advance of the entire one-hundred-year period. More than twenty million Americans suffer from alcohol addiction in various stages.

There was not a generally accepted method of healing or recovery before AA. The organization began in 1934 when a man named Bill sought out another drunk named Bob to talk about his personal struggles with drinking. Bob, disarmed by Bill only speaking about his own shortcomings, grew courageous enough to admit that he had done some of the same things that Bill related. So Bob started opening up about his own failings, and finally he began talking to Bill about his own drinking. That was the birth of AA: one drunk sharing experiences, strength, and hope with another who also suffers and can empathize—a process of coming clean and breaking down the wall of denial by sharing one thing at a time, in private with one other person or with a group. By the process of opening up, the one sharing cannot help but reveal himself or herself to his or her own conscious mind.

That kind of opening up is precisely what happened to me. In twelve-step programs, I learned to be introspective, so I could find the answers to problems in myself, in my mind and emotions, and in memories that were held even deeper, at a cellular level. I became open to new ideas.

Ideas are different from money. If you and I each have a dollar and we exchange dollars, we each still have one dollar. But if we each have an idea and we exchange ideas, we each then have two ideas.

Furthermore, if I need to say my idea out loud to another, my ego will endeavor to make it sound sensible; I will not skip steps or take shortcuts, because I might look foolish. So sharing is a sure way for me to not con myself. Explaining my thinking keeps me from jiving myself because I do not want to be caught deceiving you. Writing out my thoughts is similar. When I put experiences on paper, it is as if someone else may read them. My ego thereby forces me to try to write in a way that makes sense. If it does not make sense, I might be fooling myself, and that is not healthy.

You can tell I love AA. It saved my life. Without AA, I would not be drunk today; I would be dead. My successful recovery from alcohol addiction through AA has influenced me in my subsequent recoveries to look within to find what drives me and causes me to think and act the way I do. This way, I can uncover specific things to change if I need to, including my thinking, which is greatly influenced by my emotions. I usually have to first heal the associated emotions, which are always normal emotions that were wounded by certain events. My goal is to ensure that my emotions are helpful indicators of how I am doing in life. I do not want my emotions to hurt. And I always want my thinking to make sense, to be real and logical.

In the same way that I love AA—and with almost as much fervor—I love Codependents Anonymous, which made my sober life worth living. Without CoDA, I would be a lonely, angry old man, just withering away and waiting to die all alone. But because of CoDA, I am—at seventy-three years old—happier than ever. I have the silver lining of an exciting life behind me and ahead of me. I also have the golden lining of the peace and satisfaction of knowing I did the best I could at the time. And when my best wasn't good enough, I found a way to improve with the help of the principles and people in CoDA and the gift of introspection they gave me. That introspection was necessary because my path of recovery was through understanding my emotions, including the wounded emotions, and their history in me, and then healing them.

My primary disease is actually codependence. I am sure I drank because of codependence, and my anger was related to codependence also. I did not become codependent because of drinking. Like my history of anger, I was codependent from a young age, but I did not start drinking until I was eighteen.

So this book is about how I got my life back, the life I lost as a very small child. I do not believe that at birth I was anything less than a perfectly imperfect infant, that is, a healthy, precious child. I had wounded emotions long before I drank, but not at birth, so I had to look back at my childhood. That looking back was a very long process, and it was scary and painful at times. But it did not harm me; it only helped me and soon became fun.

In that process of reflection, I stumbled onto a cure for my anger. The cure is simple and easy to tell, but I think the process of how I got to it is important. Readers can skip to the cure, but it may not make sense taken out of context. To be honest, I don't know if it will work at all for anyone else. I just know how and why it worked for me, and that understanding requires knowing the whole story of how I got my life back—the life I lost years before I started drinking, back when the seeds of anger were sown.

[1]   "Twelve-Step Program," *Wikipedia*, last updated November 27, 2015, https:// en.wikipedia.org/wiki/Twelve-step_program.

3

CONFUSION OF PROBLEMS

Looking back to about mid-November 2007, my anger had cost me, but I had no idea how much. The cost would not have seemed devastating at that time had I set it against my perceived benefits of anger (feeling power and control). I just know my life would have been much better if I had not had so much anger in me, but it was not so bad as to frighten me into action against anger.

I had always had my anger, at least since high school, when I first became cognizant of it. I would snap at any friend or associate, even teachers or others, if it was safe. I rarely popped off at anyone who could hurt me in any way, but I knew no bounds with others.

Once in high school another boy and I went to a drive-in movie without dates. In the popcorn line an old woman, probably all of forty years old, shoved ahead of me in line. I called her a name loud enough that she could hear. Later, when I was back in the car enjoying my popcorn, an out-of-uniform police officer tapped on the window with his heavy flashlight, which would have made a mean weapon, and berated me for disrespecting his mother. It was intimidating, which he probably meant it to be. My friend saved me by having the presence of mind to ask for and write down the officer's badge number. The cop settled down and left after my friend got his number. It was the late '50s, and in that simpler time I had never heard of police abusing authority, but I was very frightened. I think he and his mother may have been out of line, but I know I sure was. But by calling her a name out loud, I asserted myself, and it felt good.

In college I had a sharp tongue even with instructors if I could get away with it. This behavior was an expression of my anger and frustration. I even popped off to the head of the physics department at registration when I transferred to a local university for a year after being barred for one year from my prestigious university for poor grades. He would not register me with the classes I had chosen, so I made a demeaning remark to his face as a parting shot. Getting the last word in felt good, although I knew at the time it was not proper. That is the way most of my "wins" or "triumphs" with anger were. I had a feeling of winning and being on top. I rarely actually got my way using anger, but the good feeling was enough.

I returned to the prestigious university after that one year and graduated the next year with a bachelor of science in physics. I got a very good job in research at a small aerospace company. Within one or two years I became the second or third author on three technical papers published in admired scientific and engineering journals because of my contribution to the work reported. Within four years I became the first author on two papers I wrote myself about electric propulsion, specifically the cesium (propellant) electron bombardment ion engine, also known as a gas discharge thruster. Xenon, an inert gas and not at all nasty like the extremely reactive liquid metal cesium, is now the preferred propellant, but the principles are the same. I worked hard and deserved the credit, but it was luck and my degree from the prestigious university that got me that particular job with only a 2.3 grade point average.

I don't remember getting in trouble at work with my temper, but I am sure I got angry and mouthed off many times. I behaved in that manner to get my way or to feel good, and usually my way at work meant what was good for the company, for the project, and for the contract I was working on, which was good for the government customer, my boss, and finally for me. I would use that sharp tongue to get things done, to get equipment, to get orders for supplies in on time, and to get technician or other support help, but I always managed to have good enough boundaries to not get called on it. Even with my anger I consistently got good raises and promotions. But my point is my anger always helped me feel good, powerful, and in control.

I was pretty gutsy though, and occasionally had fun with mock anger. One day I got a memo, like everyone did, that I had to turn in the key to my office and labs. The small company of about 1,100 employees had lost control of the keys in my new building, and it was as good a way as any to reestablish control. We would register our keys and then get them back. But just to have fun, in mock anger I stormed into my boss's office, threw the memo on his desk with the keys, and said, "That's a pretty crappy way to tell a guy he's fired!"

He actually apologized and explained I was not being fired, and I managed not to laugh long enough to let him explain. I had known my reputation for anger would precede me.

After four and a half years in 1969 I resigned with five published technical papers to my credit and in charge of my own $891,000 contract. That's not a large contract by today's standards, but as reference my annual salary was less than $11,000.

Nearly twenty-five years later I was in an undergraduate class at another university to take a BASIC programming course, which I needed for an advanced degree in electrical engineering. I was already proficient with BASIC, having taught myself. The first week of class I asked the instructor if I could get credit for the class if instead of turning in assigned work I wrote a program for my Apple II+ computer at home, and he agreed. I had written and published a paper on orbit analysis showing the feasibility of the use of electric propulsion to make a particular orbit maneuver with incremental pulses over six months, but I had made the calculations with a handheld programmable calculator. I now wanted to make more-precise calculations using much-smaller but many more increments. I went to class in body only and used the time to write code for that project. One day the instructor asked me a question, probably because he saw that I was doing my own special programing homework on paper in class and not paying much attention to the lecture and discussion. I said in a serious tone to this graduate teaching assistant, "Joe, I'm pretty busy here." He backed off and apologized, and I said, "No, no, I'm only kidding," and participated as he wanted.

I wrote the expanded Apple II+ paper and published it in the *Journal of Spacecraft and Rockets* and got credit for the class. I acknowledge my instructor, not out of guilt, but because he had done the right thing and had let me do the paper on school time.

The point is, if it was not going to cost me, I'd pop off to anyone—a stranger, an older woman (even a cop's mother), the head of my college department, or a teacher who was going to give me a grade.

I got married for the first time a week before I started my senior year, and we had a baby within a year. In that marriage we fought often, and I am sure I started nearly all the fights, many of them very heavy duty. We had a second child, and after nearly ten years we divorced. I knew that my anger was probably the reason for the divorce. I soon married again, and that second wife was, and still is, the love of my life. Even so my anger was a problem to the marriage. I realized that there were consequences to my anger, but I still did not make a concerted effort to get over it. It still was too valuable to me as a mood-altering activity—I was addicted to it. We were married eighteen years, and then she divorced me.

We fought over two-thirds of the time in this marriage. I make this estimate because our modus operandi was to fight for two weeks, drop from sheer exhaustion, make love for a week, and then start the fight again. I slapped her twice, maybe more, once hard enough to give her a black eye. She called the police once, but it was about 1985, and they only talked to me on the doorstep. Again I skated out of serious trouble and was able to deny the consequences of my rage.

I drank heavily for the first thirteen years of my second marriage. Then I got sober in AA, starting my recovery at age forty-one. My recovery from alcohol was rapid, and I never had any trouble not drinking again. I rapidly gained more self-understanding as well but did not do so smoothly. My understanding occurred in spurts over the next four years when the pain of specific issues got so great there was nothing left to do but change. I was often motivated by fear of the loss of my wife and her love, and in desperation I would work harder. That fear was a symptom of my relationship addiction. The outstanding manifestation of my anger was the damage it did to my relationship with my wife, who was the love of my life. Even so my denial over my anger was so strong that I could not give my anger up and dedicate myself to recovery from it.

I could erupt at anyone. I was just plain angry at the world, but I was most angry at my parents. I was especially angry at my mother and took it out on my wife because—I did not know this till well into my recovery in AA—she unintentionally did innocent things that made me unconsciously recall things my mother had done to me. I was unfairly supersensitive to my wife, who had never harmed me.

After about four years of sobriety, I heard of a therapist who I thought might help with my stormy relationship with my parents, with whom I had gone into business. I was often angry and raged at them, and my mom raged back. I had heard a story of this therapist making a remarkable discovery about a patient. Anyone that insightful was someone I wanted to help me work on my relationship with my parents and my anger toward them. But I made no progress with my anger with him, and I am sure it was not through any shortcoming of his treatment.

I saw him weekly for a year and then for a few months off and on for two or three years more. I think he used a form of cognitive behavior therapy, where the goal was to get me to think rationally about my problems, but even after all that time, although I was better with my general living patterns, my anger was unabated. He was very good for me, but my anger remained undiminished, and it was always ready to explode for more than another twenty years.

The greatest period of desperation in my recovery was when my wife left me after I had been sober five years. I really think it was because of my anger. For twenty years in AA meetings and in conversations with other recovering people or anyone else, I would talk about how troubling my anger was to me and how I was genuinely thankful that I had not gotten a rifle and gone up on a roof.

I was seeing the therapist when my second wife and I separated, and he helped me get through the separation, reconciliation, and finally a second separation and divorce. The divorce was particularly horrendous for me. I was not angry, which was very unusual for me, but I was hurt—no, crushed—to the point of being nearly debilitated. I had gone into business with my parents and continued working in my new career, but the emotional pain was terrific. I knew that I would not kill myself, but I was seriously afraid that I might die of a broken heart. I later realized the pain was extreme fear, or terror. I was afraid that I would not survive this "abandonment." I now realize this state was an extreme symptom of *relationship addiction*, or *love addiction*.

Abandonment is a loaded term to some therapists. They prefer their clients not say or think they can be abandoned as adults. Adults may have feelings of abandonment, as I had, but in actual fact, very few adults can be truly abandoned, and not by circumstances like a separation, divorce, or death. However, an adult who relies so totally on another person such that his or her dependence is emotionally unhealthy can *feel* profound abandonment and feel it so deeply and completely that it can be debilitating, as it nearly was for me. So in a sense an adult can profoundly *feel* abandoned. It is of course an error to allow yourself to become that dependent, but it happened to me, and that is a lot of my story.

I had those profound feelings of abandonment for over two years before and after the divorce was final. After the separation I continued going to a New Thought church[1] that my wife and I had attended together. We even had had a vow-renewal ceremony in it. Within a few months I changed to another church of the same denomination closer to home with more people my age. Being emotionally needy, I tried to find someone else to take care of me. I wanted to marry again—I mean fall in love, date, and spend time with other sober men and women my own age and with similar interests. All these goals were from my confusing belief system that illustrated the symptoms of love addiction. The irrational desire to marry again right away was a symptom of my relationship addiction; it was a means of *protecting my supply* (of my addictive substance, love). For years it was hard for me to quit fantasizing about meeting a gorgeous woman, taking her to dinner on a first date, and proposing marriage to her between the salad and the first course, at which time we would get married, have fantastic sex, and live happily ever after.

Such fantasies ring of the Welsh or Arthurian myth of the knight Tristan and his ill-fated romance with Princess Iseult the Fair, who was to have been King Mark of Cornwall's bride. After falling madly in love, Tristan and Iseult fled to the enchanted forest to live happily ever after. Eventually they had to leave the enchanted forest to return to the real world; that is, they had to recover. This interpretation reads the tale as a myth rather than as a legend, meaning the story is meant to convey some universal human truth through symbolic storytelling. (See the synopsis of Stephanie Covington and Liana Beckett's *Leaving the Enchanted Forest: The Path from Relationship Addiction to Intimacy* in chapter 15, "Recovery Junkie.")

This may not seem to have anything to do with anger, but to me, it did.

At the time and for years afterward, I thought everything had to do with *shame*. I had read a few books by then that absolutely fit me, and most centered on the emotion of shame. My difficulties in meeting new people, particularly women, and resultant fantasies about them were due to low self-esteem, and those books had the solution to low self-esteem. Low self-esteem is a prerequisite to being a love addict. Having terribly low self-esteem and needing someone else to feel good about you is the hallmark of love addiction.

I accepted that excessive shame was the cause of low self-esteem and eventually found that to be the truth for me. I assumed that my shame and anger were caused by childhood abuse, and they both were. So I leaped to the solution of "cure the shame" to cure the anger. If I solved my first problem, the pain of emotional immaturity and abandonment, then I could fix my inability to be alone and not in love. I hoped that my anger would disappear as a side effect of healing the shame. It was a kind of geometry theorem: "Things equal to equal things are equal." It was really a case of my assuming that things sharing a common cause would be equal. As logical as it sounded, it was not true.

Shame has both a healthy side and a harmful side. In chapter 5, "Emotions," I list several emotions, and for *shame* I give the synonyms of *embarrassed, unworthy, inadequate,* and *chagrin.* Generally the first and last of these have a healthy aspect because they are useful to us as individuals and to society. When we goof, we are embarrassed, and a mistake can cause us to feel and act with chagrin. These effects of shame lead to us establishing personal boundaries or self-containment limits to avoid embarrassment and chagrin. The gifts of shame are then humility, spirituality, boundaries, and self-containment. But in the extreme, excess shame heaped upon us by others can cause self-degradation, self-derision, self-contempt, and low self-esteem, and the effects can be calamitous to individuals, families, and society.

A healthy adult can only be shamed so much by others. He or she can slough off the shame and reject its effects. But children cannot slough off the shame dumped on them by parents or other caregivers on whom they are dependent. Children are very susceptible to being shamed by their parents or caregivers. This is important to the anger part of my story, but I did not realize it for a long time.

My problems in living were more complex than just not being in love.

The extreme effects of shame caused me to have a *perceived need* to be in love, as if I could not care for myself on my own. I just did not perceive myself as being whole or worthwhile without being in a loving relationship. My codependence meant I got my value from external sources, other people, and my relationship addiction meant I sought that external validation from romantic relationships.

I did not consider anger at that time to be my outstanding problem. It may have been a problem to others, but to me it was still my solution, my power. It was the way I coped with some stresses. At that time being alone without a woman to "fix" me was my big problem. So I proceeded to work on excess shame with the goal of having a woman in my life. As an afterthought, I assumed that curing such shame would cure my anger as well, which would allow us to live happily ever after.

This assumption was not totally senseless. When I first heard about shame in *Bradshaw on: the Family* TV series, I was struck by how exaggerated shame explained so many of my shortcomings, and how healing shame offered hope for a solution to a great many of my problems in living, including relationship problems, low self-esteem, and other issues that I later learned were symptoms of codependence. It was natural and not totally fanciful to hope and think that if I could heal my shame, I might heal my anger as well as all the other symptoms Bradshaw lectured about in the series. Later all the fine recovery books I read seemed to point the same way. Now in rereading them I see I was self-deluded, but I was desperate enough to hope that shame was the path to healing me of my rage. I can point to only a few fleeting instances in my books where unhealthy shame seems to be involved directly with anger or rage. But upon reflection now, I can see that in those instances the shame triggered another emotion that caused the anger.

But at that time shame was the emotion that got nearly all the attention in the popular recovery literature and in the programs I attended. It was held out to be the outstanding emotion that led to problems in living. All other emotions with negative aspects were rarely mentioned. Shame seemed to me to be the culprit. And since my work following those recovery sources, books, and talks seemed to be yielding good personal results in many areas, I had no reason to doubt that if I completely healed shame, all my problems, including anger, would be cured.

So I continued to work on my unbalanced shame. When I did get seriously involved with other women, I soon found myself seeing other therapists because of the poor quality of the relationships. Generally, the women I attracted were financially needy, and I was emotionally needy. While that made a tight match, it was always an unhealthy match. And through it all, I tended to be emotionally abusive—that is, angry. And even though I was learning to deal with my shame, my anger got no better and perhaps even got worse. Eventually I was able to cast shame off, but my anger remained.

My therapy sessions with all those women were about the dysfunctional relationships, with the primary goal being addressing my abusive nature and anger. The other therapeutic goals could wait. As a "perpetrator," I stuck out like a sore thumb compared to the "victim" I attracted (and was attracted to), so it was not at all strange that I should be the primary client. I accepted this, not out of guilt, but out of reasonableness. I thought I was bad and knew it was bad living with me, and I wanted that to change. I was unknowingly resistant to change though, because I did not want to give up the power I felt when I got angry. I was not conscious of this roadblock until I found the ultimate cure, but now I can see it clearly.

I think all the therapy I paid for worked to get me to rationally face my problems, but anger was never a primary topic. Shame was also not a topic, and I should have known that something was missing or that shame might not have been the key I thought it was. Yet the supposed shame connection was seductive—it worked so well with self-esteem and my love addiction problems.

So for years I assumed toxic shame had led to my anger, as it had led to my dysfunctional relationships. I knew shame caused my pain and bad relationships, so why not the anger also? I had it so intertwined as one tapestry that I never considered that the thread of shame and dysfunctional relationships was not at all connected to the thread of anger and dysfunctional relationships. It seemed to me that all three—shame, dysfunctional relationships, and anger—must be linearly interrelated. So cure shame, cure anger, right? I do not recall any therapist trying to correct this thinking, if they indeed even saw that was my thinking. I certainly did not voice it; it seemed so logical that I assumed they also thought that my anger was caused by shame. Looking back, I think they probably did not. In defense of all those therapists, I was incapable of voicing that wrong theory of shame leading to all my ills, so they had little chance to correct me and thus make progress with me.

In criticism of those therapists, they seemed hell-bent on curing my behavior by changing my thinking. I now believe I had emotional problems, and I went to see them for help with those emotional problems. They seemed to think I had behavioral problems, which I did, but they thought the solution was to change the thinking to change the behavior. I now believe, as I did then, that the solution was to heal the emotion to change the behavior. But even so, I was working on the wrong emotion, and I do not recall ever working on the right emotion. I will give my personal opinion on this question of rational control of emotions and its usefulness in therapy in chapter 10, "Rational Control of Emotions." In defense of all those therapists, I never specifically asked that we work on my emotions. I assumed that they were correct and that their rational approach was best. I doubt that I ever thought about a rational approach versus an emotional approach, and that failing is clearly mine.

I got my view of the importance of emotions in driving my dysfunction from the recovery books I devoured. As will become clear, my primary hope and source for healing help was from recovery books, and they came down clearly and unequivocally on the side of healing the emotions. Rational training to change or retrain behavior was a failure for me, and I think it was because rational methods are powerless over *deeply* held emotions. Furthermore, because my damaged emotions were so firmly ingrained from childhood at an age when I was not yet rational, I had to be extremely motivated to change them. As I will relate, that motivation did not come about for a very long time. Finally, I held on to the anger because it was so important to me in an addictive, mood-altering sense. It was my best friend that I could always rely on in times of feeling helpless. Like alcohol had been earlier, anger was available on demand to make me feel better and in control.

This therapeutic disconnect between me and my therapists went on for about four years. During this time I dated other women. I lived with one woman for eighteen months, was engaged to another until four days before our wedding, and lived with another one for over a year before we got married.

My anger was a factor in all these relationships. During all these relationships I was often in therapy with different therapists with these women.
The rational approach was always the first line of attack to my problems or
our problems, even as I was keenly aware that it was not *us* but our inner children who were fighting. This idea is apparent if you can consider the on-the-
surface hokey idea that as a dysfunctional person I still had an emotionally
wounded child within me. Those wounds were from childhood abuse. The
crux of the idea of the wounded child within is that very old and immature
ideas the child made up about that abuse are retained by the adult. The child
within has a powerful effect on the (apparent) adult. To the adult, occurrences that just happen as life goes along can appear similar to those painful
instances of abusive treatment as a child. These occurrences trigger the old
pain, and it is felt anew. This pain can cause many harmful emotions—sadness, depression, fear, hate, and, in my case, anger—to surface and sap the
adult's ability to maintain healthy boundaries, both boundaries to protect
oneself and boundaries to prevent intruding on the rights of others. At the
time I knew this to be true, and most of the women I got involved with knew
it, but we were powerless to change the resultant oversensitive reactions that
sparked our mutual bad behaviors because we tried to rationally work out
explanations. These rational approaches certainly made sense, but they failed
at salving the internalized feelings of the still-vital but damaged child within.
That failure was because we tried the rational approach of changing our
thinking by changing our behavior when we had emotional problems that
looked like behavioral problems. What we needed to heal was the emotions
themselves. The rational mind is overmatched in healing the behavior when
ingrained childhood emotions are the problem.

Between marriages, especially during divorces, I made great spiritual
progress. Because I was emotionally needy and thought I needed a woman to
complete me, I was driven by a fear of loneliness, that is, by my abandonment
issues. I think it is true that there are no atheists in foxholes, so I made spiritual progress. This spiritual work and codependence work together solved
my problems with shame and its effects. But my anger remained as bad as
or worse than ever, though it was not for lack of trying.

By spiritual progress I mean a discovery of the spiritual part of my inner
self and its connection to a higher power—a oneness of my higher self with

that higher power. I came to believe that I was not a physical person having a spiritual experience but a spiritual person having a physical experience. The spiritual experience had little to do with morals or ethics, which to me are properly religious issues. Other than raging, I never had ethical or moral problems.

In the popular psychology of recovery, shame has had a thorough treatment and deservedly so. Before I go into the subject of shame from the point of view of a recovering person, let me digress for one chapter to define what I mean by *recovery* and what it means to me to be a *recovering person.*

[1]   See "New Thought," *Wikipedia,* last updated November 28, 2015, http://en.wikipedia.org/wiki/New_Thought.

[2]   Stephanie Covington and Liana Beckett, *Leaving the Enchanted Forest: The Path from Relationship Addiction to Intimacy* (San Francisco: Harper & Row, 1988).

4

RECOVERY VERSUS CURED

Recovery, as I always use it in this book, means "recovery from addiction." It is based on recovery as meant in AA and other twelve-step fellowship groups, which generally have the purpose of recovery from a particular addiction. In recovery, one is never "cured." An alcoholic will always be an alcoholic, perhaps even subject to a relapse of drinking, drunkenness, and craving alcohol. But alcoholics can "recover"—that is, not drink and be restored to normalcy. To do so, they must practice total abstinence, and then, sober, they can improve their lives immeasurably in all ways—relationships, finances, job performance, social interactions, and so on. They just cannot drink, and successful recovery makes the desire to drink practically nil. So recovery in the twelve-step meaning is to not practice your addiction and to improve your life in all other ways through not practicing that addiction. The addiction is still present in the addict as a potential activity; it is just not practiced.

As for my addiction to anger, I wanted to not have extreme anger, or rage. I recognized that it might always be a potential, but I wanted it to be so unattractive that I did not have to manage it. I did not want it to come up as a problem at all, so that management would be a moot point. Not drinking is a moot point to me—I never worry about it or have to control it, *ever*. I only have to remember I am still an alcoholic who no longer practices his addiction.

I wanted anger to be the same for me. I relished the idea of being a non-practicing anger addict. The only management of my anger that I wanted was vigilance of the fact that I would always be a rageaholic, just one that no longer raged, like I no longer drank. I did not care what they called me, just as long as I did not do it!

To an alcoholic recovering in AA, having a drink is a "slip." About all we do is avoid "slippery" places like bars, clubs, and parties unless we have a good (nondrinking) reason to be there—the music, the company, or friends. And if they get too drunk, we leave, because someone who has imbibed too much is actually unpleasant to be around.

As a recovering anger addict I wanted to live comfortably without worrying about slipping into extreme, controlling, or manipulative anger or rage.

It's a mistake to think that not allowing an addiction to be practiced is a matter of will or self-control. It is not. That can be proven by considering how much control it takes to drink a fifth of gin a day plus extra on special days for fifteen years like I did. There were days following extremely heavy drinking far in excess of one fifth that I really did not want to drink, yet I was driven to. I did not understand this compulsion until I got to AA and learned that despite the bad feelings of being a drunk, being inebriated was better than the bad feelings of being sober—I simply could not cope with life while sober. So it takes a lot of control, discipline, and willpower to drink that much for that long! If willpower could cure an addiction, all addicts would have it made, because they do have willpower. It is just misdirected by the compulsion.

Since compulsive drinking or compulsive raging is not about willpower, could it be that these addictions are about emotions? The compulsion is caused by the feel-good benefits that are not available in any other way. Furthermore, and this is all important, the availability of the good feelings is instant and on demand. Those benefits entail a changing of reality by modifying the emotions of the addict to a more pleasurable state. When I was sad, I drank to feel happy. When I was happy, I drank to feel it more. When I was frightened, I drank to feel secure and numb my fear. When I was tired, I drank to feel energetic. When I was emotional or nervous, I drank to relax. I was not capable of moderating my own feelings without the help of alcohol.

Anger worked for me in exactly the same ways. If my lovers did not do what I wanted them to do, or did not make me look good, or if it felt to me (due to childish emotions left as a result of childhood abuse) as if I was going to lose the love I needed to feel good, I attempted to gain control to protect my supply (like a drug stash) by manipulating my significant others with my anger. Note the centrality of *losses* in the above. My anger always was based on perceived or threatened losses or the fear of such a loss. The converse was not always true—a loss did not always cause anger, but if anger came, it was founded on a perceived or potential loss.

The use of alcohol to moderate emotions is obvious. The dependence on other people to moderate feelings (codependence) is much less apparent or understandable, as is using anger to feel better. A definition of addiction may help clarify. John Bradshaw's "working definition," as he called it, of addiction is "a pathological relationship with a mood-altering experience that has life-damaging consequences."[1]

"Pathological" means the relationship involves disease or morbidity, or at least the relationship with the addictive substance or activity is extreme, excessive, or markedly abnormal.

The "mood-altering experience" could be anything—an ingested chemical, an activity, or even people or relationships, as with codependence and love addiction.

The "life-damaging consequences" are very numerous and obvious for booze but are generally more subtle for codependence, but in not a few cases morbidity is involved, and the disease aspect should be self-evident even for subtle effects.

The subtleness of codependence and relationship addiction is complicated in that codependent activities and behaviors are in some ill-defined specific amounts normal and admirable qualities. But in excess, codependence and love addiction can involve control, manipulation, enmeshment, low self-esteem, arrogance, dominance, and a host of life-damaging consequences and these are just the emotional ones. Physical abuse, psychosomatic-based diseases, stress-related diseases, violence, and more make these addictions potentially as damaging as drugs or alcohol, albeit much slower acting. The exact mechanisms of the life-damaging consequences of codependence and relationship addiction are detailed in chapters 11 and 12, "Pia Mellody" and "Pia Mellody's Theory Summarized," and they are touched upon in chapters prior to those.

The pathological and life-damaging consequences of anger are obvious and well documented in books about anger, but the mood-altering effects that make it addictive are usually overlooked. The literature makes a strong case warning against anger as a cause of physical disease, including coronary heart disease and a host of other stress-related health problems, and as a factor in other addictions, both ingestive addictions (alcohol, cigarettes, inhalants, other drugs, and so on) and activity addictions (codependence, gambling, risk taking, extreme sports, and so on). All these addictions modify feelings such that the emotions are more acceptable under the influence than when abstaining. Addiction to anger directly modifies emotions, seemingly improving the angry person's feelings.

The problem with only demonstrating the harmful effects of anger and ignoring the mood-altering effects is that relating such effects, while edifying, causes fear and dread, so the need for mood alteration may be increased. When I was shown gruesome photos of auto accidents due to drinking, it scared me so much I needed a drink. I advocate in this book a process of healing the underlying emotions that lead to anger so that the need to feel better by raging is no longer necessary.

In recovery the addiction symptoms decline or ideally disappear eventually. Using twelve step programs this life change is achieved by a remarkably simple but profound set of twelve steps that have a definite progression and set of goals to lead the addict to a better life of sobriety, *sobriety* meaning the addict is free of practicing his or her addiction. My recovery from anger was an even more remarkably simple process and was not due to a twelve-step program. There is not a nationwide program available for rageaholics, although there is a group in Los Angeles that has a website.

The recovery movement started in Akron, Ohio, when Bill Wilson went to see Dr. Robert (Bob) Holbrook Smith at the home of Henrietta Sciberling. Bill was from New York City and on business in Akron. He was suddenly again struggling to stay sober after getting drunk and blowing yet another big business deal he had put together, and in desperation he called a phone number on a lobby sign in the Mayflower Hotel in Akron. The number was for a local doctor, Dr. Tunks, and Bill "suddenly realized that he needed to talk to another drunk in order to keep from drinking himself."[2] He made the call, and Dr. Tunks gave him a list of ten names. The ninth name was Norman Sheppard, who was a close friend of Henrietta Seiberling.

Mr. Sheppard had to go to New York that evening but suggested Bill call Henrietta, a confidant of Dr. Bob, who was a fine doctor but also a drunk. Dr. Bob was too drunk to meet anyone that night, but his wife, Anne, convinced him to go to Henrietta's the next day, though Bob would only agree to fifteen minutes of "this stuff." As Dr. Bob writes in *Dr. Bob and the Good Oldtimers*, "We got there at five o'clock and it was 11:15 when we left." Bill came to stay with Anne and Dr. Bob the next day, and they started to work on other alcoholics.

There is little concrete evidence about what was said between them in that first six hours. Each man has given his own version. The two versions are similar but with different emphases. In *Dr. Bob and the Good Oldtimers* Bill is quoted as describing their talk as "a completely *mutual* thing." Bill said, "I had quit preaching. I knew that I needed this alcoholic as much as he needed me. *This was it.* And this mutual give-and-take is at the very heart of all of A. A.'s Twelfth Step work today."[3] The twelfth step of AA is a promise to carry the message of AA recovery to others who still suffer.

That is recovery in AA as I mean it: one drunk helping another in a process of *mutual* sharing of each person's experiences, strength, and hope. It has nothing to do with judgmental talk or preaching or advice or "you should do this …" Twelve-step adherents do not generally approve of "shoulding on" each other. And in the general sense, the process means recovery in the same mold, a mutual sharing: "Well, when that happened to me, I did this …" The implication is that I have no idea what you should do; I only know and share what worked for me. It is an easy thing to extend this sense of recovery to any other addiction.

What about anger? Is it really an addiction? I did not consider it so until I started to write this book, which forced me to look closely at a lot of things. During that process I came to see that anger fit Bradshaw's working definition of an addiction. Anger was certainly pathological in me; it smacked of disease. I had a loving relationship with anger. It was a mood-altering activity and behavior, and it had life-damaging consequences. So I had to accept it as another addiction.

Then I reexamined my recovery books and found scattered references of anger as an addiction. I was at first chagrinned at not seeing these references over a twenty-five-year period, but then I realized that denial had caused me to overlook them. Then I felt relief! Perhaps I was not a bad person trying to be better but a sick one trying to get well!

Writing this book forced me to look closely at a lot of things. Writing about oneself, like sharing with another person, is introspective. When I started this book, I assumed my original epiphany about losses and pain had cured my anger, and I meant to share that. I was truly less angry and more at ease with others. The trouble was, I had had about three subsequent bouts of very serious anger and several others of abnormally intense anger. I could not explain those; my anger was not gone, and I certainly was not about to publish a book that made me a hypocrite. But after that epiphany, there was a definite change in me. Then I read on many websites about anger management when applied to spousal abuse considers that anger is not a behavior pattern but a strategy to exert control in a relationship. Zing! That was absolutely true for me. And as I wrote and wrote, I realized that anger made me feel good—it made me feel powerful and in control where without it I felt helpless. *Anger was a mood-altering activity for me!* From there it was a small step, using Bradshaw's definition of an addiction, to see I was addicted to anger.

That process is quintessentially what I mean about the recovery process. It is a self-examination and analysis that leads to new ideas and then to an adjustment of one's emotions first and then finally one's thinking and behavior.

---

[1]   Bradshaw, *Healing the Shame*, 15. John includes this definition in many of his books.

[2]   *Dr. Bob and the Good Oldtimers* (New York: Alcoholics Anonymous World Services, 1980) 63. This book is presented as an biography of Dr. Bob Smith, but there is no author on the title page in order to follow the AA tradition of anonymity.

[3]   Ibid., 68.

5

EMOTIONS

Here comes the scary part: emotions!

Before I continue with my story of how I tried to heal my unhealthy shame and anger, let me clear up some myths about emotions in general.

1. Myth: Emotions are bad.
    Truth: Emotions are neither good nor bad. They just are. They are neutral. How you act them out is good or bad or neutral.

    Consider anger: Anger is the source of our power. Perhaps we need a painted school crossing and sign at an intersection so one of our kids doesn't get run over. If we get angry, that anger gives us power to work for that crossing. But if you act out your anger in a harmful way, you end up hurting someone and/or yourself.

2. Myth: Emotions must be controlled.
    Truth: It is often thought that emotions need to be controlled because they are bad. But since emotions are neutral, only the acting out of emotions needs to be controlled.

Emotional actions must be controlled because they can hurt despite their utility. They don't have to hurt, though. Continuing the anger example, if you work within the rules, you can get the school crossing in an orderly and respectful way. Or you can throw a tantrum and cuss and scream at the next planning commission meeting and get thrown out and be embarrassed. So yes, anger has to be managed and channeled to get the best out of it, not the worst.

But can one learn by rational thought to control or manage anger? That is the sixty-four-dollar question that is discussed in chapter 10, "Rational Control of Emotions."

3. Myth: Being emotional is being weak.
    Truth: Emotions are the gauges on the dashboard of life. They tell us how we are performing and reacting to life's good and bad events.

    If we do not have our emotions available, we have no independent and reliable way to know how we are doing. We cannot always trust others to tell us or show us. But if we break into a crying jag every time we burn the toast, maybe we are too sensitive. If the burnt toast never bothers us, maybe we are depressed.

4. Myth: Being unemotional is being strong.
    Truth: Being unemotional is being insensitive, depressed, numb, indifferent, or any of a number of things that are not very admirable and probably bad for your physical health.

5. Myth: Emotions are useless.
    Truth: With their dual natures emotions all have gifts, but in the extreme they also have downsides.

What are some common emotions? It is sad (an emotion) that we have to sit down and think to come up with a decent list of emotions. From many sources, I have collected a short list of common emotions and their synonyms, gifts, extreme forms, and effects. This is not meant to be a complete list, and it does not match the list of six basic emotions of Paul Ekman (happiness, anger, surprise, fear, sadness, and disgust) or other authoritative theoretical lists. There are many such lists as this in psychological literature, some shorter, some longer, implying that there is no officially and generally accepted list of emotions. But this list is complete enough for this book.

- **anger**
  - synonyms: frustration, resentment, irritation, displeasure, outrage
  - gifts: strength, assertiveness, energy, courage, fortitude, vigor
  - extreme forms: rage, frenzy, mania, fury
  - effects: tenseness all over the body and in all muscles, hot flashes
- **fear**
  - synonyms: alarm, dread, apprehension, anxiety
  - gifts: safety, protection, wisdom
  - extreme forms: panic, paranoia, phobia, hysteria
  - effects: sinking feeling in the pit of the stomach, tightness in the chest, faintness, suffocation
- **pain**
  - synonyms: sadness, loneliness, hurt, discomfort
  - gifts: awareness, realizations, growth, healing
  - extreme forms: self-pity, victimization, melancholy, rage, helplessness, hopelessness
  - effects: aching in the chest and heart
- **sadness**
  - synonyms: dismalness, bitterness, heartbreak, loss, sorrow
  - gifts: appreciation, growth, acknowledgment
  - extreme forms: pessimism, wistfulness, somberness, melancholy
  - effects: depression, bleak outlook, hopelessness

- **joy**
    - synonyms: happiness, elation, serenity
    - gifts: contentment, gratitude, hope, well-being
    - extreme forms: hysteria, rapture, revelry, regalement
    - effects: all-over-the-body lightness and freedom
- **passion**
    - synonyms: enthusiasm, zest, dedication, spiritedness, energization
    - gifts: excitement, interest, energy, ambition
    - extreme forms: zealotry, ecstasy, paroxysm
    - effects: all-over-the-body energy
- **love**
    - synonyms: affection, fondness, devotion, cherishing
    - gifts: connection to others or things loved, compassion, spirituality
    - extreme forms: lust, desire, craving, greed, longing
    - effects: lightness in heart, warmth all over, fulfillment
- **hate**
    - synonyms: dislike, abhorrence, animosity, loathing, disgust
    - gifts: aversion to distastefulness and evil, avoidance of sin, perfect hatred (Psalm 139)
    - extreme forms: prejudice, violence, brutishness
    - effects: rage, violence, enmity, alienation, estrangement, bitterness
- **guilt**
    - synonyms: regret, contrition, remorse, culpability
    - gifts: values, amends, reforms, remedies
    - extreme forms: stigma, dereliction, dishonor, sense of being sinful
    - effects: self-loathing, depression, borderline personality disorder
- **shame**
    - synonyms: embarrassed, unworthy, inadequate, chagrin
    - gifts: humility, spirituality, boundaries, self-containment

- ✦ extreme forms: self-degradation, self-derision, self-contempt, disesteem
- ✦ effects: hollowness and emptiness in the stomach

In my experience with these ten emotions, anger has a lot to do with four of them and little to do with shame, as I supposed some books were telling me. I grant that I probably got it wrong in studying those books, but my anger was so pervasive that I was desperate. I will address shame in Part II.

Based on the attributes I list for these emotions, they are clearly perfectly normal and occur at least occasionally in us all. Therefore, there is no reason to avoid or hide emotions inside of us. In fact, it is usually harmful to do so.

PART II:
WHAT HAPPENED

Have you learned the lessons only of those who admired you, and were tender with you, and stood aside for you? Have you not learned great lessons from those who braced themselves against you, and disputed passage with you?

—Walt Whitman

6

ACKNOWLEDGING ANGER
AS A PROBLEM

When I first got to Alcoholics Anonymous, anger was a common topic in meetings. Many alkies were angry and freely shared in meetings about their angry moments. Sharing in AA meetings is an orderly process with each person speaking about the topic or whatever is bothering him or her at the time for a few minutes, usually less than five. There is no cross talk or interruptions and no direct reference to other speakers by those who follow. People get to share or speak only once each meeting. It is a format that cuts away almost all judgment and hostility and promotes self-control, tolerance, and introspection. Sharing makes up about 90 percent of the meeting, so everyone is under unspoken peer pressure to just sit and listen.

All that sharing about various problems helped me. I realized I was not the only one with outlandish thoughts and attitudes or weighty burdens, and often hearing others voice the same problems made me realize how common or even trivial some of mine were. About the only advice given was an indirect "Well, when that happened to me, here's what I did …"

Hearing about all that anger, I could admit that I was angry also and could examine it and see to some extent how it worked in my life. I had to admit that it caused me many of the same problems in my marriage and with my parents as others related.

> Some of the following parts of this book may shock or offend you. They are not meant to do so, certainly not for dramatic or sensational purposes, and no malice or revenge is intended.
>
> I have absolutely zero intent in this book to harm anyone's memory—either that of my dead parents or the living reader's. In my parents' case such would be a complete waste of time and utterly pointless. In the reader's case there may be some discomfort, even pain, stirred up, but that is unintended. I found that such discomfort and pain was part of my healing process, very much like stretching an overworked and sore muscle just enough to heal it back to limberness. This book relates how I stretched my emotions to promote emotional health, and the book's message is how healing that can be for an angry person.
>
> I must detail my childhood experiences because they were the beginning of all the pain that led to my anger. All through my adult years, I might get angry at someone or something, and in each case the underlying feelings I experienced were traceable to some painful event in my early childhood. There were only a few such events, but it seemed to me they recurred over and over again, like reenactments, right up into adulthood. Thus, in a book about my anger, and perhaps about the anger of a great many people, such early events are worth examining. Such analysis, I hope, will illuminate similar events in the early lives of others, and such a correspondence between my experiences and theirs may be enlightening. In short, I do not believe I am unique, and neither should anyone else.

I soon became cognizant that I was angrier with my parents than with anyone else. I had recently joined their business. Since high school I had had constant hard feelings toward them and heated words with them, especially my mother. She was wonderful in many ways, and I owe her greatly for a lot of good lessons about work and how to achieve, but she was an overbearing, aggressive, and dominating person, especially to me and to my wives. The friction extended to my father, who played the role of the nice guy, but I knew she was the designated bad guy for the two of them. Nothing happened without his tacit approval, though. He and I rarely had words, but he supported her by his silence. Years later as she aged with Alzheimer's disease, he had to become the bad guy without her to play that role. Such was his concealed anger.

Mom was physically abusive to me when I was young. I got very hard and frequent spankings with an implement up until about twelve years old. One day at about that age she was chasing me from the kitchen to the bedroom with a straight broom. I fell over the bed and kicked out at her instinctively in defense. She was a little woman, so at twelve I was as big as she was. The spankings stopped that day.

I was spanked with a small stick or board hard to the point of being beaten when she was angry. She was also verbally and emotionally abusive with her frequent raging and sharp tongue. The words she used and the attitude and control she exerted hurt more deeply than the beatings. Dad's acquiescence was equally abusive and a strong form of abandonment.

Around the time I started therapy with my first therapist, the doctor asked me if I had ever thought I was about to die. I posed the question to my parents, and Dad got up and left the room—I suppose because we were going to talk about feelings. But on the way out he ventured, "Only when you were on your way to the bathroom with your mother [did you think you were going to die]." The bathroom was where she took me as a toddler and small boy to spank me with an eighteen-inch heavy wooden ruler. Being into sarcasm at that time, I thought it a nifty thing for him to say.

A few minutes later Dad and I were alone in a car to go to the store, and I said, "Tell me about the bathroom."

"I was afraid she might kill you sometime," he said without hesitation.

It never occurred to me to ask him why he didn't stop her. I never got around to asking him or her about the abuse, even nineteen years later up to when he died. Like all other abused children, I honored my abusers. I did, however, realize that he was okay with her beating me.

Dad's part in the abuse was mainly his failure to protect me from Mom's temper and physical abuse, and he probably felt that was the way to raise children. I have indirect evidence that corporal punishment, judgmental treatment, and shaming were the ways he was raised. In recovery, I came to think he may have resented my birth, which came after eight years of marriage. Prior to that they were poor, dust bowl Depression poor, and lived following the few jobs available—fruit picking, topping beets, coal mining, truck driving, carpentry, pipe fitting, and any other blue-collar labor he could get.

Mom would tell a story about Dad starting to leave her for good during an argument. She said she "protected" me by taking me in her arms, sitting in the car, and saying, "You're not going to leave *me*." It was *me* with each telling, never *us*.

Another time, when I was four or five, Dad and I were peeing in the toilet at the same time, and he peed on my hand. He thought it very funny, especially when I looked up at him, six feet and 190 pounds of farm boy and manual laborer, and said in real anger, "You pee on my hand again, and I slap you right in the face." This was another family story that was told more than once without shame as if it were funny. It was supposed to express my value as cute. I actually felt as valued as a piece of toilet paper.

As John Bradshaw lectures, to a helpless, defenseless three-year-old, parents are like gods. If they are wrong, even in getting beat, it means to the child that his or her survival is in even more jeopardy than the beating. In the child's mind he or she cannot survive alone if the parents are not perfect. Since the child must depend on them, to the child they must be considered to be right, or the child has no chance to survive.

My failure to confront my father or mother in my adulthood was just that type of loyalty to them, and anyway, there was no point in trying to change either. Such a discussion would have sounded like blame to them and would have only resulted in a pointless confrontation—I knew what had been done to me and did not need anyone to come clean or apologize. More than that, it was a dramatic example of my family's don't-talk rule of family silence, the old "don't wash your linen in public."

Long after Mom's death, I had a cousin tell me that his father, my mother's younger brother, had also been afraid that she might kill me. When we were adults, another cousin expressed how hard she and her siblings thought I had it. I imagine my spankings were common knowledge in our extended family—Mom was one of eighteen children, including full siblings, half siblings, and stepsiblings. The relevant recovery cliché is "There is an elephant in the living room." But the whole family ignored it, stepped around it, and just pretended it didn't exist.

The last few years of Mom's life saw her Alzheimer's disease withering her away to skin and bones, a barely sentient shell of her formerly brilliant self. Dad preceded her in death by two years. In the six or eight years before that time I became their caregiver and took great care to not abuse them, although Dad was sure I was abusive to him. I did what I thought was best and hired caregivers for them. I built a new house with room for my wife, her adult daughter, Mom and Dad, and two caregivers. Without Mom as the hit man, Dad had to do his own dirty work. His anger came out strongly, and he became the verbally and emotionally abusive parent. It was a lousy job, but someone had to do it in our matriarchal-turned-patriarchal family.

I digress about my family not out of resentment—resentment is like taking poison and expecting the other person to die—but out of illustration. It was a real learning and proving experience for me. I lived in the cauldron of a severely dysfunctional family all my life until first Dad and then Mom died, both at ninety-three years old, two years apart. They were universally liked and respected, much loved, and very financially successful coming from extremely humble beginnings, and I loved and respected them. But they were hard for me to like completely. I grew up to have my own mind and life, and that was unacceptable to them. It was hard for them to accept me as being my own person. My job was to be their servant, minion, and drudge while they were the rightful matriarch and patriarch. I just was an abject failure at my job of subservient son. Naturally, I found this a hard role to fulfill.

An important point that I make more fully in chapter 16, "Family History and Personal Growth," is that they were not bad people who should have been better. They were a product of *their* upbringing. By those standards they were fine parents and citizens, and I grant them that without rancor. Their upbringing was the *poisonous pedagogy* Alice Miller wrote so much about. "The concept was first introduced by German educator Katharina Rutschky in her 1977 work *Schwarze Pädagogik. Quellen zur Naturgeschichte der bürgerlichen Erziehung* [literally *Black Pedagogy, Sources on the Natural History of Civic Education*]. The psychologist Alice Miller used the concept to describe child-raising approaches that, she believed, damage a child's emotional development, but which are wholly accepted and admired by society. Miller claims that this alleged emotional damage promotes adult behavior harmful to individuals."[1]

To be clear, Miller meant the damaging child-rearing methods adults use that end up being harmful to those children as adults. The children may appear to forget about the abusive methods, but the memory does not just disappear from their minds. It remains as a poisoning set of painful emotions that get acted out in many harmful ways damaging the child through adulthood, and damaging society as a whole. Each of Miller's thirteen books specializes in a way the pain comes back, as hurting behavior, disease, or even criminal behavior. There is more about Alice Miller's many books about child abuse in chapter 15, "Recovery Junkie."

The most important point is that for me my experiences are proof of the theories I espouse—for today's world, if not for my parents'.

Mom's domineering behavior only ended with her dementia and Alzheimer's disease. Her domineering had continued from my childhood until after I went away to school and on to when I was married with a wife and two boys of my own. It was still present while I divorced and remarried at thirty-two years old, bringing me two stepsons of twelve and fourteen. Her anger and domineering and my anger continued on and beyond when I was newly sober at forty-one years old and when I went back into business with my parents for the second time in my mid forties. I was in recovery at over forty-five years old, growing in AA and looking at my life differently. And I was looking at my emotions seriously for the first time. I could not help but pay attention to my anger in a new way. I had a tumultuous marriage and a hostile business relationship with my folks, and now that I was sober, the possibilities for success seemed limitless. I wanted all life had to offer—financial abundance, peace, and happiness. Most of all I wanted health abundance. I wanted to end the dysfunction in my family with my generation so as not to harm my four sons! To do so I needed to get over a lot of dysfunctional family ways. And I needed to get over my anger to do that. But nothing seemed to help with my anger.

Everything else was getting better. My wife and I had the bills paid off and money in the bank. We were not only saving; we were also investing in California real estate and doing well (like everyone else in California in 1983). But my anger held me back. My wife and I still fought too much, and the situation with my folks was tempestuous. I was not yet aware of the codependence issues we were all mired in and would not be for about five more years, but the anger looked like something I should deal with.

---

[1] "Poisonous Pedagogy," *Wikipedia*, last updated September 17, 2015, en.wikipedia.org/wiki/Poisonous pedagogy.

7

JOHN BRADSHAW,
BRADSHAW ON: THE FAMILY

I got sober, the AA expression for when I quit drinking, in June 1983 at forty-one years old. Enthused over my new sober life, my second wife and I heard about a marvelous television program about the family and family systems on PBS by a fellow named John Bradshaw. It was *Bradshaw on: the Family*, and *Bradshaw On: The Family: A Revolutionary Way of Self Discovery* was published as a companion book.[1] Other than *Alcoholics Anonymous*, the so-called Big Book of AA, *Bradshaw on: the Family* was the first recovery book I ever read. I agree with Carol Burnett, who wrote in the foreword, "For me, the material in this book on families as rule-bound systems was a real eye-opener. If I understand it correctly, it means that we must always look at emotional illness as a social crisis. Everyone in the family is involved. I like that. It puts responsibility on everyone but eliminates blame."[2]

In watching the PBS TV series and reading the book, I remembered well my mother's anger and beatings and the humiliation she caused me, and I could identify with the abuse in my family. I was as equally struck with the realization of the manipulation and hidden messages of my family's rules and behavior. Things were not open, clear, and honest but murky, cloudy, and duplicitous. Bradshaw's TV show and book were tremendously important to me and to my recovery. They opened the door to childhood and family issues and showed me there was a reason beyond the results of my drinking for why I thought the way I thought, felt the way I felt, and acted the way I acted. In fact I have come to believe my childhood and family issues were the reason *for* my drinking. I have read through *Bradshaw on: the Family* many times after watching the TV show and reruns of it. There is a great abundance of material in the book, and in all Bradshaw's books, that my brief summaries can only begin to convey. And after all, my focus is only on anger, but I got much more out of Bradshaw's work than just a viewpoint on rage. Whether you are serious or just curious about recovery, this book is a must, in my opinion.

Seeing Bradshaw's dynamic speaking on TV and reading his book changed my life even more profoundly than getting sober in AA and reading the Big Book. AA and the Big Book changed my life dramatically, but the change was one that I desired and hoped for. I had envisioned living without drink—without being drunk 24-7—for at least two or three years but was abhorred by the prospect. Nevertheless it was obvious that I had to somehow quit drinking and live sober. Sobriety was potentially and actually only a change of living without alcohol, without being constantly drunk. I could picture everything else being pretty much the same. And it was. I had the same problems, but I had a chance to solve them sober. So it was a big and important change but not a revolutionary one.

The new total outlook on life I gained from Bradshaw and his message changed my life fundamentally, profoundly, and radically. I had gone away to school for four years with students from all over the world. I had had foreign roommates and Nobel Laureates for instructors and had listened to and talked to world leaders at intimate coffee seminars who actually addressed each student as an important individual. I had had blue-collar jobs. I was the son of a skilled blue-collar union member. I had been in business for myself with fifty or more employees. I had done research as a physicist and published papers in scientific journals. I had been a drunkard and now was sober, but all that and no other experiences prepared me for the sudden and elemental, drastic and vivid new view of myself and other people. That new view demanded a radical change in my lifestyle and behavior. Until that time people and their foibles, myself included, had been like an iceberg with only the top 10 percent visible. Suddenly, so many of my problems—my crazy (I believed) thinking; my quirks, failings, and sufferings; and those of the world—seemed to burst open as if split in two to reveal a new set of causes and, better yet, to suggest new feasible remedies.

I am certain that AA saved my life. I was killing myself slowly and was also courting a sudden, violent death by driving drunk and being angry as well as drunk. I risked killing others or being killed because of those factors. To paraphrase Woody Hayes when he was the football coach at Ohio State and rarely had his teams pass the football, "Three things can happen when you pass, and two of them are bad." Many things can occur when you drink like I did, and all but one of them are bad. I was lucky. The one possible good thing happened to me: I got sober.

The profundity of Bradshaw's message went right to the core of my being and provided me with the beginning of a new deep, subtle, and thorough understanding of myself. It seemed to explain, at least for a time, everything about me, what I was, and how I had become the way I was.

I quickly came to recognize that my whole attitude of life and method of living stemmed from my background and all that came before the present moment, right back to infancy. Bradshaw presented this concept in a nonjudgmental manner—focusing on responsibility, as Carol Burnett said. With the theory presented in that way, I accepted it as fact, like the theory of gravity is fact, that it is so apparent as to be obvious.

The key word in *Bradshaw on: the Family* was *shame*. Bradshaw brought the emotion of shame out of the shadows, defined it, made it recognizable, and showed its effects. I recall hearing once that even Freud only mentioned shame twice in all his writings.* When I checked for myself, I found only two index entries for *shame* in my copy of the 1,001-page, two-volume copy of *The Basic Writings of Sigmund Freud*.[3] Therefore, recovery from the effects of shame was a broadside to my consciousness and gave me great hope where before there had been only despair. Up until that time I had thought I was a bad person. Now there was hope that I was merely ill, and that I could heal myself.

Bradshaw did not start to differentiate between healthy shame and unhealthy shame until his later books. It was probably first in *Healing the Shame That Binds You*, which I describe in some detail in chapter 14, "Shame in Depth: John Bradshaw, *Healing the Shame That Binds You*." As shown in chapter 5, "Emotions," shame, like all emotions, has a healthy and useful side.

---

* I think I heard John Bradshaw say this on TV, but I am not sure it was he.

For the remainder of this chapter I will maintain Bradshaw's terminology of using *shame* generally, although his later term *toxic shame* would be better.

Bradshaw starts by giving a few rules of families that have been passed down to us through many generations. He claims that those rules make families dysfunctional:

> My thesis is that these rules are abusive and shaming [and cause dysfunction in families]. They destroy the children's inner identity. They result in shame. According to Gershen Kaufman in his book *SHAME*, shame is "... a sickness of the soul. It is the most poignant experience of the self by the self, whether felt in humiliation or cowardice, or in a sense of failure to cope successfully with challenge. Shame is a wound felt from the inside, dividing us both from ourselves and from one another."[4]

Bradshaw continues,

> According to Kaufman, shame is the source of most of the disturbing inner states which deny full human life. Depression, alienation, self-doubt, isolating loneliness, paranoid and schizoid phenomena, compulsive disorders, splitting of the self, perfectionism, a deep sense of inferiority, inadequacy or failure, the so-called borderline conditions and disorder of narcissism, all result from shame. Shame is a kind of soul murder. Once shame is internalized, it is characterized by a kind of psychic numbness, which becomes the foundation for a kind of death in life. Forged in the matrix of our source relationships, shame conditions every other relationship in our lives. Shame is a total non-self-acceptance.[5]

The rules Bradshaw refers to are in essence the poisonous pedagogy of Katharina Rutschky and Alice Miller on the family level. Bradshaw's rules are summarized in footnote 6 of this chapter.[6]

At some level I must have believed that anger was also caused by shame, since everything else seemed to be, indeed "most of the disturbing inner states which deny full human life."

Bradshaw continues in the next section, "Shame is a being wound and differs greatly from the feeling of guilt. Guilt says I've *done* something wrong; shame says there is something wrong with me. Guilt says I've *made* a mistake; Shame says I *am* a mistake. Guilt says what I *did* was not good; shame says I *am* no good."[7]

Notice that not once in these quotes does John Bradshaw mention anger. But he did not miss many of man's shortcomings. And since I could see he was right by my own reckoning of what my family was like and how I was raised, I jumped at the opportunity to fix all by starting a program to cure my obvious (toxic) shame. I started that program eagerly and hopefully, because he claimed there was a solution. In ten years of working on my shame, I learned that solution and how to use it, and he was right.

Except it did not work on my anger.

I had the same experience with many other recovery books, most of which seemed to focus on shame, and I made the same assumption that curing toxic shame would work on my anger.

But then, Bradshaw or the others rarely specifically said "anger." But upon encountering Bradshaw two years into sobriety and through the time when I studied the other books and everything else was getting so much better so fast, the prospects of curing shame to cure anger looked so very good! I had even stopped getting colds and the flu! Of course, I laughed, I was not drunk 24-7, and so my resistance to germs and viruses was better. But everything got better, and I was sure it was because I was sober and was carrying less toxic shame! Why not anger? I was sure this must be it: shame—cure it and be healed. I did not say it, but that was my unspoken and silent hope: curing shame could and should cure my anger as well as everything else.

And why not? If you lose yourself by being shamed, would not that make you angry? If you were belittled by one parent's beatings and the other parent's ignoring of the beatings, if your very high grades and accomplishments were denigrated as still inadequate, if you were beaten and put down by your beloved parents, your *caregivers*, for goodness' sake, would that not lead to anger? I was hopeful and probably more desperate than realistic, but

I thought shame led to anger. The abuse caused shame, and shame must lead to anger. It seemed to lead everything else.

But the anger remained unresolved even as all the other effects of shame dissipated with the shame. I had no idea that something was missing.

It was many years before I found out what was missing in my incomplete shame equation of

$$\text{Abuse} \rightarrow \underline{\quad\text{fill in blank}\quad} \rightarrow \text{anger.} \tag{1}$$

I had no idea that the blank even existed to be filled in. The books, which were not about anger but shame and low self-esteem and alienation from self and other problems, seemed silent on a path of anger. Now I can see the very occasional and cursory hints and direct statements. But anger was not addressed directly and instead presented like ancillary information.

I did miss quite a bit of direct information about anger in Bradshaw's later book *Healing the Shame That Binds You*. It is clear and in the open, and it is direct. I can only speculate why I missed it in 1991, not long after my divorce from my second wife, when I first read it. Bradshaw's third book *Homecoming: Reclaiming and Championing Your Inner Child*, which I read in 1992, also contains much more information on anger and its connection to shame, and this book is even more direct and applicable to me. For more about this oversight of mine, see the afterword.

There can be only one reason for these oversights: denial. As bad as I knew my anger was and as much as I believed and was certain that my anger had sabotaged my marriage to the Love Of My Life, I missed it in my books. Anger was too necessary and precious to me to give it up. I fooled myself through blindness into thinking that healing toxic shame would heal my anger. And besides, healing shame would make me so wonderful that a replacement love would result. And so I worked on shame exclusively. These two thoughts will be a theme throughout most of the remainder of my story.

So I continued for years to work on healing the shame, and it paid dividends, immediately and long range. There were the immediate dividends of healing my low self-esteem and the feeling of separation from others due to that low self-esteem. If I believed I was inadequate, broken in a way that couldn't be fixed, not truly whole and complete, then why wouldn't I feel less than, separated, inferior, and worthless? And why wouldn't I act arrogant and be a braggart to compensate? It all made sense to work on shame. But my secret, even from myself, was I was not about to give up my anger, which was my power.

Having been so shamed in childhood, why wouldn't I be angry? It seemed to make perfect sense. Except that I was still angry, no matter how much the toxic shame receded from my being.

I was still "lying in the gutter, looking down at the world," even though I was no longer in the gutter of drunkenness, emotional neediness, toxic shame, and general dysfunction. Now, although I did not realize it, I was "looking down on the world" because of anger, resentment, and arrogance instead of the toxic shame that caused low self-esteem and the compensating arrogance in me.

I continued to see my anger jump up and bite me and others and cause a lot of trouble. Still I held it close to me. My anger seemed completely resistant to healing when all else had seemed to heal so well. I had no idea that something was missing.

[1]   John Bradshaw, *Bradshaw on: the Family: A Revolutionary Way of Self-Discovery* (Deerfield Beach, FL: Health Communications, 1988).

[2]   Ibid., vi–vii.

[3]   Dr. A. A. Brill, ed., *The Basic Writings of Sigmund Freund* (The Modern Library, New York, 1938), Translated and Edited, with and Introduction by Dr. Brill. I found no index references for *shame* in my three-volume set (1,447 pages) of Ernest Jones, *The Life and Work of Sigmund Freud* (New York: Basic Books, 1957).

[4]   Bradshaw, *Bradshaw on: the Family, A Revolutionary Way of Self-Discovery*, 2.

[5]   Ibid.

[6]   Ibid. The full text of the rules is on page 80–82 and well worth studying, but here is a brief summary:

1. Be in control of all interactions, feelings, and personal behavior at all times.
2. Always be "right" in everything you do (avoid the bad, which is breaking the rules).
3. If things go wrong, blame yourself or others. Someone must be wrong to cover the shame.
4. Deny feelings, perceptions, thoughts, wants, and imaginings, especially the negative ones like fear, loneliness, sadness, hurt, rejection, and dependency needs.

5. Don't talk openly about feelings, thoughts, or experiences that focus on the dysfunctionality.
6. Practice myth-making: always look on the bright side, and reframe negative emotions to distract from the hurt.
7. Keep fights and disagreements going for years by either chronic fighting and conflict without resolution or by enmeshment and confluence—agreeing to never disagree. Have either conflict or confluence but never contact. Stay permanently upset.
8. Don't expect reliability in relationships. Don't trust anyone so you will never be disappointed. Be both aloof and independent (needless) or needy and dependent.

7   Ibid.

8

Emotions and Me and AA

In my recovery from anger, the parallels of my experiences of recovery from my other addictions, alcoholism, codependence, and love addiction to my experiences in recovery from rage are striking. These similarities are impossible to ignore. For that reason my narrative continually weaves back and forth from the more familiar addictions, particularly alcoholism, to my anger addiction to show those parallels. It will be seen that my recovery from all my addictions followed the same general path with the same mileposts along the way, but for simplicity, I will concentrate on alcoholism as the most direct and recognizable model for comparison to anger addiction. Similar and obvious parallels can be made to my codependence and love addiction, both of which are addictions, but the parallels with alcoholism are probably the most recognizable to the average reader.

My primary battleground in recovery from alcoholism and the other addictions was the emotional front. I may have had it wrong, but, as I have said, in the many fine books I read about recovery from all my "dis-eases," I took *toxic shame* to be the big monster on that battleground. When I first stopped drinking, toxic shame was in an emotional closet, but it had recently been brought out of that closet by Bradshaw. Finally I could face it directly. As I dealt with my toxic shame to recover from codependence and improve my sober life, I assumed I was on a path to address my anger. Recovering from my shame was a logical step to improving my emotional health. It turns out recovery from shame was not a remedy for my anger, but in a way I was on the right path to relieve my anger. This is illustrated by equation (1) in the last chapter, but it was a few years before I could fill in the blank in that equation.

I have been using many different qualifiers with the word *shame* to distinguish between healthy shame, which we should value, and unhealthy shame, which harms us. I now will switch to a much-preferred terminology of *shame* for "healthy shame" and *toxic shame* for "excessive or unbalanced shame." *Toxic shame* is the term John Bradshaw uses, except in *Bradshaw on: the Family*. It should be remembered that there is both healthy shame and excessive or toxic shame. Shame is a difficult emotion to position on the range from healthy to toxic. The healthy results of shame, such as embarrassment or chagrin, seem mildly painful, but some thought reveals their socially valuable effects. Humility, spirituality, and boundaries are also effects of healthy shame and are generally high-value traits. At the unhealthy end are self-degradation, self-derision, self-contempt, and low self-esteem. Between the extremes, the effects of shame blend together, but just where is the line between humility and self-derision? This general difficulty in feeling and evaluating healthy versus toxic shame makes shame a difficult emotion.

In my recovery trek I accepted that emotions were okay and normal and that people were not human without them. It was what I did with my emotions that made them good or bad. I was naturally emotional and tended not to hold my emotions in. When I did subconsciously hold them in, I often did so in a way that was harmful to my *inner self*. I learned this in AA meetings listening to others share and identifying with what they said. The openness of others there helped me overcome my reluctance to bring my emotions out into the open where I could deal with them in a healthy manner. After going to many AA meetings within a short time, it became fairly easy for me to bring my emotions out, address them, embrace them, accept them, and deal with them, as opposed to emoting them in an uncontrolled manner. This was much more healthy that holding them in.

Except, this didn't work with shame. Shame took stronger medicine, and it took the big shock of the loss of my marriage to find that medicine, which was Codependents Anonymous, another twelve-step fellowship (see chapter 9, "The Twelve-Step Program of Codependents Anonymous and Me").

Anger was even more resistant than shame because it was an addiction for me. I had to master shame and toxic shame on the path to the core emotions that caused and fed that anger addiction. Chapters 9 through 17 describe this path to discover the core emotions that had to be healed to recover from my anger. Those core emotions are what belong in the blank in equation (1).

As an aside, was my shame an addiction? I certainly had a pathological relationship to shame, and it had life damaging consequences. And it was mood-altering, but the alteration in mood was towards pain, not strength or power or another enjoyable emotional state. Therefore, there was no impulse to practice shame or use it to cover over or hide from an emotionally painful situation. A better feeling emotional state caused by the use of an addictive substance or activity is always the basis of the compulsive use of that substance or activity. Without such a better emotional state, I believe toxic shame is a dysfunctional state. It would be strange for an emotion to be an addiction, so this belief makes sense. As I will show later, shame leads to addictions, but is not itself an addiction.

But the discovery of the path of core emotions leading to my anger was in the future. Only much later could I fill in the blank in last chapter's equation (1) with those emotions. For the present I was busy just discovering, identifying, and understanding toxic shame as a first step in eliminating it. It seemed that all the self-help books stressed toxic shame, and I tried to mend my toxic shame as a path to healing codependence. I had success overcoming toxic shame but not with healing anger.

After I quit drinking, I immediately became a "very grateful alcoholic," as we call ourselves in AA. And why not? In AA meetings several people had said during sharing that an alcoholic will either die an untimely death from the disease, go alcoholically insane, or get sober. And I was one of the lucky ones who got sober. In my final year of drinking I could not figure out why such a guy as me, lucky in so many ways—so well educated and smart, with such a good family and such a great wife and kids—could be a drunk. Why couldn't I simply drink moderately like other people? That last year of drinking I was in hell—I could not get drunk, and I could not get sober. By that I mean booze had quit working. It no longer killed the pain. What pain? The pain of living, which was mostly codependence, a behavior from a dysfunctional emotion: toxic shame. During that last year, although my finances were poor, they were not horrendous, and I still had a good job.

I was performing well in my job, and my kids had no behavior or school problems. But my anger toward my parents, which spilled over to my wife, was not a bit better.

I told myself that everyone had the normal ups and downs of living on life's terms. But I had dealt with that by killing the painful emotions with booze. And now, just before getting sober, liquor had quit working, and all that was left was the pain of living plus the pain of being drunk, of being a practicing alcoholic.

In the first few months of sobriety, my life got better. After six weeks of abstinence the alcohol had finally been eliminated from my system. After that I was no longer physically drunk, and the pain of being continually drunk was gone. But the codependence fed by shame, and the turbulent marriage remained. I was just as angry as ever.

Why did I not just "straighten up and fly right?" If I could have willed myself by logical and right thinking, I am sure I would have. But such thinking was unavailable to me—it was buried under multiple layers of emotional turmoil, all of which *felt* like the only possible reality. To just think myself out was impossible—the emotional fog was too powerful and all consuming.

The simple logic as I heard it in in AA meetings was "Quit drinking, go to meetings, work the steps, and it will get better." But to just wait and not directly address, for my own betterment, the unhealthy emotions I was learning about sounded preposterous to me. I found that I could not think myself to a happy and peaceful life. The others in those rooms talked a lot about emotions, and they seemed happy. I wanted what they had, so I was willing to emulate them and talk about feelings also. But that meant I had to learn what my feelings were and learn to identify them, quantify them, and qualify them. That was what they seemed to be doing, and they promised what I knew I deserved: a better, more pain-free life. So I put my faith in learning about feelings, and I got closer to a part of my inner self, my emotions.

At this early stage of recovery, working directly on anger was not a priority. I had a lot of emotional shame-based problems to work on, and from habit anger still made me feel better. My anger was an addiction, and I was not yet willing to give it up, because, bad as my anger was, I had not hit bottom yet. Hitting bottom is when an addiction gets so bad you realize you must do something about it, and usually that something is to get help. Hitting bottom can only be so simply defined if one does get help and starts recovery; otherwise, apparent bottoms that do not result in getting help can continue in a worsening cascade of bottoms. Perhaps the only bottom that can occur without getting help is death.

This is where the valuable concept of *surrender* enters. It is AA dogma (indeed surrender is the First Step of the twelve). I found that until I surrendered to my anger, that is, to its devastating consequences, there was no hope of my recovery from it. This was exactly parallel to my AA experience with alcohol. Actually, someone else surrendered me; he was wearing a uniform and carried a badge and he took me away in handcuffs in a black and white car. There is no doubt that I was surrendered that day.

As I had listened to others share in AA, I wanted what they had, and my ego was so big that I figured if they did it, so could I. Besides, they promised to show me how they did it. And they meant it. I could see they meant it. They were a bunch of recovering alcoholics talking to other people in the same boat, and I was in that boat with them. I could not help but see that they were genuine and that they cared. So I knew there was such a thing as recovery, and that belief served me well later with my anger, after I was arrested, which was my bottom.

So I had been okay with emotions, and I had worked to learn to recognize and understand my own emotions and those of others. I had learned what my emotions did to me and for me (except anger—that failing of *denial*). I got to know myself, and it was fun. I had actually started to accept myself, and I almost liked myself. I did not make the common mistake of using my disease of alcoholism as an excuse—I had "alcoholic thinking," sure, but it was not innate in me. I knew I could change that thinking, which was only a behavior driven by emotions. I knew I must change, if I was to fully recover. But to change my thinking, I had to heal my emotions. I knew that the unhealthy aspects of my emotions were learned and not innate. I believed that my thinking would change only after I changed (by healing) my emotions. Such attention to my emotions had worked before for all of my problems.

Anger was the exception. Anger was actually my worst and biggest remaining problem, even though I was in denial and could not accept it fully as a problem. In my denial I accepted and kept my anger. I clung to my anger like I had clung to my drinking. Anger became my best and most reliable *friend* replacing alcohol. Anger now seemed to work to ameliorate my painful emotions, and I had no other way to deal with them.

But everything else was getting better following the surrender to each in my alcoholism recovery. I was happy sober. I learned to dance and to make love sober. I drank milk and iced tea with dinner again.

But I kept fighting with my parents and my second wife, and I generally had a chip on my shoulder. My anger was not getting better. But since everything else had, I was optimistic.

Then suddenly, after four and a half years of sobriety, when everything in my life but my anger was improving, the love of my life left me. I came home one day at noon for lunch, eager to see her, but she was gone with all her things. She left only some keys, some credit card receipts, and a dry-cleaning ticket. This event was to lead to my second divorce.

9

THE TWELVE-STEP PROGRAM OF CODEPENDENTS ANONYMOUS AND ME

A few weeks after my separation, I ran into an old friend in an AA meeting. He had had a tumultuous relationship with his girlfriend, who was also in AA, and in those meetings and over coffee afterward I had gotten to hear all about it from both of them. There seemed to be genuine passion between them, but there also seemed to be sensitive feelings and perhaps hostility and anger. I asked him where he had been, and he said he had moved 120 miles to another city as a separation from her.

I told him my wife and I were separated and that I was crushed and in great pain. He must have recognized by the way I told him that the pain was manifesting itself in fear—no, panic—because I could not take care of myself emotionally. That had been her job. I'd tried to do my part, but she had had to take care of me. I would often say, "I'll take care of the outside world; you take care of the inside world," broadly meaning that she was to take care of the housework, meals, shopping, and the four boys as well as care for my emotions, relationships with others, and social life, while I earned a living and fixed the cars and house.

I do not think I expressed those things to my alcoholic friend, at least not in that specific way, because at that point I was incapable of doing so. But somehow he could tell what was going on inside me. He said, "Heck, you're just codependent."

I questioned him because I thought codependency was limited to a long-suffering spouse, family member, or friend of an alcoholic who took on the drunk's problems in a misguided effort to help, like calling in sick for the alcoholic, making excuses, covering and lying for the alcoholic, and pretending that nothing was wrong, so that the family could pretend to lead an ideal TV-sitcom family life. By the new definition he was using, codependency was all those things and more but did not necessarily involve alcoholic drinking.

"No," he said and started to explain. Then he said, "Meet me at this church tomorrow night at 8:00 p.m., and I'll take you to a CoDA meeting."

CoDA's first step is the same *surrender* step as AA's: "We admitted we were powerless over others, that our lives had become unmanageable" (with *others* substituted for *alcohol*). That sure sounded like my problem. As would be confirmed soon, I was a control freak. Those other folks just would not get in step and do what I wanted, so my life was unmanageable. And since I was so bloody wonderful to my wife, wouldn't she be responsible for my emotions and always make me feel good on demand? In a sense I had made my wife my drug of choice.

I had had the same relationship with alcohol. It was responsible for my emotions and supposed to make me feel good on demand. I was addicted to my separated wife as I had been to alcohol; she was supposed to make me feel good on demand. Alcohol did not seem to mind that burden, but she must have. Now I began to realize that she had left me for other good reasons beyond my anger, although I still think my anger was the biggest reason.

I later realized that I had a similar relationship with anger. It was also supposed to make me feel good on demand.

Skipping ahead in the story, CoDA taught me that my life was unmanageable not because of what *they* would not do but because of *my expectations* and *my dependence* on other people fulfilling my needs. That type of thinking speaks to a lot of character flaws, but most important, it is an expectation of the impossible—why in the world should *they* be responsible for my happiness? I was to learn that it was my job to accept others, not change them. I was to love and care about them without getting so involved that I became enmeshed with them and dependent on their actions for my happiness. I was also not to be overly responsible for them, their happiness, or their well-being. They had a right to live their lives, as I had a responsibility to live mine.

Enmeshed is an excellent description for a codependent relationship between two people. Each loses himself or herself in the other, and they become enmeshed because their own selves become indistinguishable from the others'. My self-identity was wrapped up in my wife—what she looked like and acted like, her social presence and other attributes. Because she looked good in many ways, I felt better about myself. Enmeshed persons also tend to adopt the other's persona and traits and use the other person to supply their wants and needs. They do this unknowingly, unbidden by anything other than their own need to control and be needed. By feeling needed they thus feel loved and useful. By such actions for another, even when not asked to, an enmeshed person gains some twisted sense of self-esteem and self-worth, as if self-worth were earned and not inherent.

As for codependence, notice the difference between self-esteem and self-worth. Self-esteem is your opinion of yourself; self-worth is your intrinsic value independent of anyone's opinion.

For the longest time I thought these codependent behaviors of mine, driven by shame, must be causing my anger, so still I clung to the error that healing shame or the behavior of codependence would lessen or heal my anger. I still had not recognized anger as an addiction, and that I was in denial about my anger. That shame-anger connection error persisted throughout my work to heal my codependence and the emotion of shame. But as I indicated in the previous chapter, I was not on the wrong path by working on shame and codependence; the path was just much longer than I had hoped or imagined. There were other emotions that needed attention to cure anger, those missing in equation (1). The way I did my recovery, they naturally came only after I had toxic shame and codependence under control.

In CoDA and its principles I thought I had found the answer to my problems of pain and manageability in my life, although I did not focus at all on anger. Codependence was another revelation going even further beyond Bradshaw's precepts about the family. Like all my recovery efforts to date, if I thought of anger at all, I assumed that the solutions to anger would fall out of the process or that I would stumble onto the specific solution in time. Looking back, I never talked about my anger in any meetings as a core problem, and I think it was because of shame of it—that is, my embarrassment that I had so little self-control. Another reason was denial—I never talked about my anger in meetings or in therapy. Anger was not my problem, I believed; it was my solution. And I was unwilling to give that solution up. It gave me power and control when I felt powerless. Before getting sober, I considered alcohol my solution, and not my problem.

I now realize that my embarrassment over my anger, while appropriate, meant that I thought I could control my anger. But unknown to me at that time, anger was an addiction like my addiction to alcohol. While I was practicing either addiction, I had no control over them. I could not drink in moderation, because it was an addiction. And my anger was usually out of control. Both addictions required, for me, an emotional change that led to the desired behavioral change.

If I thought in terms of lack of self-control, I was thinking of my anger as bad behavior. Today my view is that my anger was an addiction, or sick behavior. There is a big psychological improvement in thinking of myself as a sick person trying to get well rather than a bad person trying to act better. Bad is so much harder to fix than illness.

Power and control were all-important to me even as I worked through my codependence. I was afflicted, I now know, by a sense of helplessness and hopelessness from a core of pain. Helplessness and hopelessness are some of the extreme effects of pain I listed in chapter 5, "Emotions." I assumed anger was lack of self-control, but as I used it, it was a tool to establish control. I think such a need and fixation on control and power over others is one of the more common characteristics of a codependent person. I worked hard to recover from my codependence, and I fooled myself into thinking that a cure for anger would follow. The faultiness of this reasoning is that not all codependents are angry.

Manipulation is another control strategy a codependent may use, and I was no different. If that failed, I was prone to resorting to anger. The decisions to resort to either manipulation or anger were not conscious decisions. They were habitual behaviors that I found worked to make me feel more comfortable, as did alcohol for a long time. The fact that neither alcohol nor anger worked on the actual problem was not nearly as important as the good feelings I got from them, as each masked the bad feelings of the actual problem.

Also at this period I thought anger was a self-control problem because all the therapists treated my general behavior as a self-control problem, and anger was an outstanding quality of my behavior. The messages they gave me was, if I could only control myself (count to ten, think it through, replace those thoughts that led up to exploding with alternate thoughts and plans, or otherwise use more-rational thinking), I would not get so angry. I will go into the type of therapy that teaches rational control of emotions in chapter 10, "Rational Control of Emotions." There is also information on this issue in Appendix II.

Except for my anger, I was making great progress in CoDA on my low self-esteem and compensating arrogance and was gaining healthy confidence as opposed to arrogance. I definitely fit the five CoDA patterns, as listed below. From the full CoDA listing of characteristics of these patterns, I've listed the characteristics that apply most to me and their impact on my anger.

+ *Denial:* I had trouble identifying what I was feeling and minimized my feelings, often substituting one feeling for another. My anger was substituted for my fear or for my pain, for example.
+ *Low self-esteem:* I thought I was never good enough; I was worth less or inadequate in a way that could not be fixed. At the same time I compensated by feeling and acting superior. The low self-esteem was painful and anger provoking, and the arrogance gave me permission to get angry.
+ *Control:* I tried to control what others thought or did. I had to feel needed to have a relationship and expected others to take care of my needs. Anger fit right in with being a control freak.
+ *Avoidance:* I judged others harshly if they did not agree with me and expressed anger toward them when other behaviors would have been more appropriate.

Like Bradshaw's delineation of family problems and, by extension, society's problems, CoDA looked exactly like the perfect description of my personal problems, and it was, if I was accurate in including anger as a trait to be changed. It was easy to extrapolate such personal problems to have their origin in my family, so it fit right in with *Bradshaw on: the Family.* The recognition of my codependence fit right in with my growing sense of how I had been living my life, and CoDA showed me how to change it for the better. This period of recognition is when I started to assume that my anger, which was pervasive in my life, was caused by my codependence, which was caused by toxic shame. However, the connection between my shame and anger was more complex, and healing the toxic shame did not relieve my anger.

I started going to two or three CoDA meetings a week. I also went to at least one AA meeting a week, even though I had been sober five years and was in no apparent danger of drinking again; I had no drinking thoughts or despair that drinking would help in any way. But I knew that I was an alcoholic and that I could drink again, even with no outward warning. But CoDA became my primary program for a time because it seemed to be the most critical current problem. I clearly was not focused on anger as a problem, because I did not see the subtle effects of codependence that led to anger. I was still in ignorance about the missing emotions in equation (1).

I did not discuss CoDA principles in AA meetings, because I feared outright ostracization. I have always taken the position that I have no business bringing the subject of codependence up to someone else, unless they have asked me privately about a problem they are having and it seems germane. I guard against being controlling, and I will not discuss codependence with an alkie if his sobriety is shaky. Not to minimize the difficulty of getting and staying sober, but recovering from alcohol compared to codependence, for me, was like comparing high school to a postdoctoral fellowship. Codependence was really, really difficult for me because the patterns of codependence *in moderation* are so socially valued and necessary in society. The line between excessive use of these patterns (codependence) and friendly, loving, and caring use of them (healthiness) is broad and blurred. Furthermore, in a committed or other important relationship, dysfunctional codependence (unhealthy reliance on another) can merge into interdependence (mutual and presumably fair reliance on another). Those healthy and fine lines are hard to discern and to maintain, especially if a person did not grow up in a family where those were the norms.

So I went to CoDA meetings. I shared at every meeting, and I paid attention. I identified with how others described themselves and their dysfunctional behaviors and thinking. I called men I met in meetings and talked and listened to them. I had the poor judgment to occasionally call women in the program as well. I did it for female companionship and sympathy and because I had the misguided need for a relationship with a woman, even though I was incapable of defining what a healthy or functional relationship was. So now there was a different dimension to the problem of getting a girl-friend—now I could identify both the woman's flaws and my own in relation to my neediness for just any woman! I had a yardstick of CoDA symptoms to gauge us both by, and neither of us looked attractive to the other. The reason I saw no healthy and attractive ladies was undoubtedly not because they were not there but because I could not recognize them, or because they simply did not appeal to me. I was so sick I could not relate to women with a healthy outlook. The solution was to not date or get into a relationship until I had recovered quite a bit, but this seemed very unattractive.

As for the men, I opened up to them during these phone calls, and I listened to them patiently. But it was hard to listen. After a few weeks of CoDA meetings and calls, I hung up at the end of one call, and it hit me that I was willing to listen to other men only because I wanted them to listen to me. That was the price I would pay, and that manipulation was pure codependence.

This entire period was a painful time of my life. Being able to see and identify the characteristics of codependence within me was painful, and I did not yet have the abilities to escape that pain. The recognition of the losses in my life came crashing down upon me, and I had no escape from them except to struggle on and walk or crawl through them.

Recovery from codependence is, in my opinion, very much more difficult than recovery from alcoholism, or at least it was for me. Alcoholism is easy in the sense that it is obvious when you have repercussions where the problem is. For example, if you have an auto accident, you get arrested and thrown in the drunk tank, or you miss work because of hangovers, it is easy to see where the problem is. With codependence, it is much more difficult to recognize CoDA patterns as problems. In moderation, all those patterns are admirable, loving, caring qualities. Well, I suppose drinking in moderation is okay and maybe even admirable, but the difference between moderate and severe drinking is usually clear. It is hard to wreck your car while drunk and make it appear admirable. Even those mysterious scratches and bent bumpers I would see the next day were not admirable. Codependence is such an insidious and pervasive disease that it is very hard to recognize it and to recover from it.

Even after some CoDA experience, toxic shame remained the primary symptom that I thought needed treating. With CoDA, as with the principles in *Bradshaw on: the Family*, I was working on my inner self. And my hope was lurking still that an answer to my anger would emerge from the work on my inner self. I relate the specific things I did to combat my codependence in chapter 11, "Pia Mellody."

10

RATIONAL CONTROL OF EMOTIONS—DID IT WORK FOR ME?

Genuine feelings cannot be produced, nor can they be
eradicated. We can only repress them, delude ourselves,
and deceive our bodies. The body sticks to the facts.
—Alice Miller

You can't heal what you can't feel.
— Recovery axiom in many books and twelve-step programs

Up to this point in my life, before and through my discovery and study of Bradshaw and through my discovery of codependence and CoDA, I had been in therapy with at least three therapists. I went in joint sessions with my wife until she left me, and then I had sessions alone. She was my source of self-esteem and happiness, and I had lost her. I could not provide those necessary commodities for myself. Besides this codependence, I was an angry man.

As I look back, it seems that all those therapists tried to fix my behavior and my emotions by channeling my thinking to both repower me away from the low self-esteem thinking and to defuse the angry thoughts I had. If I could just learn to think about events in a healthy manner, as those therapists seemed to believe and attempted to help me do, I would act and feel better.

That is the subject of this chapter. This discussion interrupts the flow of my recovery, but it is important to grasp how my therapists honestly tried to help me and to consider how well it worked for me.

I saw the same therapist steadily and off and on for about three years before and after my second wife left me. He helped me a lot and was a great source of support in adverse times, but I never made much progress with my codependence or anger. I faithfully attended sessions, usually two hours a week, and I sincerely tried to learn new thinking methods. In fact I did learn a lot of new thinking, but even with much more healthy thinking, I still made only marginal progress if any. Finally, perhaps out of desperation, he gave me *A New Guide to Rational Living* by Albert Ellis and Robert A. Harper, both PhDs.[1] I still have the book, which he inscribed to me on June 12, 1990. The book presents itself as a self-help book using rational emotive therapy (RET). The RET premise is that people do *not* "get *made* disturbed by early influence,"[2] and therefore they do *not*

> have to get restructured or reconditioned by an outside, parentlike therapist who somehow forces them into new patterns of behaving. It follows, instead, the humanistic, educative model which asserts that people, even in their early lives have a great many more *choices* than they tend to recognize; that most of their "conditioning" actually consists of *self*-conditioning; and that a therapist, a teacher, or even a book can help them see much more clearly their range of alternatives and thereby to *choose* to reeducate and retrain themselves so that they surrender most of their serious self-*created* emotional difficulties.[3]

In other words, no one else, including your parents, did it to you; you do it to yourself. Therefore, you can be taught how to quit doing it. In my personal experience through thirty-two years of therapy and recovery, it did not work that way for me. I was unable to "surrender most of my self-*created* emotional difficulties." This was either because they were not self-created or I did not believe them to be self-created.

Ellis and Harper continue with laudatory comments on their method, which I am sure in many cases is fully justified:

> People *tell themselves* various sane and crazy things. Their beliefs, attitudes, opinions, and philosophies largely (though hardly exclusively) take the form of *internalized sentences* or *self-talk*. Consequently, one of the most powerful and elegant modalities they can use to change themselves, and particularly to modify their self-defeating emotions and sabotaging behaviors, consists of their clearly seeing, understanding, disputing, altering, and acting against their internal verbalizations.[4]

I take issue with the claim that people's beliefs and so on "take the form of *internalized sentences* or *self-talk*." This may be true of beliefs and so on that are formed when a person is verbally mature—that is, after he or she learns to talk—but what of attitudes and so on that were formed in very early life. The first quote I provided of Ellis and Harper does say "even in their early lives." Are we to believe people can adapt attitudes and beliefs prior to being verbal and then put those memories into verbal sentences?

They then give a few examples of revised semantics to replace such internalized sentences:

> When clients state ... "I must work harder at the office," or "I *should not* hate my mate," we frequently interrupt them with: "You mean, "It *would prove better* if you worked harder at the office," or "You *preferably* should not hate your mate." [*sic*: quotation marks][5]

They continue with over a full page of such examples. *Notably, all are situations that adults would find themselves in and that adults would have difficulty tracing back to childhood origins.* The situations have to do with working, worrying, participating in social affairs, losing a job, being rejected, acting incompetently, treating others badly, behaving immorally and badly, acting animal like, being poor at arithmetic, racial stereotyping or being un-American, needing love, desiring a high standard of living, thinking rationally, stealing, having anxiety, being angry, and more. It is striking that none of these are primary concerns of children (except being rejected and not being loved). These are adult problems encountered in an adult world. Those few that do apply to children, like treating others badly and being angry, are at times normal behaviors for children. These behaviors are serious problems primarily in adulthood.

I can give only one example in my case where a rational change in thinking about an emotional problem made a positive difference. I was feeling abandoned by my girlfriend because I had inappropriately misjudged an out of town party we were supposed going to as only a party. But it turned out to be a task of her job, and she was busy working all evening. I felt childishly hurt and abandoned, and she reacted intensely to my immature behavior. I went alone to see our therapist about my extreme depression and sadness over these feelings. My down mood was a blatant example of an immature reaction to a rather ordinary disappointment. Near the end of the session the therapist told me in the best rational-therapy manner that I should try to identify the self-talk when these depressive events started. I said, "Oh, I know exactly what I tell myself: 'Nobody loves me; nobody cares.' And I say it over and over."

The relationship died, but that was the last such shame-pain spiral I ever had to go into. I could always stop them after that by saying to myself, "Well, I love me, and God loves me, and I care, and God cares, and that is enough at this moment. It does not matter at this moment that it feels like nobody loves me or cares." That was an affirmation (a rational method) that I was finally able to apply to an emotional reexperiencing of childhood emotions, but it took years for me to arrive at that intense emotional moment when a caring professional had reminded me, in effect, to apply the rational truth which I was able to accept only after years of work on my codependence, that is my emotions.

Learning and the ability to apply the rational thinking solution to shame-pain spirals was extremely valuable. But I missed the important role of pain and apparent loss in the creation of such spirals, and that was even more important to my anger. This whole episode hit me so (irrationally) hard, that even my old friend, anger, was unavailable to help me; I went right to helplessness and depression, which I call a shame-pain spiral.

More important to this event was that the mantra "Nobody loves me; nobody cares" had been with me for as long as I could remember, and I mean since early childhood. I learned that self-talk from the shame of my childhood abuse, which started before I could talk or reason rationally (about eight years old, generally). My episodic depression was an adult emotional situation only on the surface. Those feelings of not being loved and of being abandoned and neglected, although far, far more intense than they should have been for a fifty-something-year-old man, were a reenactment of feelings I occasionally had had all my life in roughly similar situations. The mantra, "Nobody loves me; nobody cares," was verbalized after I started to feel that way. It was in fact a verbalization of unresolved childhood feelings that still affected me in adulthood—I was acting as an *adult child*. (I first came across this term in Pia Mellody's book *Facing Codependence*, which I will discuss in detail in chapters 11 and 12, "Pia Mellody" and "Pia Mellody's Theory Summarized.")

So I do believe that such RET-like educative actions can work and that they work by the sufferer adopting a revised statement that he or she believes. In the case I just cited, I had spent years working on my codependence and healing toxic shame and its effects on me prior to this shame-pain spiral event. When I walked out of that therapist's office, and it suddenly occurred to me to tell myself that I loved myself and that God loved me, it was the culmination of years of work in that direction. Before this time I had heard this affirmation about self-love and God's love and had even used it for years to little effect. The therapist's suggestion was merely the trigger to use the affirmation, and. I finally took it up and wholly owned it finally at that moment *because I was in pain and I was ready right then*. Without the previous laborious work of reading, studying, praying, meditating, reciting affirmations, attending meetings and programs, and living the situation of extreme pain, I would never have been able to apply the positive affirmation to replace the negative self-talk as the therapist suggested. And without years of work on codependence and shame issues, I would not have been ready to do so, because I would not have been able to even consider loving myself. Prior to my emotional shame work, I was loathsome to myself, and if asked, I would have answered that God probably felt the same toward me.

I think that this is the failing of rational-therapy techniques. It took far more for me than a therapist, no matter how respected or revered, to suggest with one or two sentences that I change my thinking and for that to make a difference. It is too much to expect a major change from a one or two hour session once a week after thirty to sixty years of my hearing and *living* internally the opposing negative message, *which I picked up as a nonrational and perhaps nonverbal child. When it comes to childhood attitudes preserved in adulthood*, I have always had to come to a place through intense and long emotional work where I believe for myself the new thinking. Then and only then can such suggestive therapy take hold in my mind. It is a case of Wayne Dyers's "You'll see it when you believe it." (See chapter 15, "Recovery Junkie.")

In Appendix IV I list my favorite quotes about the perennial wisdom of the power of the mind that goes back at least to Epicurus (341–270 BC). That power does not work in me by just hearing and then dumbly repeating even excellent advice. I have to sincerely believe at the deepest cellular level, and then great things can come to pass. It might be wonderful if a totally rational authority could reprogram me in just a few minutes or sessions (although I doubt such a 1984 world would be wonderful), but as a therapy client, I am not a computer or machine. I am a human being, with valuable emotional characteristics, and those emotional characteristics have evolved to protect and serve me. And that protection is often in the form of blocking information that is new and generally assumed, due to decades of belief in the opposite, to be harmful, no matter how erroneous that assumption is. It has been my experience that when emotions do go astray, for example as a result of childhood abuse, they are just as powerful in forming negative self-talk, and overcoming them is a formidable task. I have not found such engrained self-talk so easy to overcome as these RET authors assert or such therapy apparently assumes.

Furthermore, I cannot recall one other instance in my life of such a grand epiphany that surmounted such a torturous belief being triggered or learned from *new and sudden* rational thinking. But the party disappointment was vastly overblown emotionally by the adult me, and I think it was because I often felt abandoned and profoundly alone and deserted as a child and as I did at that party.

Years later In thinking of this party event, and much further along in my recovery, I am amazed at the gravity and force this rather trivial disappointment had on me. I almost want to cry out, "Grow up!" And then I remember with compassion, at that moment of epiphany growing up is exactly what I was doing.

I had a lot of childhood trauma that led to pain and despair, and in adulthood my resultant negative emotions that remained from those events always remained steadfastly resistant to logical or rational change. Goofy as those childhood ideas were, they were my reality; I knew no other reality in childhood, and I carried that reality into adulthood. My shame-pain spiral over the misunderstood party harkened back to my abandoned inner child, abandoned by spankings and neglect that made me feel profoundly unloved and uncared for, and I reacted like a child who was being so neglected again. The sudden cure came only after years of working on just that issue of abandonment and desertion, and it came through a conscious adaption of many affirmations I had used over the years during my recovery from low self-esteem. The solution to my low self-esteem is *to be my own parent*, that is, to grow emotionally to supply my own emotional needs. This is exactly what all the books say, and I finally started doing it with that epiphany.

Over the years I had many different affirmations for the problem—"I am enough," "I will never abandon me," and so on. I often wrote those affirmations on three-inch square sticky notes and taped over them with clear packing tape. I would carry them in my shirt pocket and take them out to review them often as the day progressed. For days at a time I would say them to myself in an attempt to retrace the neural pathways of my mind. The affirmation "I love me, and God loves me, and that is enough" was one I had often used. The therapist just reminded me of that affirmation in this exact situation of a shame-pain spiral, and in a crisis (in my adult-child mind) that affirmation finally became my truth and not just a saying. The affirmation was readily available when needed due to years of work on such affirmations. Its good effect was not instant and new to me when a therapist suggested it. In fact the therapist only suggested I develop alternate thinking after I told her exactly what my flawed thinking was. It was easy to adopt the better thoughts I had already developed and tried to make my reality for years previously, probably because I was in such pain and stress.

Therefore, I believe that I as a patient suffered from self-talk and that harmful behavior resulting from that self-talk could be corrected by changing the damaging thinking to creative and healthful thinking. But I disagree that my responsibility in learning that self-talk was mine alone, since it went back to childhood. However, I accept the responsibility to recognize and discard such old negative self-talk learned in childhood now that I am an adult. But it is not as quick and easy as presented in the RET book.

The self-talk that I adopted at a very young age, before I developed my rational mind, was very hard to change; at least I found it so. In fact, much of my childhood self-talk became self-talk only when I learned to talk, so young was I when much of the abuse happened! That means the self-talk became such from self-images, impressions, emotions, odors, sounds, and body feelings. So it is understandable that I am poor at changing this self-talk by better rational thinking which is advised to be done in words even when it was learned before I had words.

This self-analysis is *not* to say that I think psychotherapy is useless or to be avoided. Quite the opposite is true. It was very useful as one of the many ways I prepared myself to change my thinking and indeed gave me useful insight about what healthy thinking really was. That knowledge did me a lot of good, but when the harmful self-talk originated in childhood, in order to finally achieve fully healthy behavior and thinking in adulthood, I had to reexperience my emotions as an adult and then make the proper adjustment. Changing the thinking alone never worked for me.

Up to this point in the discussion I have written this from the point of view of what I wanted out of therapy and my recovery: recovery as complete and total as possible. Obviously, as with any human endeavor, perfection is not a viable goal, but, darn it, I wanted to be well. I wanted to "just step out easily," as I heard it put once on an AA tape. I wanted to be comfortable, to like other people, and for them to like me, because I was a likable guy. I knew I was going through life in constant stress and tension, pretty much always on edge, as if I did not fit in and never would. And I was extremely unsatisfied to be this way. To be *better* or *nearly* well was not enough. I wanted to be *well*.

It occurred to me a few days before I wrote this that the goal of self-improvement for many may not always be to be *well* or even *very well*. Perhaps some just want or need to be *well enough*, and the definition of that is an individual thing. Likewise, some people's goals for anger recovery may not be as high as mine; some may want to just be somewhat better, so that they are not always skirting trouble and tension. I wanted the space between anger, as I lived it, and freedom from anger and tension to be so wide that it was hardly ever a problem, so wide that whenever I got angry, I could *easily* rein myself in without artificial or rational, conscious exercises to block and lessen my episodes. I wanted my anger gone or very nearly so!

Basically then I wanted the anger *and its root causes* to be banished from my life. I did not want to rid myself of the memories of it or the causes, but I wanted to eliminate it as a determining factor in my behavior. I wanted to expunge toxic anger, or rage, as differentiated from usual healthy anger, from my life. To get to this point, I am convinced that I had to discover and then expunge the causes of my anger; otherwise those causes would always sabotage me, since I clearly carried them with me in my subconscious.

If someone does not want to go to this trouble and is content with consciously applying rational tricks to lessen the impact of inflaming or vexing incidents, and if such half measures, as I judge them to be for me, are sufficient to reach his or her comfort level or that of society, then perhaps that person will find such measures adequate.

We all get to choose. My choice was the whole enchilada.

Therefore, I think I know why my behaviors were so resistant to treatment: (1) anger was my friend, as I have established, so I was not ready to give it up, and (2) I was not sufficiently motivated by need for rational thought to have much effect, so, for both reasons, I never really gave such methods a chance. But most of all, I wanted more than mere "control" of my anger; I wanted it gone, or at least as gone as possible.

I went to see several more therapists through the years with wives and girlfriends to try to calm the waters of turbulent relationships, and I think that all those therapists used some form of rational retraining, informing, or leading to help me retrain my thinking. Maybe I was just too dumb or stubborn, but it never worked, except that one time with the depressive spiral, after I had readied myself with lots of emotional and spiritual work.

It seems the problems for which I sought help in therapy were outside the purview of rationality, at least for the elimination of, as opposed to control of, toxic anger. I now know that all my problems that this book deals with were originally childhood problems. And for the most part they probably first became problems before I was rational, that is, at or before six to eight years old. Because of this, it may have been unreasonable to expect that rational thought could change what had never been rational.

I seem to be able to deal effectively with all the problems I have *that developed in adult life*. I do have other problems, adult problems, like everyone, but I can handle them in a rational, measured, and effective way. I have no complaints there.

But it remains: my problems I discuss in this book had their origins in childhood, and those origins were emotional in nature. That is to say those origins were a damaging or distorting of my healthy and normal childhood emotions. I made great advances in healing these emotional problems through the help of many different therapists and books, and there was some help and comfort in the rational ideas offered. But at no time did a rational, non-emotional solution or recommendation alone lead to a breakthrough, major or minor, in my emotional health. Therefore, little help was realized in my anger through rational therapy.

John Bradshaw came to much the same conclusion about the power of inner child work in his book *Homecoming: Reclaiming and Championing Your Inner Child*. He says of the workshop on inner child work he founded, "The workshop has convinced me that the inner child work is the quickest and most powerful way to effect therapeutic change in people. This almost-immediate effect continues to amaze me."[6] He then notes how skeptical he was about such a quick fix but details how this method seemed to begin a process of lasting transformation and how participants in his workshop wrote to tell him how much it had changed their lives for the better. Happy for the good results but confused about how they had happened, he formed a sense about how and why this method worked. Bradshaw then goes into detail about how ego defenses work, which is by enlisting the rational neocortex to marshal-thinking types of defenses: "rationalizing, analyzing, … and minimizing."[7] Quoting R. L. Isaacson, he says that the gating system of the neocortex functions "to overcome the habits and memories of the past … the neocortex is profoundly concerned with suppressing the past."[8] Bradshaw says,

So the ego defenses bypass the tension and pain, but the tension and pain remain. They are registered subcortically as an imbalance, an aborted action sequence awaiting release and integration. The energy of the original trauma remains like an electrical storm that reverberates tension throughout the biological system. People with seemingly rational adult lives may continue to live *stormy emotional lives*. Their storms continue because their original pain is unresolved.[9]

Bradshaw continues under the immediately following heading "Original Pain Work,"

Original pain work involves actually experiencing the original repressed feelings. I call it the uncovery process. *It is the only thing that will bring about "second-order change," the kind of deep change that truly resolves feelings* [emphasis added]. In first-order change, you change one compulsion from another compulsion. In second-order change you stop being compulsive. That was what I needed to heal my compulsivity. I acted out compulsively because my lonely, wounded inner child had never discharged his original distress. I went to 12 Step programs and controlled my alcoholism, but I kept acting out. I stayed in my head as a professor, theologian and therapist, but I kept acting out. I read every new book I could get my hands on, and I discussed my problems in therapy, but I kept acting out. I pursued higher consciousness; learned the ways of the ancient shamans; learned energy healing; studied *A Course in Miracles*; meditated and prayed (sometimes for hours), but I kept acting out. I was compulsive even about higher consciousness. What I didn't know was that I needed to embrace my heartbroken little boy's loneliness and unresolved grief about his lost father, his lost family, and his lost childhood.

I had to embrace my original pain. This is the legitimate suffering Carl Jung spoke about.[10]

Bradshaw clearly believes that only a deep emotional recovery can heal repressed feelings, and such feelings were the basis of my anger (from losses to pain to anger). The rest of the book presents a self-help program that is consistent with his workshop.

I did not do all the exercises in Bradshaw's book. Indeed, I only read it closely when I was researching this book. If I had, I believe I may have saved myself a lot of trouble and gotten over my anger much sooner, even though *Homecoming's* focus is toxic shame, not anger. I definitely recommend the whole book and its program.

Why did I not do the program when I first got the book and save myself that grief? Because at that time I had not reached my bottom; I had not been arrested and had not gone to jail. And anger was still my friend and source of power and relief over the feelings of helplessness and pain I had carried since my childhood. I was in denial. My life was tolerable—not great but good enough that I was able to deny that I had a problem. In short I was not ready. When I reread *Homecoming* thoroughly, I discovered that I had done my own form of "original pain" work.

The above quoted passage gave me comfort when I finally read it, because even John Bradshaw had to go through the same process I did. At times, I had to resist beating myself up emotionally for not getting to it sooner. Like Bradshaw, I went to AA, CoDA, ACA, and SA (Adult Children of Alcoholics and Sex Anonymous), and they controlled my addictions but could not heal my wounded emotions, which they, of course, were not meant to do. And like Bradshaw, I was in my head (extremely rational) as a physicist, mathematician, and businessman. One time my sponsor in AA chided me, "One day you are going to walk in and tell me you have a formula for this whole sobriety deal." I also read every book I could and spent hundreds of hours in therapy *talking* about my problems. I journaled and worked my steps numerous times. I studied, prayed, meditated, drummed, Sufi danced, sang devotional songs, did tai chi, went to many other spiritual activities, and studied *A Course in Miracles*[11] while pursuing higher consciousness. And finally a therapist led me to the last piece, which was to embrace my little boy's unresolved grief, my pain about my losses. To heal I had to embrace my original pain. Therefore, I definitely recommend *Homecoming: Reclaiming and Championing Your Inner Child* as a source to work on original pain. And I recommend you read further in this book to see exactly how I did my deep emotional work.

The epigraph of this chapter by Alice Miller, legendary exposer of childhood abuse and formerly a Freudian psychoanalyst is in direct conflict with the ideas of Doctors Ellis and Harper. Because of my experience of recovery by reexperiencing my feelings, the concurrent failure of rational behavior therapies, and my body memories, I have to side with Miller.

Miller also said, "The results of any traumatic experience, such as abuse, can only be resolved by experiencing, articulating, and judging every facet of the original experience within a process of careful therapeutic disclosure."[12] By therapeutic disclosure Miller means a reliable and sympathetic person to listen interestedly to your recollections of childhood abuse, which in the beginning probably will not sound real. But with the hearing of those disclosures they take on reality and gain meaning and become understandable; they become therapeutic. Much of the therapeutic disclosure I did was in journaling, meditating, and talking at great length with other knowledgeable and understanding fellow recovery travelers as well as in therapy, hospitals, and formal programs. Miller also said, "It is possible to resolve childhood repression safely and without confusion—something that has always been disputed by the most respected schools of thought."[13]

Another influential and standard book in the recovery world is Charles Whitfield's *Healing the Child Within: Discovery and Recovery for Adult Children of Dysfunctional Families.* This 1987 book was my formal introduction to the *inner child* concept, and it is still in print and being sold to victims of child abuse who have remained wounded into adulthood by their upbringing. Dr. Whitfield describes the *child within* as "the part of us that is ultimately alive, energetic, creative and fulfilled."[14] It is a person's *true self* as differentiated from a person's *false self* that the abuse creates through the child's adaption to the dysfunction and chaos of his or her upbringing. Whitfield advocates integrating this true self into awareness as a healing process. The first step is discovering the true self, identifying your personal needs, and then practicing to supply them yourself as the only adult capable of doing so on a full-time basis. This involves identifying and reexperiencing the pain of childhood losses. This *grieving* of losses and pain is precisely what Bradshaw, Miller, and I advocate as a healing process. It is precisely what I did. And I add my doubt that the healing process can be done with rational intervention alone—at least I could not.

Whitfield also wrote the excellent companion workbook *A Gift to Myself*.[15] In it he covers many details of the gift of recovery: the gift of your true self to yourself. He notes that no one can give us this gift—we have to do it for ourselves. He talks about needs and who it is safe to talk to, about determining the truth of our childhoods, about rigid rules we may have been raised under, and about feelings, yes, emotions. And he says we must reexperience the losses and pain to grieve them properly.

Another workbook with the same theme of grieving is *The Inner Child Workbook* by Cathryn L. Taylor.[16] She points out that we have many children within, one for each of the many stages of life: infant, toddler, young child, grade-school child, and more up to the young inner adult. For a variety of reasons, most children from dysfunctional families do not experience proper, healthy maturation steps. This lack results in unmet needs and losses and pain—the child grows up emotionally handicapped. Taylor's book addresses these different needs of each age. This is another *reparenting* book, where adults learn to become their own parents to care for themselves emotionally.

The common theme of all these books, and of all inner-child work, is *emotional*. I have found no authority on recovery from childhood issues that says you can rationally talk yourself to adult emotional health, that is, *functional* health.

CONSISTENCY

As is detailed in the previous section, I have found that, for me, rationally based therapies that concentrate on classification and identification of events and feelings, at least the rational description of feelings, with the goal of healing those painful feelings by more-constructive thinking about myself and present events has been of little use in helping me with both my codependence and anger. These therapies may lessen the intensity of these emotions to where they are socially acceptable and less trouble, but I personally found that inadequate. I wanted such toxic feelings to be ejected and banished from my life without being repressed or otherwise stuffed into my unconscious, where they could arise anew in other forms. The sense of my self and my place in the world—which seems to be the result of my emotional reactions to events in my life, particularly my childhood trauma—was entirely resistant to attempts at reorganizing and adopting more-helpful rational thinking. The suppressed emotions that caused that thinking and that I had always carried were simply too powerful. Sooner or later these suppressed emotions always found a destructive way to reveal themselves and to treacherously sabotage me.

I do not deny the power of the mind. In fact, due to my pioneer parents and the can-do attitude they instilled in me, I really do believe that all things are possible *if you believe you can do them.* This is a belief inspired and based upon New Thought philosophy and faith that resonates with my family background. (New Thought as a philosophy or religion is a movement that began in the 19th century, but the central idea of New Thought is ancient: *believing makes it possible.*) That belief has resulted in remarkable accomplishments that should have not been possible for me. The problem is that sometimes I have been unable to believe I can do a thing, and then surely I cannot do it. The can't-do power of the mind is just as powerful as the can-do power. As a record of notable people who believed in this power of the mind, this positive thinking—no, *positive knowing*—see Appendix III, "Mind."

So the question is one of consistency. Why wouldn't the mind with its creative power be useful to change my thinking and heal my emotions? After all, if the debilitating feelings of low self-esteem and personal boundary problems, as well as most of the other negative thoughts and feelings that are symptoms of codependence and of anger, are just a distortion of a functional world outlook and one's place in that world, why shouldn't the mind be able to heal one's thinking and alleviate the painful effects of trauma, which I claim lead to codependence and a lot of anger?

The answer is that there are other ways of knowing something than knowing it mentally, or rationally. I have found that there are three ways of our being human. There is the rational way, which developed in us last; the emotional way; and then the most fundamental, even cellular way of being: body feelings, or body memories. Body feelings may have developed in us first.

But again, if the rational mind is a later development than the emotional mind and much later than the ability to store memories as body feelings, perhaps it should be useful in creating or recreating our reality, by which I mean our concept of ourselves in the world. But my experience comes down firmly on the side of the rational mind's *inability* to heal emotions, even when the rational mind has relearned the thoughts and attitudes that lead to the symptoms.

I first describe body feelings that I had in chapter 15, "Recovery Junkie," as I relate my experience reading Janet Woititz's *Adult Children of Alcoholics*. I will further discuss body feelings and how to use them in chapter 22, "A Simple Course of Treatment," but for now, I will say that I have had to overcome and utilize body feelings in my recovery. There can be only two places of origin for my body feelings: being born with them—that seems unlikely, even hokey or supernatural—or learning them at a very young age, before I could talk, understand, and reason and perhaps before I could even fully perceive all input. Yet there was knowledge or at least information there, memories that I could feel and had to overcome to recover. And for all I know, they provide good knowledge necessary to function, like balance, intuition, how to see and hear, and so on. But who is to say there are no painful and fearful ones lurking within?

The consistency question is then, if I believe the mind can work wonders in extending our abilities beyond what we formerly believed we could do, what do I have against rational-therapy methods, and why did they fail me as a recovery method? The answer for me is that there are some memories, some knowledge, beyond the mind that we carry in our bodies, and if harmful and dysfunctional, these irrational, emotional body memories are not accessible to change by logical, talking-in-sentences means. Before you pooh-pooh this, recall an instance where some sight or sound or recollection tingled you deep in your body, right down to your bones, to your very being, just a momentary sensation of recognition of some feeling or vague event in the far past. I am sure you have had such an occurrence. Have you every turned a corner in late dusk and nearly stepped on a garden hose and jumped back shaken to your core thinking it was a snake? The series of body-memory jolts I had reading Janet Woititz's *Adult Children of Alcoholics* absolutely convinces me of this idea. (See chapter 15, "Recovery Junkie," Janet Woititz.)

I am convinced that for deeply held emotional feelings, similar to so-called emotional intelligence[17] those emotional memories always are more powerful than rational thinking in determining our behavior. This is a strong statement, but in addition it should be considered that the emotional memories I am talking about were formed in our systems before we were rational. With this in mind, it is little wonder that rational thinking, made of words forming rational sentences, would be of little use in changing those old behaviors. Furthermore, the reinforcement of those early childhood behaviors from emotional memories later in life is just that, a *reinforcement* of old emotional memories, not new rational memories.[18]

For example, the extreme distress and debilitation I experienced after the love of my life left me was, to me, a reenactment and reinforcement of the extreme losses I felt when my mother punished me and left me alone in the bathroom with the door closed because "Nobody wants to hear you cry." Indeed crying was useless, even if my father was home. As a very small child it was demonstrated abundantly to me that I was inadequate as a human being; my body was useless and of no value, and my emotions and paroxysms of pain and anguish were of no interest or concern to anyone. In fact, it seemed that others were totally disinterested in my suffering. As an adult, when the love of my life left me, I *felt* abandoned, just as I had felt in that bathroom—alone, helpless, and terrified of my lack of value due to having been discarded to perish, for every very small child knows intuitively that without protectors and providers he or she will perish.

Empirically I have found that the rational approach to healing emotions was useless for me, but then it must be remembered that I wanted it all. Stronger medicine was required to be truly well. I found I had to fight fire with fire. I had to heal harmful emotions with other emotions.

---

1   Albert Ellis and Robert A. Harper, *A New Guide to Rational Living* (North Hollywood, CA: Melvin Powers Wilshire, 1975).

2   Ibid., x.

3   Ibid.

4   Ibid.

5   Ibid., xi.

6   John Bradshaw, *Homecoming: Reclaiming and Championing Your Inner Child* (New York: Bantam Books, 1992), xii.

7   Ibid., 75.

8   Ibid.

9   Ibid.

10   Ibid., 75–76. Dr. Carl Jung's famous quote is "Neurosis is always a substitute for legitimate suffering."

11   *A Course in Miracles: Combined Volume* (Glen Ellen, CA: Foundation for Inner Peace, 1992).

12   "Alice Miller Quotes," BrainyQuote.com, accessed December, 26, 2015, http://www.brainyquote.com/quotes/authors/a/alice_miller.htm.

13   Ibid.

14   Charles L. Whitfield, *Healing the Child Within: Discovery and Recovery for Adult Children of Dysfunctional Families* (Deerfield Beach, FL: Health Communications, 2006), vii.

15   Charles L. Whitfield, *A Gift to Myself: A Personal Workbook and Guide to the Bestselling* Healing the Child Within (Deerfield Beach, FL: Health Communications, 1990).

16   Cathryn L. Taylor, *The Inner Child Workbook* (New York,: Jeremy P. Tarcher/Putnam, 1991).

17   Daniel Goleman, *Emotional Intelligence: Why It Can Matter More Than IQ* (New York: Bantam Books, 1995).

18   Bradshaw, *Healing The Shame*, 56.

11

PIA MELLODY

I left my recovery story in chapter 9, "The Twelve-Step Program of Codependents Anonymous and Me," just as I had discovered I was codependent, and Codependents Anonymous (CoDA) promised to help. If my acknowledged codependence had a root cause in toxic shame, I looked for ways to heal it. I vaguely felt healing shame would lead to a healing of my anger because in a way they were the same thing. I believed shame was the cause, and codependence was the effect. Everything else seemed to be caused by toxic shame, and because of my denial anger was a trivial problem to me, if not to others. Anger seemed to be an incidental problem compared to my low self-esteem, my neediness for a woman to love and to have love me, and my difficulty in attracting an acceptable woman. Therefore, I reasoned (erroneously) that my problems, anger included, must stem from shame. My belief in this assumed causality will become clear in this chapter as I relate how I processed new evidence to demonstrate, if not prove this idea.

Pia Mellody's book *Facing Codependence*[1] was one of the three most important books to my recovery. In it she identifies and organizes the extremely confusing and baffling symptoms and characteristics of codependence, the origins of codependence, and how these origins translate into dysfunctional behaviors throughout life. I have read and studied this book at least six times.

When I first read it, I was overwhelmed by its applications to me and my life. It just seemed to fit, and its explanatory power was astounding. Where Bradshaw's *Bradshaw on: the Family* had revealed the dynamics of my family in its dysfunction, *Facing Codependence* detailed and ordered the personal dynamics of a child like me who suffered abuse and explained the effects of that abuse that were carried into adulthood. I was so overwhelmed by it throughout my first reading that I only understood about one-third of it. Here in one easy-to-read book was my life as it had actually unfolded. It confirmed what I knew and thought I knew about my past and my present and made sense of them. I say "easy to read" in reference to the words, the sentences, and the structure. It is extremely well written. Nevertheless, it was largely beyond me initially because of its profundity for me and my experience and because I carried a lot of denial of and blindness to my own reality.

Within a year of first reading *Facing Codependence* I saw a fellow in an AA meeting that I had seen only one other time six months before. We had seemed to connect then; we had nodded, smiled, and laughed at the same times during others' sharing, as if we understood these things in the same way. We'd made eye contact to signal to each other that we understood and identified with what was being said. I don't remember if we talked after that first meeting, but when I saw him across the room at that second meeting six months later, I sure remembered him. He was now sharing about his new marriage, his sixth, a remarriage to his second wife. Six months before he had been grateful to AA to be sober and to deserve her in his life again. He had just come out from the southeast to remarry her, and he was on cloud nine.

Now six months later, he gave a drastically different evaluation of her and their relationship. Naturally, after the meeting I asked him what had happened to make her suddenly seem so bad for him. His response was the typical "Let's get a cup of coffee," which means "Let's sit down privately and really talk"—the real meeting after the AA meeting. After the coffee came, he opened up. She was this; she was that. And, worse, he was now this, and he was now that, and it was getting worse. I listened a few minutes, and then when he paused, I said what my friend had said to me after my separation from my second wife: "Heck, you're just codependent."

He had the same response I had had when told the same thing. I told him that the new view of codependence was not just about those problems in relationships induced from the effects of drinking but about uncontrollable relationships in general. We talked late again, and I told him about CoDA and Pia Mellody (as I understood them at that time). It was definitely the blind leading the blind, but that is the way twelve-step programs work—in them, as in life, you learn by doing and making mistakes and especially by analyzing your mistakes with others who have made them also. I said, as had been said to me, "I'll take you to a CoDA meeting." That is also how twelve-step programs work: one person willing to share the program to keep it. As CoDA had been given to me, I wanted to give it someone else, so I could keep it.

We went to a CoDA meeting the next night, had coffee afterward, and talked about the meeting and all that had been shared, about how he had done that and I had too, and about how I had done this and so had he.

If anyone asks you how twelve-step programs work, you can tell them "really well" or give a summary of that last paragraph. It is the connection, the commonality, and the honestly and humility of coming clean out loud one on one with another person in a meeting after the meeting in an all-night coffee shop while you are still wired from the coffee in the meeting. Seeing another person being humble and honest about his or her character defects promotes honesty and humility in your own mind and heart—especially since that person never points a finger at you and strictly sticks to his or her own experience, strength, and hope. It is self-examination, not advice. That self-examination is open and free, before another and out loud, and you can't skip steps and jive yourself as you do when talking to yourself while stuck in your own head. Self-examination is good for the soul, the heart, and the head.

A few days later, his wife called me from her work and went on and on about he did this and he did that and couldn't I do something about him? This fellow was about 6'9", weighed about 350 pounds, and was ten years younger than me. Then there was the twelve-step doctrine about only sharing my own stuff and not giving advice unless asked for it. For both reasons I was not about to "do something about him."

Immediately, I called him at their home and, without any small talk first, said, "Hey. I'm supposed to fix you."

He said, "Let's get a cup of coffee." We met and talked CoDA and some AA all afternoon. I was in the midst of my divorce and was staying alone in our big five-bedroom home—all four kids were grown and had moved out. Looking back, I see that it was probably codependent of me, but when he said he was going to move out of his wife's house but had no place to go, I offered him a place to stay with me. I thought it would be a good opportunity for us to work on our problems together, me and my codependence and him and his codependence. I told him about Pia Mellody's book and asked him if we could read it out loud together, one paragraph at a time, to study it and work our program that way. He said he'd have to think about that but that he would really like to talk to me about codependence and could see I wanted to also. Heck, we both needed to badly. We were really sick.

He moved in the next day, and I suggested I drive him over to the bookstore so he could buy the book. He acted a bit shy and then looked at me and said he was nearly broke and that eight dollars or so was a lot of money to him at that time. And, by the way, he was dyslexic and had a hard time reading because he saw words mixed up on the page, and because he had so much trouble reading, he had a personal vow never to start a book without finishing it. I knew he was not dumb but very smart. I was touched, but I had vowed to myself that I would not buy him a book. That was very stupid of me, but I was trying to not be codependent—it was his program, after all. But I had bought guys the Big Book of AA before. What was the difference? My boundaries were all screwed up, I guess. Anyway, the next day we drove to a bookstore, and he bought himself a copy of Mellody's book. We returned to the house and started reading to each other right away. I'd read a paragraph, and he'd read one.

We did finish the book. It took three or four months—not because of slow reading, but because each page took an hour or more with all the stories we told each other about our childhoods, marriages, parents, jobs, and relationships. In between these compulsive sessions of recovery work, we would go to CoDA and AA meetings together and even to some Adult Children of Alcoholics (ACA) meetings, even though we agreed none of our parents were alcoholic. They just had the dysfunctional traits that ACA deals with so well, and in trying to deal with our parents, especially our attitudes and recollections of them and our own learned dysfunctional behaviors, we found ACA a good program. We also occasionally played pool, and I worked some—I was self-employed, so I did not have to work unless I wanted to eat. But mostly we talked about our childhoods, teen years, married lives, his military service, and our work lives.

One day after we had finished the book, he said, "I think I should go home to the other coast." I knew what he meant. We were getting well, and it was best for him to leave before we got codependent with each other. Neither of us said it, but in a few days, he left. I felt a lot of sadness over his leaving, but it was best. He was well enough to do what was best for him. And I was well enough not to try to control him, and for me, that was progress.

[1]   Pia Mellody, Pia, *Facing Codependence: What It Is, Where It Comes from, How It Sabotages Our Lives* (San Francisco: Perennial Library, 1989).

12

PIA MELLODY'S THEORY SUMMARIZED

I admire Pia Mellody and her books very much and rate them at the top of the list of books that were important to my recovery. This section should *not* be taken as a substitute for reading her books and studying them thoroughly. I have read *Facing Codependence* six times, and each time I got still more out of it. So there is no way that this brief summary can do it justice. There is a great deal more in the book in both detail and additional subject matter than this short chapter can relate.

This is what got my friend and me to a higher state of wellness. Mellody's favorite number is five. Bill Wilson, who wrote the Big Book and *Twelve Steps and Twelve Traditions* of AA, always had lists of twelve steps, traditions, promises, and so on. Mellody always has lists in fives. This is not a criticism; rather this method probably helped them organize their thinking and writing, and it helps me remember all the points.

Mellody writes first about what codependence is. She gives five symptoms of codependence:

1. Difficulty experiencing appropriate levels of self-esteem
2. Difficulty setting functional boundaries (protective limits we set for ourselves or to limit ourselves to protect others)
3. Difficulty owning our own reality
4. Difficulty acknowledging and meeting our own needs and wants
5. Difficulty experiencing and expressing our reality moderately[1]

In each section on each symptom she describes the problem, where it comes from in our past, and what the problem looks like. The problem comes from, in Mellody's system, childhood abuse. And I agree that is true for me.

Codependence is caused by childhood abuse, also called childhood trauma. By *trauma* I mean a physical or psychological occurrence or wound that causes the victim extreme psychological injury or pain, that *seems to the victim to be so serious that the victim presumes or feels that his or her life is in danger or nearly so.* By *childhood* I mean before or around the ages of six to ten, but the age is not as important as the dependency of the victim on the abuser, for childhood abuse is typically inflicted by caregivers, parents, teachers, clergy members, older siblings, or other people who are supposed to take care of the child and not harm him or her. Note the flexibility of the definition of childhood abuse. It is *how the individual child experiences an event* and the resulting psychological damage that makes the experience traumatic, or *apparently so to the child.* This means that two children can experience the exact same treatment and have it affect them differently. This is why one adult who was beaten as a child feels no dysfunctional repercussions from it while another adult may still be traumatized by the same severity of spankings or beatings. It depends on how the child perceived the event at the time, and that depends on the child's sensitivity and other personality traits and a host of other personal and environmental factors.

The same is true of the trauma from war for soldiers and of the trauma as a victim of crime or an accident. Two or more people may go through the same horrific experience, but one is traumatized while others are not. There is no doubt that adult trauma from accidents, battles in wars, shootings or mayhem, and many other causes can be similarly traumatizing or not, and that trauma can stay with the victim for a very long time while others are relatively unaffected. The parallels are clear between adults being traumatized, which we accept as real, and childhood trauma, which we tend to minimize or even deny. To do so is a grave error for both traumatized children and adults who were traumatized as children. I submit that childhood trauma is a serious reality in the population in general, and in my story it is central, particularly with its long-lasting effects. Furthermore it is the ultimate cause of my anger, but not how I first imagined.

The surfacing of vast numbers of childhood abuse cases in the twenty-first century is shocking. Two things stand out besides the sheer numbers. First the magnitude of the emotional damage from that abuse is astounding. Grown-up victims have told of the long-term effects these events have had on them, and these stories confirm Alice Miller's reports in her many books from the 1980s to the present. The extent of damage is further verified by the massive monetary awards to the victims in larger institutional cases, speaking of real and lasting damage to the abused youngsters. Second, the victims' outrage shows no sign of abating, even as more cash awards and apologies are given. It is as if no matter how much is paid and how many apologies are made, these offerings are still insufficient to adequately help the victims. No matter how much denial our society has, child abuse is real, and there are more victims than ever imagined.

Mellody defines the following five types of childhood abuse.[2] I have noted examples in each case in parenthesis.

1. Physical (spanking, beating, hitting, burning)
2. Sexual (inappropriate touching, jokes, sexual language, exposure to others having sex, actual sexual contact)
3. Intellectual (degrading statements like "You're so dumb" and "Where did you learn such a thing?" educational deprivation, false information given as real, telling a child he or she is exceptionally bright when he or she is not)
4. Emotional (raging, belittling, humiliating, asking or making a child do tasks far beyond his or her emotional maturity, like taking care of Mommy, which is using the child as a *surrogate spouse*)
5. Spiritual (statements meant to frighten or as punishment or a threat like "God will get you for that," "You will burn in hell," and "If you are not a good little boy, God will punish you"; denial or overemphasis of the importance of spiritual or religious experience to a child; distortion of such experiences)

For each type she describes the child in a functional family as a precious child, that is perfectly imperfect or undamaged, based on her list of innate characteristics of all children:[3]

1. Valuable
2. Vulnerable
3. Imperfect
4. Dependent
5. Immature

These, she says, are natural. They are the way kids are, and functional parents should nurture and allow their children to be this way "so they arrive at adulthood as mature, functional adults who feel good about themselves."[4] I sure did not identify with that mythical family that allows its children these natural characteristics. I recognized these as natural and important for childhood, but I had a great deal of trouble associating any of these characteristics as being accepted in my family. I was not raised as if it was okay for me to be any of these. My parents expected either less or more of each from me.

Mellody then goes on to show how childhood abuse violates these natural characteristics and causes dysfunctionality in adults so that some of us grow up to be *adult children*, all due to the shaming that childhood abuse causes. As John Bradshaw wrote, children look up to their parents or caregivers as gods—if Mommy and Daddy are wrong when they are whipping you, you have no hope, no future. You, as a five- or six-year-old, know that you cannot feed or clothe yourself, cannot protect yourself, and cannot provide yourself warmth and shelter or any of the other necessities of life. So the parents cannot be "wrong" in your eyes. They are gods, providers of all. In a child's mind his or her future depends on the caregivers being upstanding, just, and right. Therefore, "It must be me," says the child, and the child grows up with distorted or dysfunctional views of reality. "I must be wrong," the child says.[5] The child thinks that he or she must be, as Bobby Earll says, "fundamentally bad, inadequate, defective, unworthy, or not fully valid as a human being."[6]

That could have been me Bob Earll is describing. I got those feelings and ideas and acted them out starting when I was a baby. Many children who were more badly abused than I was did not grow up so wounded, but I did. As I said above, it is not the amount, frequency, or severity of abuse but the child's perception and interpretation of it. So not only were my parents unmindful of the devastating trauma they were causing me, but I also contributed by believing the shame I felt. Even though I am willing to take on my share of responsibility, my parents were not blameless. At any rate, I decided when I was a child that I was broken in a way that could not be fixed. I grew up with extremely low self-esteem.

To accept responsibility for my faults, which were, after all, normal childhood shortcomings, was not a rational decision that I made. I was only an immature, not-yet-rational child. It *was* done to me in my case, despite what Doctors Ellis and Harper write. As a child I had the sense that I was flawed and imperfect. I assumed that all my imperfections and flaws that my parents emphasized were true to guarantee my security, to keep their care of me going. That is the insidious nature of child abuse: the child assumes all the blame and responsibility and internalizes it as his or her own (false) identity—the child sees himself or herself as worthless and flawed, and, in ways that can't be fixed, his or her spirit is broken. A big part of recovery is to assign proper and realistic responsibility and culpability for the harmful effects of the childhood trauma. Many recovery books try to gloss over this by saying it is not about blame but about responsibility. But responsibility is about blame. The first definition of *responsibility* from Dictionary.com is "to hold responsible," and the second definition is "to place the responsibility for (a fault, error, etc.)." Only by the proper understanding of what happened can there be hope of recovery, and that means placing blame. The common admonition to not blame the parents is a holdover from the poisonous pedagogy rules that dictate that the child is always wrong and that the parents are always right and therefore justified in any actions—all for the child's own good.

My parents were responsible for what they did, and that realization was *part of the rational understanding I needed as an adult to start recovery.* I had those five innate characteristics that Mellody listed and also the normal child's security-first reaction to rejection by my parents. Only after accepting my parents' role could I *become responsible for the way I took that rejection in their abuse of me.*

The first time I read *Facing Codependence,* I highlighted it and marked it up, but as I said, I probably understood only about one-third of it that time. When I read it with the other fellow, I highlighted and marked it up again with a different color of ink and highlighter and dated the colors. I went to a renowned recovery center and studied it again in a thirty-day program there, marking it up once again in yet another color. Through the years I read it three more times, each time marking it up with different colors, each of which I dated. My book is a mess, but finally, I am not. With my study of Pia Mellody and hard work over twenty years to put her wisdom and that of others about codependence into practice, I recovered from the effects of childhood abuse and the toxic shame it caused me, ridding myself of low self-esteem and the feeling—no, the *knowing*—that I was unworthy and inadequate in ways that could never be fixed.

But that long and gradual recovery from codependence went on for many years. In the beginning of my codependence work, I was only aware of low self-esteem as a major problem. I was aware of my anger, but tended to relegate it as a minor problem—I was still in denial.

My progress against codependence was steady. My relationship problems seemed to me to be my greatest problems in life, and I judged those to be paramount. So I worked exclusively on codependence, which is, healing from toxic shame.

The relationship problems could also be viewed as anger problems, but unwilling to give up anger because of my denial, I thought or hoped curing the shame resulting from childhood abuse would be a path to cure not only my relationships but also my anger. I accepted that I was shame based, that is, my behavior reflected the effects of the toxic shame still remaining in me. As time went on the toxic shame level dropped steadily, but the anger did not.

On those occasions when I did consider my anger I would say, "After all, look at my abusive childhood. It is no wonder I am angry. How dare my mother do those things to me—demanding perfection, giving me hard spankings, subjecting me to intellectual abuse. She told everyone I was a genius—I guess because that made her one. And then my father allowed that abuse … " and on and on. This was logical on the surface, but it was wrong. I was angry because of the abuse, but there were still two missing emotions in equation (1), the same two as always.

Therefore, with responsibility and reality in hand, it was my plan to cure the shame and in the process I would cure the anger. I guess I deluded myself that when the effects of toxic shame were finally banished, my relationships would be very good, and I would not be angry. I neglected to consider why I was still as angry with people I was not in a romantic relationship with, other drivers, store clerks, and all the others.

During my recovery from codependence I did assign responsibility, but I never wanted revenge on my parents. I did, however, have a large measure of revenge through the anger I felt for my parents, but that was not my purpose. My purpose was to feel better, in control, not helpless. I held them responsible, but I did not expect them to change. I had a vain hope that they would see the light, but of course they never did.

I had an antagonistic attitude toward them until they got so old that I became their caregiver. Then, thank goodness, I had recovered from most of the codependence but not the anger. Thankfully, I was not mean to them. I still had a great deal of anger inside up until their deaths and even afterward, but I did not take it out on them late in their lives. Unfortunately for my third ex-wife, I took it out on her. And that is proof that although I was less dysfunctional in a codependent way, I was still an angry man.

Facing Codependence, many other books and lectures, and a lot of work and practice on my inner self fixed my low self-esteem caused by the shame that started with childhood abuse. Compared to before, I was reasonably well in that way, even though eventually I again was in a codependent marriage. I was just not as codependent as before.

But I was still angry. That got no better. Being a type A personality, I told myself that I just needed to work harder and it would come.

---

[1]   Pia Mellody, *Facing Codependence*, 7–42.

[2]   Ibid., 137–93.

[3]   Ibid., 61.

[4]   Ibid.

[5]   Bradshaw, *Healing the Shame*, 47.

[6]   Bob Earll, *I Got Tired of Pretending* (Tucson, AZ: STEM Publications, 1989), 46.

13

INDUCED OR CARRIED EMOTIONS

I t seemed to me, even years ago, that my anger was far more intense than
it should have been. My first few years in AA, when I first started to seriously consider my emotions and how they caused me to behave, my anger
seemed excessively more volatile and powerful than was warranted by my
childhood trauma, which was not nearly as severe as others had suffered. I
accepted that a little childhood abuse was sufficient to wound a child, but
still it seemed that my maladjusted behavior, especially anger, was far out
of proportion from what I expected. My other emotions seemed perhaps
excessive in some cases also, although I rationalized that I was just naturally
emotional and wore my emotions on my sleeve. Certainly toxic shame fit this
description, but nevertheless I just accepted myself as I was, more emotional
than average.

I have come to know that a lot of the anger and toxic shame that I had
was passed down to me from my family of origin, including all the generations before me but particularly my parents, since they were the main pipe-
line between my antecedents to me. My progenitors had the same shame.
I simply learned and adopted the toxic shame, anger, and certain other
feelings that my family had. It is neither polite nor loyal toward your parents
to believe this and certainly not to say it, but a little introspection makes it
obvious. Their traits, behaviors, and beliefs tended to become mine. Only
in rebellion did I reject those qualities and only after I left the nest to go to
school and live 450 miles away. In college I learned a new set of values. There
were other instances of separation from my parents' values of course, but the

primary shift followed the abrupt change of going to college and living on campus. My daily family contact was replaced by a whole world of books and lectures, ideas, philosophies, educational pursuits offered in an intellectual community, and people—both other students from around the world and learned professors and instructors. My world suddenly was not uniform and homogeneous or inflexible. It was varied and shaded with a great variety of ways to look at things and of methods for accomplishing life's tasks.

My mother liked to tell others in my hearing that college ruined me. Since it was the start of my separation from my parents' ideas, I guess I can see her (codependent) point.

After I went away to college, I began to examine and evaluate the values of my family against those values presented by the new experiences and associations at school as I met and roomed with students from all over the world. In college, I had to accept that what I had thought I knew until then was not necessarily so. Later, when I started examining my dysfunctional family and my own dysfunctional life in my mid forties, I again had to accept this. Then, comparing the intensity of my feelings, particularly anger and shame, to what appeared to be average, I could not help but see that I shared not only my parents' values and attitudes but also a great deal of their behaviors. Mom was angry, and so was I, a fact I became conscious of at about fourteen years old.

Mom and Dad were very proud, more so than necessary, prideful even, as if it was a cover for some self-perceived shortcomings. Later, Dad openly talked about when he was a child, his father had pointed out men in their small Ohio town and assessed their worthiness based on their station in life: "He's a laborer," my grandfather would say in a downturned voice, full of sympathy. "That man's a businessman," he'd say in an exalted tone, and, "That man's a *banker*," he'd say in a way that obviously meant the man was very special. Assigning value to others (or one's self) because of a profession or wealth is a clear sign of toxic shame. I adopted that thinking inspired by toxic shame, or rather it was unconsciously passed to me, and I did not reject it for years. My parents modeled toxic shame, and I picked it up as the way to be. After all, these were my parents, and early in life, they were all-important and godlike to me. Because I was an only child, I got the full measure of abuse and had no one to commensurate with or to compare myself with, and there were no other models of such power in my young life. I had, in Alice Miller's terminology, no "sympathetic advocate" with which to share my troubles.*

Mom was angry, and she was quick to lash out with an acid tongue. She could be cuttingly sharp, modeling anger and that behavior for me. It seemed to work for her, and I admired and worshiped her, so why not emulate her? I felt helpless, useless, and powerless because of toxic shame, both the shame from my abuse and the shame that was frozen in my family as carried or induced emotions, so if anger worked, I used it.

I use the word *frozen* because another common name for induced or carried emotions in the recovery community is *frozen emotions*, so called because the emotions are frozen in time, permanent and rigid so as to never change, and are forced to fit all circumstances no matter how awkwardly.

Brenda Stanton, on her website, writes on the *Claim Your Worth!* Section, (I have added my own interpretation in parenthesis—note the twisted logic for anger),

> Carried shame is when you are holding onto to someone else's stuff (*pain or sense of loss*). It's a feeling of overwhelming responsibility for something that you feel guilty of (*hurt over*) – but you aren't sure what you did that was so wrong (*made you so angry*).
>
> You just know that you don't feel worthy – and that you need to avoid being fully seen and claiming what you truly desire because of this underlying shame that you feel.

---

* Alice Miller stresses in many of her books that therapists should act as advocates or sympathetic confidants while listening to their clients' recollections of childhood trauma, for their clients may have no one else to turn to and to be open with in telling their dark secrets. For example, in *Thou Shalt Not Be Aware: Society's Betrayal of the Child*, chapter 1, "Two Psychoanalytic Approaches," Miller first presents analysis by a strict Freudian who adheres to the needs of the parents and tends to protect them and their reputations. Miller critiques this approach as all too accepted in society, terming it *poisonous pedagogy*, wherein the parents are flawless and the child is always wrong and to be harshly punished (abused) to be trained or even broken in spirit. She then contrasts this therapeutic attitude with that of a more humane, open, and caring therapist who is willing to believe the client's stories of abuse and help him or her to understand the abuse and resolve the resulting pain and anger. Chapter 6, "Why Does the Patient Need an Advocate in the Analyst?" carries on this theme.

Almost always any carried shame began with your family of origin and most likely it all happened unconsciously. It happened as a result of you taking on the shame of a family member (or several family members) because that is your nature – to take-on responsibility and blame – even if it wasn't your fault [the super-responsibility of a codependent].[1]

Those few substitutions above in her definition for *carried shame* makes its own twisted sense for *anger*. The whole parallel construction is,

Carried *anger* is when you are holding onto to someone else's stuff *pain or sense of loss*. It's a feeling of overwhelming responsibility for something that you feel *(hurt over)* – but you aren't sure what you did that *made you so angry*.

I modified the above lines, because all emotions can be carried from one generation to another, because the older generation may exhibit any emotion in excess and the following generation may assume a dysfunctional core mirroring that emotion. These emotions can become dysfunctional cores in any generation, especially in a later generation from induced or carried emotions. Here are some examples listed by emotion:

+ shame—A person with a core of shame can have a *sense of unworthiness* or, in reaction a *compensating behavior of either shamelessness or arrogance*
+ anger—A person with a core of anger can be a *raging* person whose anger is far beyond healthy anger
+ fear—A person with a core of fear can be prone to *panic, paranoia, phobias, or a sense of powerlessness*
+ guilt— A person with a core of guilt can feel a sense of excess *fallibility or a sense of uselessness*
+ love—A person with a core of excess love may make love into physical love always, i.e., *lust*

+ hate—A person with a core of hate may exhibit excess *anger, violence, or prejudices*

+ joy— A person with a core of excess joy may over demonstrate *satiation, revelry, intemperance, or mania*

+ passion— A person with a core of passion can show *zealotry or fanaticism*

+ pain— A person with a core of pain may be prone to *self-pity, a victim role, or rage*

+ sadness— A person with a core of sadness may be inflicted with *melancholy, depression, despondence, hopelessness, or rage*

Note than in the above list there is not an exclusive correspondence between causing emotions and the dysfunctional excess ones. In particular, rage may result from and excess of anger, pain, or sadness. And given the complexity of the human psyche, there could be other, less common paths to rage. For the remainder of this book, pain and sadness are going to be very important.

This brief chapter is a very cursory treatment of induced or carried emotions. Pia Mellody includes a lot of information about induced or carried feelings in *Facing Codependence* in the chapter "'The Nature of a Child," which describes how children grow up to be either functional or dysfunctional.[2]

John Bradshaw seems to include shame so induced or otherwise learned in his term *toxic shame*, but he is not very specific about where it comes from (see chapter 7, "John Bradshaw, *Bradshaw on: the Family*"). Throughout the first twenty pages of *Bradshaw on: the Family* he discusses at length family traits learned and adopted by children too young to have normal emotional separation from their parents.

---

[1]   Brenda Stanton, "Carried Shame & Worthiness," Claim Your Worth!, Dated April 17, 2012, http://brendastanton.com/carried-shame-worthiness.

[2]   Mellody, *Facing Codependence*, 96–103.

14

SHAME IN DEPTH: JOHN BRADSHAW, *HEALING THE SHAME THAT BINDS YOU*

Despite the broad hint and warning in the last chapter about the causes of carried rage, I return to the subject of toxic shame, because it will figure prominently in the analysis of my story. Recall that equation (1) had toxic shame leading indirectly to anger or rage.

John Bradshaw's *Healing the Shame That Binds You* is another book that helped me with my codependence and anger. I only partially summarize it here, and I heartily recommend the whole book to anyone who struggles with codependence or anger.

As a starting point I'll review the impact his book *Bradshaw on: the Family* had on me. In *Bradshaw on: the Family* (see chapter 7, "John Bradshaw, *Bradshaw on: the Family*") Bradshaw does not directly address codependence by that name. He refers to "the crisis in the family" and concentrates on *shame*, calling it a sickness of the soul. He then discusses in great detail how this sickness of shame is "a kind of soul murder" and many specific effects of it.[1] He does not say that shame, like all emotions (see chapter 5, "Emotions"), has a good and necessary side, but in later writings he differentiates between shame and *toxic shame*. At the start of *Healing the Shame That Binds You* he characterizes "shame as a healthy human emotion."[2] In typical Bradshaw style he covers healthy shame thoroughly in nearly six full pages.

In *Bradshaw on: the Family*, he takes on shame as the primary cause of people's emotional and behavioral problems, discusses its effect on the family as a system made up of those troubled people, and extends the problem to a crisis of society. Even assuming that he is always talking about toxic shame, *Bradshaw on: the Family* is a sweeping indictment of the family as a system of raising children, a criticism that my parents would have been aghast to see me considering. The exact reason my parents would have been so appalled is the *no-talk rule*, which Bradshaw discusses in his introduction to the *family rules*. The no-talk rule acts to protect the parents in the guise of protecting the family and society. I describe the no-talk rule in chapter 6, "Acknowledging Anger as a Problem," and I list all the family rules in endnote 6 of chapter 7, "John Bradshaw, *Bradshaw on: the Family.*"

Sweeping as it was, *Bradshaw on: the Family* appropriately called attention to a problem for a society made up largely by families that form the children who grow up to be future society members, and it was pragmatic in explaining the defects pervading our society. These defects become obvious by watching the nightly local and world news.

In *Healing the Shame That Binds You* Bradshaw discusses what he calls *toxic shame.* He quotes Scot Peck on the difference between neurotics and those who suffer character disorders: "The neurotic assumes too much responsibility; the person with a character disorder [assumes] not enough. When neurotics are in conflict with the world, they automatically assume that they are at fault. When those with character disorders are in conflict with the world, they automatically assume the world is at fault."[3]

John then notes that some neurotic and character disorder personality traits are common to us all, but that to be committed to a healthy life "we must be willing to commit ourselves to reality ... to have the willingness and capacity to suffer continual self-examination."[4] And this willingness is what a shame-based person does not have. Rather than limiting him or her healthily with proper boundaries and an uplifting spirituality, the shame is overblown and tells the person that he or she is flawed and intrinsically worthless. Bradshaw calls such shame *toxic shame.*

After this introduction of toxic shame, the rest of the book provides a description of all of shame's manifestations and suggestions on healing toxic shame.

I cannot recommend this book too much as a pathway out of toxic shame. I read it a second time to study it in depth after still one more personal crisis of separation, which I describe in chapter 19, "Third Marriage and Arrest." I had slipped back into toxic shame and codependence in that marriage, and I realized at that time that I needed to get back to work on myself. Bradshaw's many exercises, which I did alone with a tape recorder as he recommends, helped me greatly. They were another example of the efficacy of tackling my emotions directly and working to heal them as opposed to learning to rephrase my thinking about problems as a rational adjustment of my thinking would have had me do.

Bradshaw also discusses the "internalization of shame" and uses anger as an example:

> Any human emotion can become internalized. When internalized, an emotion stops functioning in the manner of an emotion and becomes a characterological style. You probably know someone who could be labeled "an angry person" or someone you'd call a "sad sack." In both cases the emotion has become the core of the person's character, her identity. The person doesn't have anger or melancholy, she *is* angry and melancholy [respectively].[5]

His "internalization of shame" is pretty close to induced or carried shame, but this shame is not necessarily induced from another person's shame. As I recall, Bradshaw does not talk directly about induced emotions, except in general terms such as this. In chapter 13, "Induced or Carried Emotions," I covered some emotions that young children can unintentionally pick up from their caregivers. Pia Mellody is more explicit about how children can learn emotions in a toxic form by seeing the excessive emotions mirrored in a parent or other caregiver or by other pass-through generation-to-generation means. (See the end of chapter 13 in *Facing Codependence*.)

People commonly say that someone hit or pushed their buttons, meaning someone said something that caused them distress, usually anger. Bradshaw explains that as we grow up and shaming experiences accrue, images of the memories of those events are recorded in a person's memory bank. Because the [young] victim has no time or support to grieve the pain of the broken mutuality [between him and the abuser presumed to be a trusted caregiver], his emotions are repressed and the grief is unresolved. The verbal (auditory) imprints remain in the memory as do the visual images of the shaming scenes. As each new shaming experience takes place, a new verbal imprint and visual image attach to the already existing ones forming collages of shaming memories ...*

As the years go on, very little is needed to trigger these collages of shame memories. A word, a similar facial expression or scene, can set it off. Sometimes an external stimulus is not even necessary. Just going back to an old memory can trigger an enormously painful experience. Shame as an emotion [that is toxic] has now become frozen and embedded into the core of the person's identity. Shame is deeply internalized.[6]

Here Bradshaw expresses in popular language how we are triggered when someone hits our buttons. He also explains why repetitions of the same or similar shaming events can build up to make us so sensitive and *perhaps respond with anger at the unexpressed built-up pain.* Furthermore, if events are "recorded in a person's memory bank" at a young enough age, the person has not only no "time or support" but also no logical framework to analyze and evaluate these shaming experiences and thus cannot throw them off as irrelevant. They become embedded in either carried emotions or what I call body memories.

Incidentally, the attractive or familiar characteristics of Mom (for boys) or Dad (for girls) are also so "recorded in a person's memory bank." This explains the tendency for people to romantically fall for and marry those

---

* I now can make that connection of pain and grieving ("grieve the pain" and "unresolved" grief) to anger, but I could not when I first came across it. My recovery books usually speak of healing damaged emotions, such as pain, by "resolving" them. Here is a more concrete reference to the healing process, and that is grieving pain. This is the crux of my overcoming anger. My grieving is covered in detail in chapter 22, "A Simple Course of Treatment."

with characteristics similar to their opposite-gender parent and to do so, as in my case, over and over. For me the characteristics were not necessarily attractive in a conscious sense. But the unattractive traits were familiar, and I was comfortable with them. And that was enough to make the person with those traits attractive.

Taken all together these last few paragraphs explain to me why eventually the ladies in my life finally got fed up with my anger and generally blustery, judgmental, and arrogant attitude. They may have felt comfortable around me in the beginning—"Gee, he's just like Daddy"—but in the end the collage became overwhelming, like the straw that broke the camel's back.

Bradshaw also talks about shame being the core and fuel of all addiction:

> The content of the addiction, whether it be an ingestive addiction [like alcohol or drugs] or an activity addiction (like work, buying or gambling) is an attempt at an intimate relationship. The workaholic with his work, or the alcoholic with his booze, are [sic] having a love affair. Each one mood alters to avoid the feeling of loneliness and hurt in the underbelly of shame. Each acting out creates life-damaging consequences which create more shame. The new shame fuels the cycle of addiction.[7]

Bradshaw paints many more descriptions of the effects of shame, many of them addictions, but one stands out. It is what he calls *acting-out* behavior, or *reenactment* (see, for example, Alice Miller[8]). He defines this behavior as belonging to a criminal offender who was once victimized in much the same way as he or she criminalizes. He says,

> Children from violently abusing families, children from families where high voltage abandonment takes place, suffer terrible victimization. They generally either take on a victim role or reenact it over and over again, or they identify with their offender and reenact the offense on helpless victims (as they once were). This reenactment is called "repetition compulsion"—the urge to repeat.[9]

In reading this I wonder, *How criminal does the criminal role have to be? How terrible does the victimization suffered have to be?* In asking such questions I am not at all interested in an abuse excuse. I am only interested in the pieces of the puzzle, that self-examination that Bradshaw holds so highly. And I hasten to note that as in his discussion, he rightly claims that there is not 100 percent or anything nearly like 100 percent correlation in cause and effect in such cases.

Finally, Bradshaw takes up the subject of rage as an addiction: "When we are raging, we feel unified within—no longer split. We feel powerful. Everyone cowers in our presence. We no longer feel inadequate and defective. *As long as we can get away with it,* our rage becomes our mood alterer of choice. We become rage addicts."[10] John continues in this section to describe his own raging, and it sounds a lot like mine.

I have often told how my anger was present for me whenever I needed to feel powerful and in control. It cured my feelings of inadequacy and ineffectiveness. My rage frightened those around me. It was an activity that modified my emotions and feelings. It was an addiction like alcohol, always ready to modify my emotions on demand, and it had life-damaging consequences of hurt loved ones and damaged and lost relationships. And eventually the consequences were very much more serious.

---

[1]   Bradshaw, *Bradshaw on: the Family,* 2.

[2]   John Bradshaw, *Healing The Shame,* 3.

[3]   Ibid., 9.

[4]   Ibid.

[5]   Ibid., 10.

[6]   Ibid., 12–13.

[7]   Ibid., 15.

[8]   Alice Miller, *Thou Shalt Not Be Aware, Society's Betrayal of the Child,* (New York: Meridan, Penguin Group, 1990).

[9]   Ibid., 19.

[10] Ibid., 103 (emphasis added).

15

RECOVERY JUNKIE

Keep on going, and the chances are that you will stumble on[to]
something, perhaps when you are least expecting it. I never heard
of anyone ever stumbling on[to] something sitting down.
—Charles F. Kettering

Some are sicker than others.
—Twelve-step-program cliché

It takes a lot of bricks to build a wall.
—Verryl Fosnight

In this chapter I discuss books and tapes I studied, lectures I went to
given by self-help notables, and programs I attended in my recovery and
spiritual path. I could list them in order of importance to me, but that would
not be valid for anyone else. Even for me, their relative importance varied
depending on the order I came across them and where I was emotionally
and mentally in my recovery at that particular time. I've instead organized
them by subject matter. Do *not* rely on me to work your program. It is your
life, and you should have the say and the joy and exhilaration of discovering
your own sources.

At first glance you may think this extensive collection of recovery ma-
terials is worse than whatever your own dysfunction is. "Geez, this is being
addicted to recovery," you might say. Well, yes, it is, and that is what I said

to myself in my first AA meeting: "These folks are addicted to AA." But then using Bradshaw's working definition of an addiction (see chapter 4, "Recovery versus Cured," or the "Sex and Love Addiction" section later in this chapter), I cannot identify any "life-damaging consequences" to recovery. Nevertheless I cop to being a recovery junkie. Or maybe I just want it all, all the good things the universe can provide. I probably will only have one shot at this thing called life, so why not live it to the fullest? And in recovery I have found it all, the fullest life I dreamed of. In all those addictions the joy was fleeting and hollow. But in my recovery I am me, and that is enough. I am like Goldilocks: not too much, not too little, but just right. And actually the "just right" is fuller and richer and more fun than the extremes of addiction, and I've suffered a lot of addictions, so I can say that with assurance.

Another dysfunctional thought process I had early in my recovery was that one day I would get well and be able to go on autopilot through life effortlessly and automatically without working at it. *Wrong.* I have found what my therapist told me when I expressed this wish to him to be correct: healthy people work really hard at it. There are a lot of pitfalls and rules and boundaries to observe and not violate, and it takes constant vigilance to not transgress. Still, functional living is easier than dysfunctional living by a wide margin.

Once I started my recovery, I gradually realized that I was on the most rewarding, joyous, fulfilling, profitable, and gratifying path I could ever imagine. I meet interesting, loving, helpful, and wonderful people, and I learned to seek them out because I liked them and not because I needed them. Most of all I met and grew to love one person above all whom I could rely on unashamedly and without anxiety to always care for and cherish me and who would never abandon me. That person was *me*. I was there all along—precious, whole, and complete, lacking nothing, perfectly imperfect. I am that someone whom I have needed all along to love me unconditionally and without reservation, the one and only person who will never desert or abandon me. And that is fitting and proper, for it is my life, and I am responsible for it. If someone else lived my life or was responsible for it, then I would miss a big part of the ride. As I started to feel this, I became more confident that I could do it. I could heal myself and be the person I had always wanted to be, even though I am nothing special. I just never gave up on myself, because I learned to love myself. It was not ego or pride. I just learned to love myself enough to care for me.

Here are the recovery resources I used. As I mentioned, they are not in order of importance to me or to anyone I know. They can be used as a start if you'd like, a rough guide to starting your own list.

Shame and Childhood Abuse

John Bradshaw, *Bradshaw on: the Family: A Revolutionary Way of Self-Discovery*

Bradshaw wrote this book after his seminal public-TV series in about 1985. It was my first exposure to the recovery world of self-help gurus, a term I use admiringly. I write about this book and how it changed me in chapter 7, "John Bradshaw, *Bradshaw on: the Family: A Revolutionary Way of Self-Discovery*," and chapter 8, "Shame and Me." For the first time, the fundamental idea of dysfunctional family dynamics was presented to me, and it fit my family like a glove. And by extension I could see that my dysfunctional family was central to my personal problems and shortcomings. Because it was the first self-help book I read, it is probably as important to me as the Big Book of AA.

John Bradshaw, *Healing the Shame That Binds You*

After I got my all-important start with *Bradshaw on: the Family*, I probably got as much out of this book as any of Bradshaw's others. My focus was on shame and hopefully how understanding it might help me cure my anger. This book has some excellent exercises, which I did while I was separated—I always did my best recovery work when in pain, because pain leads to growth. When I was separated, I was motivated to grow into health.

I expand on this book because of its importance to me in chapter 14, "Shame in Depth: John Bradshaw, *Healing the Shame That Binds You*."

John Bradshaw, *Homecoming: Reclaiming and Championing Your Inner Child*

This very good book is about reclaiming your inner child as a method of healing all types of dysfunction. The *inner child* is a construct of an inner self we all retain within our psyches to which we can apply our adult healing powers to heal the wounds that inner child still suffers. Hokey, you say? Hey, it works. John says that inner-child work in his workshops "is the most powerful work" he has ever done and continues, "The workshop has convinced me that the inner child work is the quickest and most powerful way to effect therapeutic change in people. This almost-immediate effect continues to amaze me."[1]

I still have three stuffed animal toys that look down on me every night from their place on the armoire in my master bedroom: a howling coyote, who is my mischievous, fun-loving, teen self; a shy beaver, Beverly Beaver, who is my feminine side; and a white teddy bear, Verryl Virgil, who sits erect and with a very suspicious, vigilant look on his face. Beverly was given to me, I guess, or left behind by my ex-wife when she left me. The coyote was left in an apartment by a tenant. Verryl Virgil, the cute but vigilant bear who I bought on a special trip to a toy store—he is the part of my inner child who does not trust those big folks, parents and other adults. But it is all right, because if he gets scared, I hug him and reassure him that I will never abandon him. It may be hokey, but it works.

I think the inner child concept works because we are an extremely visual and tactile species and are very sensitive to movement, actions, touch, and the participation in those activities. So hugging my inner child as personified by a teddy bear resonates with tens of thousands of years of evolution. It is a physical thing that I do that is right in character with my human social nature. I hug my inner child to reassure him that as an adult I will never abandon him, no matter who else may. I am actually the only one who can make this pledge to him. At some point everyone else will be tempted to abandon me, or I may imagine that they are about to, but I will never abandon myself.

In part 1 of *Homecoming* there is fine information on codependence, its symptoms, and how inner children are wounded. It gives information similar to Pia Mellody's *Facing Codependence* (see below) with fine additional discussion and other characteristics. It also contains information that I managed to overlook about the dysfunction of anger. I do not know why I missed this information several years ago, but I did. At that time I was not ready to give up the benefits of anger—the power, the apparent control, and the soothing of my feelings of helplessness. The not being ready to release my anger was denial.

John Bradshaw, *Family Secrets: The Path to Self-Acceptance and Reunion*

This book explains how to understand your family and yourself in an entirely new way. Throwing down the gauntlet, Bradshaw says to "heal your family secrets or pass them on to your children," a scary thought indeed. Early in my recovery I vowed with all my might to end this dysfunctional stuff once and for all with my generation. (I actually used another noun for that "stuff.")

John Bradshaw, *Creating Love*

In this book Bradshaw discusses relationships. Ever get the idea dysfunctional people have trouble with relationships? And our families taught us so well ...

Pia Mellody, *Facing Codependence*

For me this book is all-important, for it tells all about childhood abuse leading to shame and the resultant codependence, what they are and how they come about, and how to go about healing them. Eventually I could understand even my anger. I covered this book in the previous chapters 11 and 12 about Pia Mellody.

Bob Earll, *I Got Tired of Pretending*

When I read Bob Earll, I knew I was not alone in going beyond AA. At one time he was a favorite speaker at national conventions and other important AA events, but when he came out talking about childhood stuff, he became less popular. After I started going to CoDA and reading Mellody, I quickly learned it was better for me not to talk about childhood issues in AA meetings. I was shunned a bit when I did so, so I would only mention these issues in passing. The pain involved in looking closely at childhood issues is terrifying to feel; I would mention it peripherally in my sharing, giving it due importance but not stressing it. Very few asked about my experience, strength, and hope after meetings because they could tell I was digging that "stuff" up. Only twice did someone come up and ask me about that childhood stuff. I replied both times, "I think people should only open this can of worms when their sobriety is very secure, say at five years. The emotional material studying codependence brings up is so traumatic a person might drink to kill the pain it brings up." Then I carefully started to tell the person what it had been like for me, what I had done about it, and what it was like now for me. Both times, I got only a couple of minutes into what I had done about that pain of childhood abuse. Each time, the person interrupted me in midsentence and blurted out, "I gotta go," whirled, and walked away. This tells me that it is indeed terrifying to dig up, face, and resolve this stuff. But to me, it is scarier to leave it rotting away in the crevices of my mind and heart, to foul and besmirch and desecrate what is my holy gift, my very life and the living of it.

Claudia Black, *It Will Never Happen to Me*

It Will Never Happen to Me is a fine book about the effects of living in a family with an addicted person. It explores how the addicted person's behavior and the other family members' codependent behavior to help, or enable, that person all cause dysfunction. Because of its prevalence and conspicuousness, alcohol is the primary addiction referenced in the book, but the book is easily adaptable to any addiction or to the effects of any dysfunctional family. I was able to apply Black's principles to my own childhood situation although my parents were not alcoholics and were merely (!) dysfunctional.

Claudia Black, *Changing Course: Healing from Loss, Abandonment, and Fear*

The sequel to *It Will Never Happen to Me*, this book is about chronic loss that emanates from physical or emotional abandonment and resulting family issues. *Abandonment* is broadly defined in the book as a family life that was too chaotic, rigid, enmeshed, or disconnected and thus caused abandonment experiences. Black explains that, as a result, the sufferer's worldview has been colored by chronic loss that still dictates how that person lives his or her life today. This book was very important to me understanding my losses from my pain that led to my anger.

Janet Woititz, *Adult Children of Alcoholics*

At about three years sober I was lying on the bed in the master bedroom on a lazy Sunday afternoon and started reading this book even though my parents were not alcoholic. When I got to the section listing thirteen characteristics of adult children of alcoholics, I found it so emotionally disturbing that my breathing became ragged and my whole body agitated. I gasped for breath and broke down in halting sobs. It was probably anxiety, the fear that you don't know what you are afraid of. At about number 5 I literally threw the book across the room in panic and rage. I did not recognize what this reaction was at the time, but now I know it was extreme *body feelings*, emotions so strong that I felt and experienced them throughout my body in a series of visceral and major muscle impulses and contractions. Body feelings are profoundly more intense and are also more immediate that mere emotions; they are a direct connection to our environment. In this instance, my body feelings were so intense that I got up and paced around the large room. Finally, still shaken, I returned to reading. I threw the book across the room again in a second body-feeling attack and paced some more. After one or two more tries I finished the list of thirteen characteristics. But I was greatly agitated for some time afterward. My folks were not drinkers, having only a drink or two with company on special occasions. When I still was drinking, I would tease my mom whenever I made her a drink, telling her I had only waved the cork over the glass to make it weak enough for her. But that list of things got to me, deeply and disturbingly. I did not understand it, but I had been in AA long enough to know to pay attention to such intense feelings. Now I know them as body feelings, and they are very useful, as I shall describe in chapter 22, "A Simple Course of Treatment." I'd stumbled onto something important that Sunday; there was no doubt about it, and I knew enough to pay attention to it. I did not understand what it was, or why it was so powerful, but I was aware to watch for opportunities to understand it.

The fine book *Adult Children of Alcoholics* and the list in it were not meant to be disturbing. The list of characteristics just hit me personally with such overwhelming intensity that I experienced those body feelings.

I went to a lot of ACA meetings, and I got a lot out of them. They addressed the CoDA issues I was about to discover in the next year or two. I did not ever feel as if there was any blaming of parents in any ACA meeting or literature I ever encountered. There was honest assignment of responsibility but not going so far as to outwardly blame or punish parents. Recovery is not so much about blame as it is about realizing responsibility, and, by far, the biggest part of the responsibility is that to oneself. The responsibility to oneself is to move entirely beyond blaming or punishing and into self-healing.

Janet Woititz, *Struggle for Intimacy*

Struggle for Intimacy is a good book on codependence's effects on relationships and how to face those challenges.

Melody Beattie, *Codependent No More*

Codependent No More is another standard and seminal work on codependence, along with its contemporary *Facing Codependence*. Probably because I am a physicist, I get more out of the rigorous, structured treatment of *Facing Codependence*, from hypothesis through cause, effect, and cure. In this fine book, Beattie describes and defines codependence well in the first fifty pages. Thereafter, in part 2, "The Basics of Self-Care," she discusses the things a codependent needs to do to recover. According to Beattie, codependent people have learned or tried to solve relationship problems by taking on too many of the responsibilities of a relationship rather than doing only what is reasonable and possible. So recovery is about how to take care of oneself and not both people in the relationship. She writes from the point of view of the origins of the term *codependent*, when a codependent was the significant other of an addicted person who abrogated the responsibilities of taking care of himself or herself.

Melody Beattie, *Beyond Codependency: And Getting Better All the Time*

This book discusses the new life after recovery from codependence and certain strategies to keep the recovery going.

Anne Katherine, MA, *Boundaries, Where You End And I Begin*

This is a good book that describes different types of boundaries (protective limits one should establish and maintain for his own benefit and other personal limits to behavior toward others for their protection and privacy). It uses numerous case studies to illustrate how we are violated. There are also exercises to learn all about boundaries. These short articles illustrate guidelines, rules, and procedures that a person sets as reasonable, safe, and permissible limits for how he or she should behave around others and for how other people should behave around him or her.

Dr. Henry Cloud and Dr. John Townsend, *Boundaries, When to Say Yes, How to Say No to Take Control of Your Life*

This is a Christian-based book on the subject of boundaries, one of the main topics of any codependency book. You have poor protective boundaries if you let people walk all over you, poor limiting boundaries if you walk all over them, and so on.

Alice Miller, (1) *Prisoners of Childhood*, (2) *For Your Own Good*, (3) *Thou Shalt Not Be Aware*, (4) *Pictures of a Childhood*, (5) *The Untouched Key*, (6) *Banished Knowledge*, (7) *The Drama of the Gifted Child*, (8) *Breaking Down the Wall of Silence*, (9) *Paths of Life: Seven Scenarios*, (10) *The Truth Will Set You Free*, (11) *The Body Never Lies*, (12) *Free from Lies*, and (13) *From Rage to Courage*

Miller's books address the prevalence of child abuse and how childhood abuse is hidden by personal and societal repression. Children are "gifted" in that they innately know the needs of their parents and know how to adapt to those needs, even if the needs are less than nurturing for the children. I recommend reading at least one of Miller's books for the study of childhood abuse.

Among her books some look at particular case studies (1, 4, 7, and 9); societal rules to enable child abuse (2, 3, 6, 7, 8, and 10); effects of child abuse on the child and society, including notable child victims who become offenders like Adolf Hitler (2) child abuse of famous artists and actors; serious adult disease caused by child abuse (all of them but especially 1, 5, and 6); the hope of recovery (all of them but especially 12); personal stories and advice (most of them but especially 9 and 13); the damage to the psyche from spanking (10); and autobiographical art (4).

Alice Miller invented childhood trauma as a field of psychology and therapy and extended the trauma model of mental disorders (alternatively called *trauma models of psychopathology*), particularly in early development, as the key causal factor in the development of some or many psychiatric disorders, including increasing vulnerability for depression and anxiety and the likelihood of trauma as an adult, like PTSD. She started her career as a Freudian psychoanalyst but grew further and further away from that discipline as she recognized that its tenets contained rules that blamed the child and exonerated the parent. She devotes her book *Thou Shalt Not Be Aware* largely to a critique of psychoanalysis as a movement and particular practice and was critical of both Freud and Jung for their denial of parental blame for childhood trauma as a cause of neurosis. She agreed with Freud's 1896 paper on the etiology of hysteria being sexual abuse but identified his sudden reversal of 1897 into his theory of childhood drives as harmful to recovery and to society. She ultimately broke with psychoanalysis altogether and attempted to find a more effective analysis process. Eventually she refused to recommend anyone else but still saw patients, refusing to subscribe to sexual drives in children as a cause of emotional distress and instead making herself a "sympathetic witness" to the adult recollections of abuse that she considered to be a verified reality. In fact, all her books have this bias, which from my personal experience I believe to be helpful. Despite the difficulty and pain of reliving that trauma in adulthood, it has been my path to healing and well worth the difficulty.

RELATIONSHIPS AND SOMETIMES ANGER

My inclusion of "sometimes anger" in the heading above is recognition that if anger was dealt with directly in these books, I missed it originally. My conscious emphasis was to work on shame to cure codependence with the hope that a solution for my anger would fall out of the mix. Unconsciously, I was in denial about my own anger, and habitually overlooked it in all books.

Healthy relationships in recovery are viewed as a spiritual pursuit, the highest plane we ordinary folks can attain in our daily lives. Angeles Arrien has called a relationship the "most rigorous spiritual practice." True intimacy, not just sex, requires not only love and devotion but also a continual dedication to compassion, understanding, compromise, nurturing, respect, appreciation, fondness, allegiance, and more with an unlikely combination of freedom and commitment with devotion, all while retaining your own self and identity (boundaries). For ordinary people like me in ordinary situations, relationships are the testing ground of life and of recovery.

Pia Mellody, *Facing Love Addiction*

Mellody's website provides this summary of *Facing Love Addiction*:

> In this book, Pia describes in detail the dynamics of a co-addicted relationship, the symptoms of each partner, and the stages of addiction from attraction and fantasy to denial and obsession. She provides a practical recovery process for love addicts and their partners based on Twelve-Step work, exercises, and journaling. Pia's clear guidelines will comfort and motivate all those who seek to establish healthy love relationships.[2]

This book was required reading at a one-week workshop at a well-known recovery center I attended in 2007 during the separation leading to my third divorce (see chapter 20, "Back to the Recovery Center"). The book is excellent. Particularly interesting is Mellody's positing of the "love avoidant" who meshes with the "love addict." Both are needy individuals with low self-esteem. The love addict chases the love avoidant, who gets attention by dancing just out of reach, until the addict says to heck with it and turns and walks away figuratively. Then the needy love avoidant sees he or she is losing the partner who caters to his or her sick needs, so the love avoidant turns and pursues the love addict. The love addict then turns back, and the avoidant turns away yet again. They then together continue the cycle of approach and rejection in perfect dysfunctional, agonizing bliss. Neither can furnish satisfaction for his or her own needs to be valued and loved as a healthy person would be able to do, so each requires the other to supply those needs. The love addict desires enmeshment, and the love avoidant fears enmeshment because he or she feels smothered by it. I found this book very helpful for my relationship addiction problems.

I hasten to add that when I say I found a book helpful, I mean that I did not just read it but *intensely studied* it. I typically highlight a book, make notes all over it, and often write in a journal about my thoughts and emotions that arise as a result. I probably studied many of these books much harder than any physics or math book I had in college. The results probably reflect that: my grades versus my recovery success.

Terry Kellogg, "Relationships," address at the First Annual ACA Convention, CD or audio tape

I originally had an audio tape of this approximately thirty-minute-long talk, and I finally wore it out. I bought the CD last year on the Internet. It is a fantastic and entertaining outline of healthy relationships. Get this first, in my opinion, if you are searching for a healthy romantic relationship. He breaks healthy relationships down very thoroughly into many finely divided different levels of commitment. By contrast unhealthy relationships are illuminated.

Stephanie Covington and Liana Beckett, *Leaving the Enchanted Forest: The Path from Relationship Addiction to Intimacy*

This book is based on a retelling of the Irish folk tale of the ill-fated romance of Princess Iseult the Fair, who is betrothed to King Mark of Cornwall, and the knight Tristan, who is pledged to King Mark. Iseult and Tristan accidentally drink a magic love potion and become entranced with each other. They run from King Mark to the enchanted forest and live in unrealistic bliss, ignoring the need to leave the forest to return to real life. This book mistakenly confuses Tristan's lover, Princess Iseult, with her mother, Queen Iseult, but the lesson is valid.

Being a recovery book based on relationship addiction, it was ideal for me, and it made obvious that this malady was not limited to the modern day. As a relationship addict I struggled with the desire to be in my own enchanted forest with my own love of my life, all the while knowing it was impractical and unrealistic to ignore the real world of children, family, and career. Fortunately, I was not to find such a love sober, but I was consumed with the desire for an enmeshed relationship, much as I knew it would have been bad for me. Perhaps this was another example of rational thinking unable to surmount hard-held emotions. Who would ever want to be in an enmeshed relationship? Someone who grew up in one, that's who.

This book showed me that myths are still important to modern life in illustrating universal truths about human nature.

Earnie Larsen, *Stage II Relationships*

This book provides practical advice on how to break unhealthy patterns of relationships as a person moves forward after sobriety. It is easily adaptable to any addiction.

John Gray, *Men Are from Mars, Women Are from Venus.*

John Gray, the ex-husband of Barbara De Angelis, does not focus on dysfunction or codependence in this book but instead outlines the differences between men and women in a most entertaining manner. It is indispensable.

Douglas and Naomi Moseley, *Dancing in the Dark*

I read this early in my quest for a healthy relationship right after a separation—did I mention I was a love addict? It is a very good book, probably the best non-twelve-step type of recovery book I read for general healthy relationship principles.

John Welwood, PhD, *Journey of the Heart*

This is another good general book on relationships that is not a twelve-step type of recovery book.

GENERAL WELLNESS, ABUNDANCE, AND MYTHOLOGY

Lynne Bernfield, *When You Can, You Will*

This is a comforting book about recovery and self-help for people just trying to improve themselves. Bernfield provides compassionate advice to ease up on your quest and just relax and smell the roses along your recovery path. You'll do it when you can, that is, when you are able.

Marianne Williamson, *A Return to Love* and numerous lectures, tapes, and other books

Marianne Williamson used to have weekly free or for-a-small donation lectures at a packed theater in LA when she was not in New York. She lectured on general principles of living from *A Course in Miracles*, which is a spiritual book and program that many people swear by and that I admire. Her lectures were always an uplifting spiritual activity for me, and many times I arranged carloads of other fifty-year-old singles to go on outings to see her speak. I got a lot out of her tapes when she spoke about relationship issues, since relationships are best looked at as a spiritual pursuit. Relationships should not be a battlefield of love but the testing ground of love and of the techniques to make them workable.

Deepak Chopra, too many and too famous to name them all

Deepak Chopra's books provide a highly spiritual and practical approach to nearly all subjects, and each is a joy to read.

Joseph Campbell, *The Hero with a Thousand Faces* and the Bill Moyers interviews with him on the six-part public-television series *The Power of Myth* (available on tape and DVD)

I mentioned above why I think myths are important to man. See chapter 16, "Family History and Personal Growth" for a short discussion on Campbell's seminal work *The Hero with a Thousand Faces*. This book discusses the similarities of myths around the world, a similarity that convinced me that all men face pretty much the same problems and stages of life, regardless of the age in which they live. *The Hero with a Thousand Faces* is a very important book. While I read it, I kept a journal of my own progress along the hero's journey through life, with surprising and gratifying results.

Barbara De Angelis, PhD, *Real Moments*

Real Moments explores what the real moments of happiness are and how to recognize, cultivate, and create them, as opposed to the other mundane business of life. Barbara De Angelis recommends the advantages of enjoying these "real moments" as opposed to just trudging through ordinary life. It was a fun book for me about the practice of getting back to enjoying life by recognizing the real moments.

I also saw De Angelis speak at a New Thought church one Sunday. Her forte was relationships, and she had a lot to say about baggage, that dysfunctional stuff we bring to relationships. In the question-and-answer session, a woman rose to ask a question and started off by describing her relationship with her boyfriend and how he pushed her buttons. "It's his *job* to push your buttons," Barbara interrupted, emphasizing the word *job* loudly. Her point was that one reason to be in a relationship must be to grow. So when we pick people who push our buttons, we must want to get past those buttons, which are, after all, ours and do stick out quite far, making it easy for others to push or even bump into accidently. I love growing up.

I also got last-minute tickets to see her tape a self-help video. Now my mother did not raise any fools, and I am a relationship addict, so I called up a gorgeous lady who was a former child movie star and asked her to go with me. Sure enough she looked great, and while we were standing in line at the movie studio, a young man walked up and asked if we would come with him. He soon explained when we got a few steps away, where the rest of the line could not hear, that he wanted to put us in the front row. She was delighted, and so was I. I was happy to be seen with her and to sit in the front row, which had been my plan all along. I never saw the tape, but some friends in recovery did and mentioned seeing us on it on TV. The taping was very interesting and entertaining, and it confirmed all that I had been working on with recovery and relationships.

TRAUMA, PAIN, AND LOSS

I have placed this category of references low on the list because I came to it late in my struggle with anger, actually after I started treating my losses (see chapter 22, "A Simple Course of Treatment"). I found in trauma a whole new and fruitful field to explore and standard practices to cure it. I do not regret missing it for so long. Rather, I realized through Lynne Bernfield's *When You Can, You Will* (see above under "General Wellness") that my path was the best that I could do. I never slacked but did take a month or two off here and there to relax and enjoy the plateaus of recovery that I reached along the way. I cannot emphasize too much how enjoyable my life in recovery has been, despite the fear, disappointments, anguish, and all the hard work that I put into it. Why did I go through such a grueling ordeal? First of all it was fun and deeply satisfying, even if it was often painful. But mostly I realized early on that I was worth it to me. My low self-esteem went first after the realization of my shame, next came self-acceptance, and then I finally started to put myself first on my list of people to take care of.

Stephen Levine, *Unattended Sorrow*

My voices cracks and I nearly break out crying when I tell someone this title out loud. In a way it is the story of sixty-two years of my life. It is not about addiction recovery but about recovery from trauma in general. Stephen Levine expanded a pamphlet he wrote for the victims of 9/11 into this book. The 9/11 committee ended up not accepting the pamphlet, but the book is fantastic. It was the final piece for healing me in book form, like my excellent therapist provided the final piece as far as a therapy.

Then I discovered that trauma healing is a field all its own and is growing. Right after *Unattended Sorrow* I read the next two books on this list.

Peter A. Levine, *Waking the Tiger*

This is a fascinating book, if you can accept that we are higher animals that have a lot in common with other mammals. In this book Peter A. Levine demonstrates that animals have an instinctual capacity to heal. He asks why animals in the wild are rarely traumatized even though their lives are threatened continually. He tells of antelope narrowly escaping being killed by big cats and then, in a visible physiological process, they literally tremble and shake off the effects of the attack. Within minutes they are back with the herd grazing as if nothing had happened. From this he extrapolates to the steps for humans to similarly heal from trauma via a program he presents in *Healing Trauma*, the next book on this list.

Peter A. Levine, *Healing Trauma: A Pioneering Program for Restoring the Wisdom of Your Body*

I must admit that by that time I read this book I had found my own program by crying, and so I only skimmed the book. But I am sure it is valuable, for by utilizing my psychological/physiological processes, I healed myself.

When I blithely say, "I healed myself," I do not negate all the assistance and compassion of all the men and women in programs and therapy rooms and the authors and lecturers who contributed mightily to the cause. Of course none of them worked for free. They must have also thought I was worth it. But ultimately, I had to do the work, and no one else could do it for me.

Tian Dayton, PhD, *Heartwounds: The Impact of Unresolved Trauma and Grief on Relationships*

Tian Dayton presents a comprehensive treatment on the effects of trauma and grief on relationships in this book, and very importantly she emphasizes the concept of loss as the form pain from trauma can take. The book is sadly silent on anger, though, or I missed it. I finished reading it a few weeks before my anger miracle finally happened.

Judith Viorst, *Necessary Losses: The Loves, Illusions, Dependencies, and Impossible Expectations That All of Us Have to Give Up in Order to Grow*

This book is about the vital bond between our usual and normal losses and gains that are necessary to grow—what we give up in order to grow. In my book I also consider chronic losses, those that occur over and over in life until we heal the causes.

FEAR AND LOVE

Fear and love are often confused as opposites, but this is not so. The basic opposite of fear is courage, and the real opposite of love is indifference or hate. Nevertheless, as a path to serenity many books make a compelling case for moving from a position of fear into a position of love. I combine these two emotions in this section because of the striking association of them in the following book, which I would recommend to anyone. It is in my top five.

Gerald G. Jampolsky, MD, *Love Is Letting Go of Fear*

Love Is Letting Go of Fear is a truly feel-good book, and it is hard for me to see how anyone would not be better for reading it. Jampolsky is also a treat to see speak. It is impossible not to be swayed by the glow of love and serenity that he emits. I have read this little book four times.

SEX, LOVE, AND RELATIONSHIP ADDICTION

Anne Wilson Schaef, *Escape from Intimacy, Untangling the "Love" Addictions: Sex, Romance, Relationships*

This book allowed me to classify myself as a relationship addict. I also consider myself as a love addict, because in me, either descriptive name fits. I am both addicted to love and to being in a relationship, but the relationship must be a loving one. In other words, for the arrangement to work for me, I need to be in relationship with someone I love and who loves me.

Schaef's classification of love or relationship addiction is more specific, and probably more widely applicable. For her use of the two terms, love and relationship are not both necessary at once in each member of the couple.

Further both love and relationship addicts may not insist on sex, so they are not necessarily sex addicts.

It is a confusing situation; all combinations of symptoms may be present in a person or in a couple.

One may object that the classification of humans is somehow improper, and I would agree that to do so with a moral (or immoral) or ethical (or unethical) agenda, it is. But the first stage of any science is classification, the sorting of characteristics, causes, and results into classes. This book helped me crystallize my thinking about the dysfunctionality in my relationships. And such classification tells me I am not unique. A danger in AA is summed up by the cliché "terminally unique," meaning a new-to-the-program alkie can be, in his or her mind, so unique that it may kill him or her. There are fundamental commonalities in human beings, and identifying them with a name, even if that naming is limiting, is useful.

Patrick Carnes, PhD, *Understanding Sexual Addiction, Contrary to Love, Don't Call It Love, In the Shadows of the Net,* and many other books on sexual addiction

These books had the same value for me as the Schaef *Escape from Intimacy* book; they helped define me with my symptoms and narrow my focus to properly define my recovery program.

There is some controversy over Patrick Carnes saying that sex addiction is a true addiction, and some believe that most of what he proposes to cure the addiction is disguised social judgment. I cannot speak to this for the general population. It's a close call determining whether sex can be an addiction, but my definition of addiction, taken from John Bradshaw, is "a pathological relationship to any mood-altering experience that has life damaging consequences."[3]

Sexual activities can be so compulsive or dangerous they become diseases, and sex is certainly mood altering. And it can have life-damaging consequences, like sexually transmitted diseases, divorce, a lover's jealous spouse, and more. But many so-called sex addictions may be merely socially unacceptable behaviors to some but not all people.

RELIGIOSITY (ADDICTION TO RELIGION)

Father Leo Booth, *Breaking the Chains*
Father Leo, now Reverend Leo, a former Episcopal priest and now a Unity minister, was a don't-miss speaker on the AA circuit for his wit and ability to relate to all alcoholics as only another alkie can. His forte has been the field of religious addiction, advocating in many of his books a noncompulsive approach to religion, especially since religious belief and spirituality can be abused in recovery, and, like all addictive behavior, the result can be life damaging.

In *Breaking the Chains*, Father Leo describes the pitfalls of addiction to religion and sets people on a sane approach to it. The pitfalls are particularly dangerous to recovering people, who often exhibit tendencies toward excess.

Father Leo Booth, *The God Game: It's Your Move*
In this book Father Leo describes spiritual addiction where the assumed relationship to God is a drug to cover up problems.

John Bradshaw has also written, lectured, and made tapes on religious addiction.

ANGER AND ANGER MANAGEMENT BOOKS AND PROGRAMS

Generally speaking I found books on anger to be of two types: training of my thinking so I could rationally control my anger (anger management), or detailing of the bad health consequences of anger. I dismissed the bad-health type as trying to scare me into getting over anger, which was judging them harshly, because there are definite and serious health risks to extreme and chronic anger.

As for the anger management type of book, I never read one completely. As for anger management programs, I found them useless for me, but that was my failing. First, I had no use for them because I was addicted to anger, and as I have said, anger was my friend. For years I had gotten angry to feel better, to modify my feelings of helplessness and powerlessness. Second, when I finally got serious about getting over anger, I wanted a complete recovery from anger—that is, I wanted toxic anger completely banished from me (as I discuss in chapter 10, "Rational Control of Emotions"). I was not interested in "managing" my anger, and that is exactly what the programs I went to attempted to do—help me learn ways to *manage* my anger. But I wanted anger exiled—gone but not forgotten—from my behavior. The rational approach of anger management held no interest for me in my hopes to quit my anger altogether. I was not interested in just being a less angry and marginally better person; I wanted to be a not-angry and much-better person.

There is a fundamental flaw in anger management as a concept: it assumes anger is the bad behavior of a "bad" person; therefore, he must learn to be "better," that is, not act out his anger. First of all, this goal does not try to lessen the reservoir of emotions that fuel the anger; it only attempts to control or manage the emotion of anger. But more importantly, the underlying idea of anger management is that you as an angry person are labeled "bad." This promotes self-defeating self-talk which can be devastating.

We are what we believe ourselves to be. If we fervently believe we are "bad," we will tend to be a "bad person." And we will tend to be as bad as we assume we are. This is an ego thing. Something within us drives us to be "right," that is, "correct," rather than "incorrect," even at the expense of lessening ourselves. We would rather be right than good. So it is a monumentally poor strategy to try to correct behavior by taking the first step of labeling yourself a bad person. This sets up the potential for a "self-fulfilling prophesy." I back this thinking up by the perennial wisdom presented in Appendix III, "Mind."

Nevertheless, knowing this, I swept those ideas aside in my desperation to be "better." So I did try two different anger management classes.

There is more detail about my experiences in anger-management classes below in this chapter, and Appendix II presents research that I funded about those programs. I also point the reader to chapters 35 and 36, "Anger Management: A Survey of the Web" and "Anger Management: A Survey of the Professional Literature." The latter is an introduction to Appendix II. My personal experiences below as well as the realities behind chapters 35 and 36 and Appendix II are the basis of my opinion.

I attended two different anger-management weekly groups. They were both court-mandated programs, although I volunteered for the first. I was volunteered with a nudge from the judge to the second. In the first program I went to about eight meetings, but I got almost nothing out of them. First, I did not fit in, because everyone but me was probably there under court order. I was and am cognizant of the reality of how someone can be "too" unique (*terminally unique* as we say in AA) such that the message goes in one ear and out the other. The techniques they taught to stop the emotional rush of power to claim the high ground were logical, and at the time I was sure they would work—except I thought that they would be insufficient to work for me, as quick and as hot as my anger was. I doubted that the rational thinking could cope with how powerful my anger often seemed to be. It seemed it would be like shoveling away at a rapidly advancing avalanche. I now know I was addicted to anger. The second anger-management program was even more ineffective, and I tell about it in chapter 34, "Alternate Treatments for Anger."

I also went two different times to what I would call an abreaction program conducted by a group of psychologists. It was a three-day all volunteer session attended by about twenty people who hoped to cure or alleviate their anger or the effects of it. On Friday it started about five o'clock in the afternoon and ran until about two in the morning or until the day's work was done. In other words, no one was left in the middle of his or her work or in a crisis, and we all stayed through it. The Saturday session started at eight in the morning and ran similarly till about two in the morning. On Sunday, we started at nine in the morning and ran as late as anyone wanted, which ended up being about eight o'clock both times. The program was intense and featured a lot of acting out of our anger and confronting cushions or empty chairs as representations of people we were angry at, usually a parent or caregiver. These confrontations ran the gauntlet from talking or screaming angrily to beating the surrogate cushions with plastic Wiffle bats. The idea was to get in touch with your anger and pain and to show rage and tears with the hope that not only would you feel differently about your emotional self and effect an emotional shift but also that the anger or pain would leave when the hypothesized causal emotional energy was released. I did get a lot of good out of the experiences intellectually by paying attention to everyone's turn to work, but it did not lessen my anger. I did get further in touch with myself, and it probably helped ease my low self-esteem simply because I was in such a tightly constrained group and could not help but feel I fit in. They were not weirdoes or thugs, just ordinary people like me, and it was comforting to be accepted. It was a landmark three-day experience, the best workshop I ever went to, but I was not able to lower my anger as a result either time. Since my anger was not abated the first time, I went to it a second time less than a year later. The experience probably reinforced my self-esteem feelings, but I'd already taken the main step upward in self-esteem, so there was no very large change. Interestingly, the staff did not seem to focus on me nearly as much this second time, and I think it was because they had seen me there recently. I likewise had no discernible lessening of my anger or its effects from this second session. It did not release much anger, if any at all. Nevertheless, it was on my path to wellness, so I cannot advise against it.

I have read criticisms of this type of abreaction therapy that say it tends to increase anger rather than release it, because the client may take the extreme expression of anger in a violent way (violent toward the cushions, anyway) as socially acceptable. It might have done that to me, but I think it really had little effect on my anger, although it was one more step toward knowing my self. It is possible that the experience of beating pillows while screaming at my imagined mother allowed me to justify my anger, but it is hard to tell. I had always felt pretty justified at being angry at both of my parents, especially Mom, but now I think that justification was the relief from pain or fear of a pending loss that anger gave me, not a logical analysis of unfairness.

One way to view the experience was that it was like the controversial *aversion* methods of curing alcoholism, which all AA members laugh at and abhor. *How*, we wonder, *can you give an alcoholic all the alcohol he wants, even laced with some substance that will make him sick, and expect him to want to not drink?* Drinking is what alkies do best! And feeling sick from a hangover never deterred us. And it is hard to imagine the shame and pain that an alkie is trying to escape being better than the pain of the alcohol and substance once it is no longer administered—if you truly understand how bad that normal alcoholic's pain is.

In the workshop I experienced no aversion to anger after beating the cushions or watching others do it. After all, anger was my best friend. It always made me feel good. How could a lot more make me want to stop? At least in retrospect this seemed to be my experience.

I now wonder, if the cushion beating was to dissipate my anger, where was it supposed to go? It just stayed with me. When I beat my cushions, I was not triggered by any current shame attacks or pain attacks, so my turn at bat resulted in embarrassment. Without anything to feel helpless over—no *cushion* had ever abused me either as a child or an adult—I had no need to call forth the soothing effects of anger to effect power and control over that dastardly cushion.

It is interesting to note that in this workshop there was an assumption that the clients' anger was a result of some action or wrong done to them by whoever was the object of the anger. Thus, it was fair to assume that the remaining interaction in the form of emotions toward those folks needed to be addressed. The acting out was the recommended method. The process seems somewhat logical, but the results did not support the method for me.

My Personal Experience with Therapists

I have also been in therapy with many therapists, usually for my problems with relationships, which problems were chiefly due to my anger. I believe that during this period my anger was really residual anger at my mother directed at my wives and women friends. I was supersensitive to their actions or words that seemed to trigger me like some long-past behavior of my mother, and often I could specifically identify the behaviors of my wife or girlfriend that were similar to something my mother had done. In most cases the women were entirely innocent and never as guilty as I made them out to be. It was my childhood issues stuffed away in the dark recesses of my mind that leaped out at them in anger when I perceived "Here it comes again"—an accidental utterance or action that reminded me of one of my mom's abuses against me and triggered some residual pain.

Out of about eight therapists, only two did me any real good, but maybe I was a tough nut to crack. My wives liked the others though and were the driving force behind my continuing the sessions with them beyond all reasonable hope. If my anger was my power, the sessions can be said to have been power for my wives. I viewed the sessions as me, the perpetrator, trying to get well in a therapeutic session with my wife of the moment, the victim, trying to get me well.

I can't say these professionals my wives and I saw were bad, but their treatment did not click miraculous with me. But imagine how they probably felt. One diagnosed me as ADD, in my adulthood, after seeing us for about one and a half years. I went to a psychiatrist at the psychologist's recommendation, and he gave me a test out of a mass-market paperback and, after a twenty-minute session, prescribed Ritalin for me. It only cost me $400 every six months for another twenty-minute session and a new prescription. After about two years, another doctor knowledgeable about ADD and Ritalin scoffed at my ADD diagnosis, and that ended my Ritalin usage. I had been optimistic that maybe I was ADD, and I hoped Ritalin would be the cure for both that ADD and my anger. Hence it might save the relationship. Ritalin slows down a truly ADD person (usually), but to a non-ADD person, it is an addictive upper. And considering I was prone to anger, as well as alcoholic, it was a dangerous drug for me to take. Fortunately, I did not get addicted to it. The whole Ritalin fiasco was an indication of how severe my relationship addiction was—I was willing to go to any length to preserve it.

I went to my final therapist (see chapter 21, "Was My Therapist a Genius, Was I Ready, or Was He Tipped Off?") completely on my own while separated following my third divorce and finally had very good results.

Maybe my error was in going to all the others for someone else—my parents or a wife. The other one who did me a lot of good was the first one, but that was at three and four years sober, before I found CoDA. I went to him on my own because of my anger toward my folks and my volatile relationship with them. And I did get help on dealing with them but not on my anger. So maybe there should be a therapy principle like the AA rule "You can't get sober for anyone else, only for yourself."

HOSPITAL PROGRAMS, WORKSHOPS, AND MEETINGS

John Bradshaw, seminars

I went to John Bradshaw's first "Finishing Business with Mother" workshop. There were about four hundred people in a large convention showroom for the two-day workshop, and many therapists and caregivers roamed the aisles to assist people who swooned. I did not swoon. Although I did all the exercises to the best of my ability, I had little emotional reaction. Intellectually I got a lot out of it, though. The workshop may have been too large, but more likely I was not ready. I was definitely in denial about my anger, thinking deep down that it was not that bad (at least to me), although I wanted to get along better with my mother. I may even have been far enough into codependence recovery that the workshop did not touch me in a shocking, new way. It was geared to counter toxic shame, and not anger. At that time I had the mistaken belief that my anger was directly due to toxic shame, so I hoped work on shame would help relieve my anger toward my mother. Later as I developed, I learned that my anger was from the pain of my childhood, that is, indirectly from toxic shame. Because I went to do anger work, I was disappointed that I was unaffected, disappointed that my anger toward my mother was not miraculously healed and that I didn't at least have an epiphany or some deep insight. I had read often about "finishing business with father" but never mother. Since my business was mainly with Mom, I jumped at the chance to go to the workshop. It surely helped me with my codependence, but not my anger, which stayed far beneath the surface, totally inaccessible to treatment for reasons that are developed throughout this book.

I believe I went to this workshop after John started his inner-child work about which he writes in *Homecoming: Reclaiming and Championing Your*

Inner Child, because the workshop exercises were inner child exercises. One exercise was to write a letter to mom left handed. As he relates in that book (see above), he found the healing results for *many* miraculous compared to any other work he had previously done. I was not one of the many. But I also feel I was not a fair subject—I was there for anger, not the results of toxic shame such as low self-esteem, isolation or other symptoms. For all I know, it did help with my toxic shame which I had at that time, and those benefits just did not extend to my anger.

ALCOHOLIC ANONYMOUS

I give my second wife credit for getting me to AA, where I got sober. It was a Wednesday, and I had vowed once again to quit drinking the Saturday before. We had had a big fight, and she called me at work. Leery that the fight might continue on the phone, I took the call in my office, not in my lab where others might hear. She said brightly and with excitement, "I just called Alcoholics Anonymous, and I talked to the most wonderful woman. She was so spiritual!" My wife was talking fast like a delighted little kid.

Alcoholics Anonymous! I thought. *Geez oh me. Why didn't I think of that?*

"She was so calm and peaceful, and … I'm going to go to a meeting tonight!" She still sounded very happy.

I thought, *Oh geez, please take me with you.*

After a pause, she asked, still excited, "Do you want to go?"

"I sure do."

That's how I got to AA. My wife got us both there, and I wanted to go because I was sick and tired of being sick and tired. I'd had exactly the right amount of drinks, not one too many and not one too few.

We went to meetings, and she entered a twenty-eight-day hospital program run by a medical doctor who pioneered hospital sobriety programs. I went to the hospital to see her every day and also to all the lectures at the hospital I could, and I saw all the movies and sat and talked to her and the other patients about our drinking just like Bill and Bob had in 1935. I followed the bus in my car and went to the meeting they took the patients to every night and spent weekend days with her and the other patients. I wanted to stay sober so very bad. I took a week off from work for her family week in

the hospital program. Three days before she was to be discharged, I was going crazy. I had gone without a drink for sixty-three days since the Saturday
before the phone call she made to the volunteer at AA. After sixty-three days
I was probably finally getting sober, as my poor liver finally had assimilated
and passed the reservoir of alcohol stored in my fat tissues. I was experiencing
a classic six-week *dry drunk*. With no more booze in me to kill the feelings, I
was really squirrely. My wife got her counselor at the hospital to talk to me,
and it was not too hard for her to convince me to check in to the same hospital
program. I really wanted to stay sober. Drinking was not on my mind, and I
did not feel like I was in danger of drinking, but an alkie is always in danger
of drinking, especially a newly sober one whose emotions have finally been
released from sedation. Checking myself in was just a matter of my being
"willing to go to any length" (a line from the Big Book made into an AA cliché
describing how desperately an alcoholic should be to get sober).

   I said my wife got me to AA, and that is true. But codependence drove
me to drink and thus to AA. I was such a sick codependent with my life
history of abuse and family enmeshment that carried over to my marriage
and also my love addiction that only alcohol could have eased the pain. Five
years later I found out how bad that codependent pain could be when she
left me, and I was sober but still codependent. That pain is described in the
next chapter.

   This wife, the love of my life, left me five years after we got sober. During
those five years my anger had not gotten any better, although I was sober
and doing very well in all other ways. We divorced about two years after
the initial separation. I had discovered CoDA after the separation, but my
progress against codependence was exceedingly slow. I was single and suffered desperately from love addiction, an extreme form of codependence,
even though I was now going to CoDA and studying Pia Mellody and all the
other sources on codependence I could find. I lived with a very nice woman
and broke up with her, and in that relationship my anger was as bad as ever.
I was single for a couple of years and then engaged to be married, but that
engagement was ended when to my childhood abandonment issues surged
to the surface. About three years later I got married again to yet another
woman, and my anger was even worse. It was the same old story. My childhood issues, of which I was well aware but could not overcome, caused me to

rage often and intensely in all these relationships. And my anger was getting progressively worse.

My third wife and I were separated for six months after about four years of marriage, and I ended up in a recovery center for a one-month program that specialized in addiction recovery. I needed to recover from my anger but was put in a sex addiction program, because they considered love/relationship addiction to be a sex addiction. Still convinced that my problem was shame from my childhood issues that must have led to my anger, I tried to do my assigned program, but my heart was not in it. Naturally, I made no progress under a program I was not fully committed to. I could not adhere to my assigned program, and I do not think they had a program for anger that was based on an emotional cause (pain and losses in childhood).

As a relationship addict, who feared the loss of my relationship, I was willing to go to any length to preserve it, and if that meant trying to adhere to my assigned program, I was compliant. Viewed the other way, if I had assertively stated that I wanted to get over my anger by dealing with my childhood issues, I believe that together the organization and I would have stood a chance of my making progress. But at the time I was not aware how pain worked within me or how much of it I had. As it was, I completed my month with no progress toward my goals. I did, however, have a great deal of respect for the institution, and six or seven years later, I returned for a very successful and rewarding one-week workshop geared exactly toward relationship addiction which uncovered the pain.

Both the above one-month and the two weekend stays (at the anger-expression programs) were wasteful failures for me for the simple reason that I submitted myself, unknowingly, to programs that had no reasonable, in a theoretical sense, chances of successes. All three programs were designed to treat the wrong thing within me. The anger-expression, pillow-beating weekends seemed designed to bring hidden anger to the surface and to express it in a safe way and thus (hopefully) to dissipate it so it would no longer be a problem. This wrong program had nothing to do with what I thought was the crux of my problem, my anger rooted in my unresolved feelings from my childhood abuse.

Basically, I had attempted to cure an ailment like arthritis by taking antibiotics, as if I had a severe infection as opposed to arthritis. As I stated when I first went to AA, I *badly* wanted to get sober. It is plainly stated in the Big Book that an alcoholic cannot get sober for anyone but himself or herself—not for a significant other, a job, or kids. Likewise, when I went to beat pillows, I was attempting to heal the wrong thing; I thought maybe if I just expressed my anger it would finally dissipate. I never paused to consider that I'd had a lifetime of anger and rage expression and that those frequent expressions had never dissipated my anger. And in all my therapy, except the last, which I shall relate later, I went for someone else—to get along with my parents or my wives. Additionally in the last therapy, instead of pillow beating (anger expression) or work on shame, I reexperienced my sadness and pain of childhood. That process led to healing those emotions, and that made the anger dissipate. (See chapter 22, "A Simple Course of Treatment.") In the other therapies sessions I was intent on healing my shame, which I mistakenly thought would stop my anger.

I went to other one-day meetings, seminars, talks, and lectures given by other practitioners and organizations. If there were any that even seemed remotely likely to shed light on codependence, relationships, or anger, I would go to them, participating to the fullest extent I could. I was a full-blown recovery junkie, addicted to recovery perhaps, but I had stopped banging up cars and falling down drunk, so I was happy. And I was getting better in codependence and healthier in relationships all the time.

But that darn anger. That had to wait till my one-week workshop experience related in chapter 20, "Back to the Recovery Center."

---

[1]   Bradshaw, *Homecoming*, xii.

[2]   "Books," Pia Mellody, 2007, http://www.piamellody.com/books.html.

[3]   Bradshaw, *Healing the Shame*, 15.

16

FAMILY HISTORY AND PERSONAL GROWTH

My dad's father, Charlie Fosnight, was a hellfire-and-brimstone fundamentalist preacher down on the dryland, our family name for the prairie in southeastern Colorado. Charlie and Ella had migrated from Ohio via Oklahoma. Ella was carrying my dad when she and my grandfather left their sharecropped farm in Oklahoma in the summer of 1915 by horse and wagon with my dad's older brother and sister. Dad was to be the third of four children. Charlie was escaping a local cholera epidemic. He had heard about free land in Southeast Colorado that was opened to homesteading. The day they left, a neighbor of his, Levi Guthrie, rode up on horseback and asked him where he was going. Charlie told him, and Levi asked if they would drive slow and watch for him to catch up, so he could go back and load his family and things in his wagon and join them. Charlie agreed, and several days later, they each filed on a half section of land in Las Animas County, Colorado. Levi did not like the adjoining land, so Charlie refiled on slightly poorer land in Baca County. Levi and his wife, Eva, then filed on the land in the next half section, so they and my grandparents could be neighbors. Neighbors were at least one-half mile apart, and five or more miles was not unusual and unusual spacing. The closeness was important because horse and wagon were the only transportation. A man sometimes had to walk a mile or more for help.

Levi and Eva eventually had four children, but Levi was kicked in the head by a horse and killed about eight or nine years after homesteading. Eva stayed on and raised the children herself, and some of them stayed on the homestead to live and raise their own families there. One of Levi and Eva's descendants is still living in that country; he is a big rancher and owns about nine sections of land and leases a lot more.

Each family homesteaded a half section of land, 360 acres or one-half square mile. The large size of the plots indicated how poor the land was on the prairie. Years ago I asked a contemporary of my folks, Boyd Rose, another big-time rancher who was still living in Las Animas County on his dad's homestead, how many acres he figured for each cow. I had just read James Michener's *Centennial*. In that book one of the characters leaves his father's forty-acre farm in the rich Pennsylvania Dutch region for Colorado, and Michener describes how well the family lived on that small farm. Boyd told me he figured forty acres was needed for each cow, and in Pennsylvania Michener claimed forty cows per acre! That works out to Colorado land being 1/1,600 the quality of Pennsylvania land.

Charlie gathered rocks from the cliff of a small rise near the house and some squat trees from forty miles away to line the walls of the pit to make a dugout house with a sod roof for that first winter. The floor was about three or four feet below grade, which meant that just a little lumber or sod was needed for the above-ground walls, which were three to four feet tall up to the sod roof. There were no trees of any significant size for lumber on the prairie, and the nearest timber was about 140 miles as the crow flies, which is a good expression since there were few roads.

In November, a month after the snow started coming to that country (and by then they had probably survived at least one blizzard), Charlie delivered my father, Verryl Sr. Dad was born, of course, with Ella's help, but no other. There were probably no doctors within two hundred miles, which was how far it was to Denver. Dad told me in his late seventies that he saw his first doctor at age twenty-eight, when he was drafted in 1943. That was the way it was where they grew up from 1915 on. It was not unlike the 1880s.

Dad was born a blue baby; that is, he failed to breathe right away. Levi saw the light of the coal oil lamp from a mile away and rushed over to come upon Grandpa rocking and praying while holding his stillborn son, who suddenly howled to life.

The next year Grandpa built a new house at ground level because the original house flooded several times in the spring rains, which in those pre–Dust Bowl days came fairly often. Snakes, mice, and pack rats were a problem also, and a snake might be a diamondback rattler. Grandpa went back to his original home in Ohio and bought enough lumber to build a four-room house (kitchen, living room, and two bedrooms) and had it shipped out to Colorado in a railroad car. I do not know where the unloading point was on the railroad, but it probably was La Junta, Colorado, about sixty miles away by wagon, a two- or three-day trip. He probably had to make several trips also. It may have been sixty miles farther if the railroad only went through Pueblo. The kitchen of the house he built doubled as a store from which Grandma sold coffee, sugar, flour, and other staples that Grandpa trucked by wagon from La Junta.

One day in the store when Dad was still a baby he was crying very hard. An Indian woman asked, "What's wrong with that baby?"

Grandma said, "I don't know. He's been crying all day."

"Give him to me," the Indian said, looking in his wide-open screaming mouth. Then while holding him, she whipped off his damp diaper, wrapped the wettest spot of it around her finger, and swabbed the inside of his mouth with it. "Do that three times a day," she said and handed him back to his mother.

He recovered from trench mouth in a few days. That was doctoring on the dryland in 1915.

Mom's mother and grandmother came to Las Animas County about that same time with two wagons of all their things, about ten kids, and no men. Both had lost their husbands. Because there were no men, the land agent would not file their claims for one-half section each; to him no men meant failure to survive in that harsh land.

According to Timothy Egan's 2006 National Book Award winner, *The Worst Hard Time*, an oral history about the dust bowl centering on Baca and Animas Counties in Colorado plus the panhandle of Oklahoma and West Texas, in the land in Colorado they settled on

> The weather might display seven different moods in a year,
> and six of them were life-threatening. Droughts, blizzards,

grass fires, hailstorms, flash floods, and tornadoes tormented … A few good years, with good prices, would be followed by too many horrid years and massive die-offs from drought or winter freeze-ups.[1]

So without even one man to do the backbreaking work, the land agent said, "Well, I'm sorry, but I can't let you file your claim."

They argued.

"What are you going to do at plowing time?" the county man asked.

"That boy can plow," my grandmother said, meaning with a horse and probably a walking single-row middlebreaker.

"He's just a boy. How old is he?" the county man asked.

"Fourteen, but he can plow."

"How you gonna milk and plant your crops?"

"We can all do that, and these other children can help."

My grandmother and great-grandmother had an answer for every doubt, but finally he asked, "What're you gonna do for money?"

"Why, we'll teach school," my grandmother said.

"Oh, you're schoolteachers?" the county man said and hurriedly filed the claims.

Yes, they could teach school. Many of my mother's older sisters taught school after attending some high school. Mom and Dad did not graduate from high school until I was a small boy. The wooden one-room schools of the time were originally built by the settlers for their and neighbors' children. Later during the Great Depression, the WPA replaced many of them with stone one-room schools. The stone school building on the site of the original wood building that my dad and his brother and sisters went to is still standing and has a stone lintel over the entrance with "WPA 1934" chiseled on it. 1934 was the year my parents were married. On Sundays the wood and later the stone building was the church, and my grandfather preached there. My mother was one of the first ones of her generation on either side who graduated with a four-year college degree, and she did so from a California state college the week before I did from a prestigious university in 1964. Her younger sister graduated from nursing school in the early '40s in Denver, and that sister's husband attended the University of Colorado as a chemist.

He took all his doctorate classes but did not get his PhD because of the Depression and hard times.

This was the world my parents were born into and in which they pulled themselves up by their bootstraps. In addition to being children of the Great Depression, they were right in the center of the worst part of it, the dust bowl. At a deeper level they were children of horse-and-wagon days, almost covered-wagon pioneers. They grew up in 1915–1934, but because of place, the barren plains, and the times, their life was akin to the late 1800s when my grandparents grew up. My cousins and I were raised on those dust bowl stories about how hard times were then. My family referred to that period only as the dust bowl and never as the Depression. I think this was because no one on the dryland had more than a few dollars at any one time. Since everyone was poor, the hard part was the drought and dust storms. Otherwise, the lack of funds or goods was not at all unusual.

Thus my parents grew up in a *subsistence society*, very different from how I grew up in the mid-1950s to 1970s. In my childhood I lived in a world where I could "follow my bliss," to take Joseph Campbell's famous phrase. "If you follow your bliss, you put yourself on a kind of track that has been there all the while, waiting for you, and the life that you ought to be living is the one you are living. Wherever you are—if you are following your bliss, you are enjoying that refreshment, that life within you, all the time."[2]

That bliss was possible on the dryland during the dust bowl but only from family and managing to survive, not from any material goods, exalted stature, or great works. It was a subsistence and patriarchal society at that time and place—you did what your old man said, or someone in the family would die or the whole family would suffer. In my mother's case with her mother and grandmother migrating to that desolate land alone, it was a matriarchal family.

I have often wondered if my mother's family remained matriarchal after my grandmother remarried my maternal grandfather. He died before I was born, so I never knew him, only of him. He was dynamic and fiery but small. He came up from Texas on horseback at fourteen years old with two men whom he was not related to. My uncle, his son never knew the story, but my guess is he probably ran away from a harsh family life. That uncle's son, my cousin, told me that his dad asked our grandfather about those circumstances but that he would never talk about it.

My parents came from an inherently codependent system that was necessary and proper given the living conditions of hardscrabble dryland farming. They scraped by, just barely surviving. The main benefit was they owned their own land. When I was a young boy in the late 1940's, there were more deserted homesteads with abandoned houses and barns than families that had managed to remain there.

On the other hand, I was a small child when the United States emerged from World War II as the richest, most powerful country in the world. The world lost about sixty million people in the war, and Russia alone lost about twenty million people. In comparison, the United States had only about three hundred thousand casualties, killed and wounded. All told, the world I lived in was a paradise compared to much of the rest of the world and the extreme poverty of the dust bowl world my parents had grown up in. As a country in the late '40s and '50s, the United States was rich and powerful with a sense that anything was possible for us. Throughout my lifetime the United States went to the moon, conquered polio, and established the world's first cures for other diseases and addictions, including alcoholism and codependence. I grew up in a time when every American had a car in the garage, while other nations did not even have garages, and a TV and phone in the home and then in every room. I've now gotten to see phones we can carry with us and even phones that can connect to the World Wide Web. As a young man, I did not have to follow the jobs, riding trains as a hobo as some of my uncles did, or have to stand in block-long lines for the one job that was only occasionally available. If someone was hurt on the job in my generation, he was provided with insured care. My dad saw injured men fired and another brought in that same day, and there was no unemployment insurance for the unlucky injured man or his family.

When I was a small boy in the late '40s, my father would dress, go out and start the car, and check the tires every morning at six o'clock before breakfast to make sure he would not be late to work as a pipe fitter at the refinery, so he would not lose his job as men were known to during the Great Depression.

I graduated from college as a physicist right in the heart of the space race, so I had no trouble getting a job, and a very good one at that. As an added bonus the draft did not take physicists. There is a huge difference in the thinking and feelings between my generation and my parents', more than is usual from one generation to the next. So it is no wonder that my parents were enmeshed with each other and their family and I with them. And after going away to school and finding there was a whole new world I had never been exposed to, it is no wonder that they thought me such a rebellious kid—"spoiled" my mom called me. There was a huge generation gap between me and my parents, a gap equal to perhaps two or three generations, considering how I had grown up compared to their childhoods. The old ways of subsistence farming that my parents had grown up in had been replaced with a prosperous world where I could follow my bliss.

Mom said one day a few years before she died that Dad had to leave Ohio, where he was an electrician on the railroad, because no one would talk to him because of Grandpa's preaching. My grandfather was what I would call a religious addict. His father was an alcoholic, and he treated his shame with religious addiction. I still have a letter from him warning me not to marry my first wife, who was Catholic. Probably seeing himself as head of the family, he sent it to my mother. She showed it to me, but I blew it off, shocked as I was with my modern thinking. At the side door of the church weeks later for the wedding, Mom and Dad approached me, and she said to me with my best man standing right there, "Dad and I will go in and sit down. If you don't come in within five minutes, we'll get up and walk out." I am not often speechless, but I was at that moment. I never knew for sure why she would walk out, but she evidently felt justified in being the judgmental matriarch against my fiancé in some peculiar way. I never did ask, so I guess I was acting under the no talk rule.

Mom was barely sixteen years old and Dad barely eighteen when they got married in 1934. Dad never would go to church after they got married, because he had gotten such a strong dose of religion in his youth. We moved to California the summer before I was to start high school. That year, as part of my growing up, Mom saw to it that the three of us started going to church, I think for my own good, and I got involved in the Methodist Youth Fellowship, a high school social club with a minimum of religion. It was all very pleasant for me and a lot of fun through high school. But like my parents, I was never very religious, or at least not often.

When my second wife and I got married, she had two sons, and I had two. We put her two in a Baptist school. We were both drinking heavily at the time, and my early stages of alcoholism were dragging us down. The restaurant I owned and operated by then, where we had met in the swinging '70s, was starting to fail. We started going to church as Baptists to support the boys. My younger son was chronically ill, and we enrolled him in the same school for a more-supportive educational experience. I sold the restaurant after going broke in it and started selling real estate. Naturally, what better source of contacts than church? So I got religion and read and studied the Bible. It was my fundamentalist phase. My life was a shambles because of drinking, and financially I was making bad decisions, so I tried church. For an alcoholic it was a lot better than quitting drinking.

My wife and I went to AA and got sober. After five years of sobriety the alcohol was out of our lives, but the dysfunction of a codependent relationship and my anger got no better. I had started seeing my first therapist over my quarrels with my parents, but my wife and I also had my anger impacting our marriage, so we began to see him together. Our toxic relationship soon took over the sessions and my anger towards my parents became secondary. Soon my wife was seeing the therapist's partner, and we would have regular sessions with all four of us.

Anger was a subject in that therapy, but we never focused on it specifically by that name. It was more of a "Verryl's behavior" subject in the sessions. That is the way I remember it, but I may well have deflected any frontal assault on my anger due to my denial. As I recall, the focus was to look at situations in my marriage and in my relationship with my parents differently using a healthier and more realistic thought pattern and then to adjust my behavior accordingly. The therapist's method was rational emotive therapy (RET), and he was the one who gave me the RET book I wrote about in chapter 10, "Rational Control of Emotions—Did It Work for Me?" Perhaps rational emotive therapy should have taught me how to control my emotions and heal my relationship problems and the anger with them, but it did not as I explained in detail in chapter 10.

About one year later the love of my life left me. I continued to see the same therapist, only now it was for survival. My caregiving wife had left me, and I was totally unable to care for myself emotionally. Oh, I could work, do my laundry, clean house, brush my teeth, and put my jammies on for bed alone, but emotionally I felt devastated. I was feeling what I could only describe as fear in all its forms. I felt ordinary fear from being alone with no one to lean on emotionally, and I was anxious—the kind of fear where you do not know exactly what you are afraid of. But mostly it was far beyond fear. What is scarier than terror? And it was constant 24-7 terror. I was so fearful that I hurt, and I was so was preoccupied with that pain that I missed many freeway off-ramps while driving, often more than one a trip. I hurt. I was in severe emotional pain all over my body, in my gut and neck and limbs. I had sharp stabs of pain and a dull, oppressive aching constantly for about twenty-four months. I was barely able to take care of myself emotionally for more than two years. I knew I would not kill myself, but I was seriously concerned that the emotional pain might kill me. I truly felt I knew what it must be like to die of a broken heart.

I literally did not know who I was, and I did not know how old I was. My wife was eighteen months older than I, so I had always added two years to my age out of codependent deference to her. I had to calculate from 1942 to get my age. She had been my identity. I had been worthwhile because I had married her and because she was in my life. She was very attractive, so I had been the husband of a drop-dead gorgeous and sexy woman. I was the papers I published as a research physicist in the aerospace industry. In my mind I was only as good as the amount of money I made, the number of papers I had written, the work I did, how the kids did in school, the car I drove, the house I lived in, and how the lawn looked. I was nowhere to be found anywhere in the map of myself. I eventually found out all these were symptoms of codependence.

This is when I ran into the fellow at the AA meeting who told me I was "just codependent" and took me to a CoDA meeting the next night. I started learning about codependence, but my understanding came very slowly because of the ravages of codependency and shame. I met Pia Mellody in her books and had no doubt she was talking about me. Her books were so comforting, as were the CoDA meetings; they showed me that I was only one of many and that there was recovery, like there was for alcoholism. After all, I had been sober for five years in AA and had learned firsthand that there was recovery, so why couldn't I recover from another addiction?

I cannot express how difficult recovery from codependence is or how baffling it is for the first year or so of recovery. The hallmarks of codependence are just extremes of loving, caring, and socially approved social and familial behaviors and defective or nonexistent personal boundaries. A person's boundaries establish limits of reasonable, safe, and permissible ways for other people to behave around him or her and limits of how that person should behave around others so as to not transgress their boundaries.

As I became the recovery junkie I describe in the previous chapter, I started coming across the concept of spirituality. At first I thought it meant religion. Gosh darn, folks, I not only had been baptized in the Methodist Church while in high school but had also been baptized again, the "right way" by immersion in the Baptist Church. I had read almost the entire Bible and studied parts of it thoroughly. I even bought a 0.3 mm mechanical pencil with lead tiny enough to write notes in my King James Bible during Sunday and Wednesday-night services. What more was required?

My second wife and I got back together again after six months of separation and at her request I took her to services at a New Thought church. That first Sunday I felt like I was home. It was a perfect fit for where I was at that time. The marriage reconciliation did not last though, and we got a divorce, but I kept going to church and studying New Thought.

Within a few months and alone again, I changed to a church closer to my home. It fit even better because the congregation was more my age. The church was in a neighborhood of middle-class and working-class people my age. The minister was dating a therapist, so the emphasis was on relationships and living, in broad terms. It fit my emerging fascination with all things recovery. A few years later I switched to a very large church. As my codependence waned, I became more socially adept, so I had grown into the larger church. It was a yuppie church, and I was now seven to eight years sober and beginning to feel financially well off, so I fit right in. Besides, there were so many attractive single women. I was so spiritual!

I did get genuinely spiritual with a definite New Thought feeling of oneness with All That Is and all other folks, rejecting the separation concept of me here and God up in heaven. For me God was within, a feeling I still have today. I mean to be honest about the motivations for my spirituality: I was looking for love, finally in the right places, and would have welcomed a healthy relationship with spirituality at its core. I guess there are many paths up the mountain, for my spirituality is real still over twenty years later. Those were the years of trekking to see Marianne Williamson, visiting other churches to see other noteworthy speakers, and listening to Wayne Dyer and Deepak Chopra tapes, all of which I still have.

Along the way I discovered Joseph Campbell, the mythologist and famous and favorite professor of mythology and other ancient studies at Sarah Lawrence College. I first saw his interviews by Bill Moyers on public TV and was transfixed by his concept of a *monomyth* that sees all mythic narratives around the world and in all cultures and ages as variations of a single great story. He taught that myths were not just "ancient TV" but had four functions:

1. Metaphysical function: to awaken a sense of awe and humility before the mystery of being
2. Cosmological function: to explain the form of the universe
3. Sociological function: to validate and support the existing social order
4. Pedagogical function: to guide the individual through the stages of life[2]

The notion of the uniformity of myths from around the globe and all four of these functions fascinated me, especially the last. The last one bears directly on my recovery from the many disorders I had.

From this uniformity as taught by Campbell, it seemed as if my basic understandings, musings, and concerns had a lot of universality to them. I had spent so much of my life on the outside looking in, feeling a sense of alienation that is concordant with low self-esteem, so it was comforting to know that I was not unique. I fit in at last. My shame work was having the desired results.

I took the pedagogical function seriously. I read Campbell's first full-length book as a solo author, *The Hero with a Thousand Faces*[3] which was based on the introductory mythology class that he had been teaching at

Sarah Lawrence College on how to read myths. In this book he tells a myth from, say, India and then relates essentially the same myth from many different cultures all over the world. He uses this technique to show both the uniformity and commonality of myth and therefore all peoples. Not only is the hero the same hero in each myth, but at different stages the hero experiences the same challenges, goes through the same trials, and comes out having grown in the same ways.

At about fifty years old I started the book over with a journal in which I recorded my own matching experiences, challenges and pains, and growth as I passed each trial. I was amazed at the correlation in my experiences and mythology. I was indeed on the hero's journey, and at the end of the book when the hero crosses over the river to pure ecstasy and does not want to return to real life—I felt some of that also. But soon the hero knows he must return for unfinished business, so he reluctantly does so, only to find that he is just as comfortable on the worldly side of the river as on the nirvana side. I felt that then and still feel it now. It was a unifying idea and gave me comfort and confidence in my recovery path and in relations with others.

I was fascinated by everything I stumbled across in my recovery—my sense of *self* (my public self), my emotional self, my inner or spiritual self, other people and a new acceptance of them and by them. It was, and still is, heady stuff. And unlike some proselytizing religions, I do not feel compelled or duty bound to advocate it or convert, approve, or judge anyone else. This book, for example, is meant to be used like what is said at the end of so many twelve-step meetings: "Take what you want, and leave the rest."

Sometime in the first five years of my sobriety, a neighbor suggested that I twelve-step a friend of his who had a drinking problem. I declined three times over some months before the feeling came over me that perhaps I should approach him. I did, and it went well, and I started taking him to meetings every night. Sitting in my car in front of his house late at night after a meeting and talking about alcoholism, he suddenly said belligerently, "What are you going to do if I drink again?"

I got angry because I had not really wanted to go to three meetings in three nights, so I struck back, as I did regularly back then, saying, "I'm not going to do a damn thing. I don't care if you drink or not. That is up to you, and it is your choice. I'm doing this to keep myself sober because the twelfth step tells me 'to carry this message to alcoholics, and to practice these principles in all our affairs.' I need to work my program so *I* can stay sober. Besides, if I tell you I do something a certain way and I don't do it, that makes me a hypocrite, and I refuse to be one. So I am doing this for me. This is a selfish program. I can't make you get sober. You can only get sober for yourself."

I saw him around in quite a few meetings after that, and I guess he stayed sober. But he did not do it because of me. He had to do the work, and he had to do it for himself. The same principle worked out well for me with anger. Near the end of my story in this book it will become obvious that I finally got over anger and rage *for me*. Up to this point, it should be obvious that I had been trying to do it for someone else. My goals had been to make it easier for someone else to stay in a relationship with me. That did not work; all those people left me, and I was left with the collateral damage of being alone. But that price was not enough for me to stop being angry. Anger was still working to make me feel better, even with the losses it caused.

With all my growth in taming toxic shame, with my rise in self-esteem so that I loved myself and could therefore love others, with the increasing popularity I was finding, and with my business success, I was still angry and full of rage and would be for another fifteen years.

What in the world was the answer? I never asked that, and it is a wonder I did not. I would think I should have, but of course anger still worked for me, deluding me into thinking I had control. Perhaps I did not ask because of denial. I should have asked, but I would have had to answer, "I'll do it when I can."

[1]   Timothy Egan, *The Worst Hard Time: The Untold Story of Those Who Survived the Great American Dust Bowl* (Boston: Houghton Mifflin Company, 2006), 22.

[2]   Joseph Campbell, *The Masks of God, vol. 4: Creative Mythology* (New York: Viking, 1956), p608-624.

[3]   Joseph Campbell, *The Hero with a Thousand Faces*, 2nd ed., Bollingen Series XVII (Princeton, NJ: Princeton University Press, 1968).

17

HEALTH (NOT COUNTING RELATIONSHIP ADDICTION), ENGAGEMENT, AND BREAKUP

I was sober, I had healthy self-esteem, my relationship addiction was not so devastating that I would get involved with anyone at the drop of a hat, and I was experiencing a growing inner spiritual self as part of my emerging inner emotional self.

I would like to say that church was all about spirituality for me, but honestly I was just as much on the prowl for a relationship as to practice spirituality. Spirituality, while very important to me, was a means to get back into a relationship that was healthy for a change. I also wanted to alleviate the pain of not having a relationship. I was still a relationship addict, and without a romantic relationship I was like any addict deprived of my drug of choice, in this case the love of a woman. So spirituality was in a sense the great collateral benefit of my church experience. I was obviously a long way from being healthy.

My codependence had lessened almost entirely into being a relationship addict, or love addict, and now it was ameliorated into "*almost* any relationship, no matter how bad, is better than none." I had begun to feel complete, worthy, and adequate in life *not being* in a relationship, but I still would have much preferred to be in one. The quality of the love I wanted had changed to where my partner and I would be not only equals but also interdependent, that is, able to function well alone when not together and to function coop-eratively otherwise.

Since I was not in a relationship, my anger was not a big problem. I was always capable of erupting in rage, but it did not cause me much trouble, because few things threatened to cause a loss to me. My anger still served me as being an apparent source of power in work and career. It was still a problem in my relationship with my folks. I was full of rage toward them, even though I remained in business with them. With their advancing age, it was getting so they needed me more than I needed them, especially since I was an only child. My anger was still present in my heart, but the lack of a relationship and the resultant lack of the chance of losing what I did not have made for fewer opportunities to get angry. This may have deluded me into thinking I was healthier than I really was.

My social life blossomed with my newly gained self-esteem. After a few months I started seeing the attractive woman I took to see the taping of Barbara De Angelis's TV show. Soon we began living together, and that lasted for about eighteen months. She and I had harsh arguments with lots of anger and screaming, and I still had problems with my anger toward my parents. In fact, my anger was common toward everyone. This woman under-stood the concept of the inner child as described by Pia Mellody (see chapter 12, "Pia Mellody's Theory Summarized") where an adult has within him or her an inner identity of an immature child from childhood trauma. The inner child holds the built-up memories of pain and shame that Bradshaw discusses and that I extend to carried emotions. Consequently she and I were well aware that we did not argue and fight so much as our inner chil-dren battled. When we pushed each other's buttons, we were pushing on the sensitivities of our wounded inner children. I believe that this theory is absolutely true for me, and that all the fighting my partners and I engaged in was really our inner children battling.

Since both of us knew that, why did we fight? Rational knowledge and rational thought was powerless to help us for all the reasons I gave in chapter 10, "Rational Control of Emotions." To oversimplify, my emotions were too powerful to be moved by my rational mind, no matter how knowledgeable I was and how much rational self-talk I practiced.

I eventually broke up with this woman. Always before the women had broken up with me. In that breakup, I was actually assertive, as opposed to aggressive. I said what I needed to say to take care of myself. I did not scream it or emote all over her. I just said my truth and left, expecting her to respond. It was the most healthy relationship thing I had ever done.

As a relationship addict, that breakup was a sign of real growth for me. I had progressed to the point where I could end a relationship, and I did so in an assertive, healthy way, face-to-face, because it was not in my best interests to stay in it. And I did it without anger. I was caring for myself with minimum hurt of another.

My anger showed up in other areas thereafter like always though, particularly with my parents. Looking back, I realize I did not really want to give anger up yet. I held it close to me as my source of power in an otherwise relatively powerless existence as far as close relationships went. At work and in business, I was dynamic and successful, but those arenas seldom called forth old childhood wounds unless my parents were involved. In those situations, a triggered childhood wound could lead to my anger and even rage.

I had made progress in my recovery only through a lot of hard work in CoDA and by reading books. It was painful at times to face my newfound realities, but when a situation got too hurtful, when the fear got too big, or both, I was motivated to change my thinking to improve my lot. Only then could I get busy and do the work to improve myself.

Looking back, I know the above is true, but I could never have made progress in my recovery by just changing my thinking, as RET postulates. Analyzing the above paragraph, which I wrote carefully, it is clear that *if I tended to the underlying emotion first*, then I could change my thinking.

One day a few months later I was talking to one of those adorable little old church ladies who were blocking my way to the courtyard where the action was. The average Sunday attendance at this church was just over one hundred, but there was always a chance of a pretty woman my age showing up. And as I politely but not too patiently looked past the older woman, I saw this beautiful blonde in a sundress. At first I thought she was too tall for me, so I did not go meet her. But in church it was announced that she was resurrecting the church singles' group, which I and another woman had started two years before. It had died when I had started living with my last girlfriend. Naturally this rebirth of the singles' group fit right in with my relationship addiction program, so I went to the meeting she had arranged at the church after the service. I soon became her right-hand man in the new singles' group.

As a cousin of mine told me once when he was trying to get sober, "All I ever wanted was to be a wheel." That expression certainly fit now that this woman and I were running the singles' group together and I was its main financial benefactor. Not only was I a ladies' man, but now I was also a big wheel. And I was happy having a lot of women friends, even though I was not in a relationship. I told myself that I'd like to be in love but that I was too busy to be in a relationship, and that one would come naturally. I was a lot healthier than ever before, but this new attitude fooled me into thinking that I was totally healthy. I told myself that I had licked my relationship addiction. But I forgot that with addiction one can relapse.

The financial support was a small price to pay to be a wheel. The validation of knowing I was accepted by women as a friend and possible future boyfriend, fiancé, lover, or husband was sufficient. I had gone a long way toward being well and was definitely in recovery, but I still was counting on having a permanent full-time relationship. The only difference was that now I was more patient and willing to wait for it. This was the gift of breaking off my relationship with my last girlfriend when it was not good for me to stay in it. I had made progress, but I still had a long way to go.

Since I was not in a relationship, my anger was very much less apparent, although I sometimes got angry with the singles' group leader. Now it is obvious that those cases were when I sensed a loss similar to some ancient childhood loss. I would flare into anger, and often it was extreme. I still was in business with my parents, and anger was the same old problem there. My relationships seemed to be a field that promoted losses. I must have greatly feared those losses and associated pain. They were very powerful over me; they were largely reenactments of my childhood pain and losses rising up frequently.

Together the tall blonde woman and I directed the singles' group and started throwing parties, and she became my best friend. With her marketing skills, vivacious and outgoing manner, and good looks and with my money, my computer to make newsletters and print invitations, and my ebullient manner, soon we were throwing huge parties of up to four hundred singles. It also helped that now I was finally fully at ease in crowds and meeting new people. I was good-time Charlie and had lots of women friends and dates. I had come a very long way from the low-self-esteem, self-loathing, overcompensating, and arrogant person I had been a few years before. My recovery work was definitely paying off.

But my anger was still lurking, and I often clashed with my new best friend over managing the parties. It became more and more apparent that when we clashed, it was because she had accidentally pushed my buttons and triggering my old issues. She would say or do something that would vaguely sound like my mother, and I would go off on her. I could never in real time recognize the similarity of her actions and speech to my mother's, but afterward I could make the connection. It was like old tapes playing in my mind. This was the kind of behavior Bradshaw talks about as I relate in chapter 14, "Shame in Depth: John Bradshaw, *Healing the Shame That Binds You*."

Things were better for me than any time since my divorce; so what if I occasionally got angry? Anger still resulted in no loss for me and only increased my sense of apparent power and control.

The singles' group got bigger. The leader visited five other big churches and networked their singles together, and we sent out invitations to all six. Between Labor Day with our first beach party and the Halloween party, the guest list grew up to four hundred. We had a member who had worked at Disneyland on the Haunted Mansion and knew how to make various special effects, so we had some pretty sophisticated displays of dungeons and ghosts in mirrors, floating ghosts over my four-poster bed in the master bedroom, pressure-sensitive mats under rugs to set off tape players, and lights and fans to blow diaphanous cloths. We put on a play in the middle of the party for which I created the goofy characters and the singles' group actors played their parts by repeating the ad-libbed lines they had made up in the rehearsals. There were new attractive ladies coming through the doors each week. Life was great. I was still angry, and everyone knew it and accepted it in me, I guess. I do not remember it being a problem for anyone except my parents, my new best friend, or the occasional waitress or store clerk. And for me it was just my way of gaining power and control in painful situations. My anger felt good, at least to me.

I had no trouble meeting new women or asking for their phone numbers. After all, they were single women at a singles' event. I was not about to miss any opportunity, and neither were they. I reasoned that all the single women I met at these events must have wanted the same thing I did—a relationship—or they would not be here. I was still needy, but I had learned not to show my neediness to the opposite sex. Each dinner date did not have to be viewed as if it would require a proposal of marriage. I would say to myself, "I want a healthy relationship, but I don't have time this week," *and mean it.* That was real progress toward full recovery.

Then after the New Year's Eve party with another four hundred people, the leader quit the singles' group. I could not talk her into staying. She was convinced that I had wanted to take it over. This was not true, and the singles' club died because I did not have the time and was not capable of managing it alone. But there were other singles' events to go to, and I found them.

Soon I met and dated another woman, and I went immediately back into codependence. While I was single, I was reasonably healthy, but back in a relationship I slipped into the old habits. She and I went to see some of the old singles' gang once, but she did not like them. I was a people pleaser, so we went to the dark side of the moon and planned to get married. We fought four days before the wedding and broke up the next day. It was a codependent breakup and featured rage, not by me, but, for a change, by my partner. I thought the party was to be a romantic weekend out of town, but she had to work at the party. I went into what I misidentified as a shame spiral of depression when I was disappointed. Now I think it was a pain and shame spiral triggered by my immature sense of loss of being with her full time at the party. She had to work at the party and largely had to ignore me, so I spiraled down into shame from that pain and loss—"Nobody loves me; nobody cares." It looked like pouting to her, and in a sense it was. The next day, she came to my office to berate me, and I, the master of intimidation and anger, sat for an hour or more taking all the rage and invective she could dish out. I had one thought. *Geez oh, me! This is terrible being raged at like this.* It was karma.

After a while I suggested we put off the wedding, which was three days away, and take some time to reflect and to continue dating but not be so enmeshed. She could not get past her anger. And I knew what it was like to be an adult and to be raged at. Eventually she broke up with me that afternoon, and at that point, I did not object.

You remember that the gift of my eighteen-month living-together relationship was that I could end a relationship on my own and do it in a healthy way. That woman and I are still friends. The gift out of my relationship with my fiancée was I could be dumped and survive. I nearly had not survived my divorce from my second wife, suffering for two years. This breakup three days before the wedding was also good for me. I knew it was necessary for my own good. The minute we officially called it off, I called the tall blond singles' club woman, and she said, "Come on over. We are planning a party." She had started a new singles' club for the workers in her industry, and I was off and running again helping and financing parties.

The gift of the near-marriage relationship was that although I felt pain and was embarrassed, I knew the breakup was for the best, and I was able to go on with few lingering effects. I came to clearly realize that I had gone into that relationship as a needy man looking for a woman to fix my emotions. I was once again operating under the mantra that any relationship was better than no relationship, no matter how bad. But I survived with a healthy dose of reality that I had dodged a bullet of an unhealthy, codependent relationship. It would have had to end sooner or later, and it was better to have it end sooner.

Furthermore, I saw the part anger, hers and mine, played in this relationship. I was rarely angry with her; rather I was very submissive, which was new to me. I knew it would be useless to get angry with her, that she could not be so manipulated. But rather than acting healthy and assertive, I became compliant. Immediately after the breakup, I saw this, and I was grateful that we had split up.

I had another reaction to the breakup that was strange for me. Immediately after the breakup, I was able to care for myself and not fall into being the wounded little boy who had lost Mommy—I mean, a love. And I realized that my progress over codependence had been made only while I was not in relationship. I was healthy in theory only, as long as I had no encumbrance of commitment. I grew from this pain, and I was able to see the good side: that I was much less codependent. But if I was to be completely healthy, I would have to be healthy while in a relationship, if I ever got into another relationship. And of course now I realized that I did not have to fall in love. I truly believed that I was perfectly imperfect, whole and complete, lacking nothing. It was a wide-open field of male and female friends, and I could enjoy life single. I knew with only a little reflection that in this near-marriage relationship I had fallen back into the only ways I knew, the ones that I had learned from being enmeshed with my enmeshed parents, who had modeled to me the traits they had learned in their enmeshed pioneer families.

Actually, there was a second and very significant gift to this breakup, as I relate in chapter 10, "Rational Control of Emotions." I will repeat that gift here to put it into context. After the disappointing party and my shame spiral, my fiancée and I went to a therapy session (this was a great engagement—we were already in therapy before the wedding), and I went to a second session the next day alone. At the very end of that second session, the therapist told me, "You need to listen to your self-talk when you go into one of these depressive spirals—listen to what you are telling yourself."

"Why, I know what I tell myself," I answered. "I tell myself, 'Nobody loves me; nobody cares,' over and over."

Three minutes later as I twisted myself into my sports car, I mulled this over. *Why, Slick,* I thought, nearly saying the words out loud, *whenever you think that, you should know that it does not matter if no one loves you and no one cares at that moment. You love you, and you care; God loves you, and God cares. And at that moment, that is enough.*

It was an epiphany, and since that time, I have not been troubled by shame or such a depressive spiral. At times I have had to literally wrap my arms around myself and hug myself, but I have always been enough for me since that time.

It is important in analyzing this event to realize that the self and God love statement was *not at all* new to me at that moment; I had used it regularly for several years of codependence recovery. This time the saying took on a special meaning, and that can only be, because I had become through suffering and hard work, finally ready to make such a change. Many hundreds of hours of intense work preceded this event, and that work was predominantly emotional.

Actually, a few times over the years, happening with less and less frequency, such an emotional spiral has started to come on, and once or twice I deliberately allowed it to take over for a short while. This was an experiment to reexperience the sensation and to see if I could control it. Those times I ended it at will.

This original purgation looks at first glance like RET in successful action, but I believe that before that epiphany in the parking lot, I had already seen the behavioral and emotional results clearly and put them into rational words and thoughts. Only after suffering an emotional upheaval for nearly twenty-four hours, which I was able to handle maturely and ably because of all the work I had put in throughout the preceding years was I capable of mounting a rational, healthy self-talk response that worked. It was as if I had worked out all winter and yet more in spring training, and then and only then was I able to get in the game and hit a home run. The presentation of RET that I have read about and experienced is that it is a much-faster, more streamlined process of a reformulation of some stinkin' thinkin,' followed by a quick acceptance of the new thought process that leads to a sudden and immediate catharsis. My belief and contention is that my catharsis took years to effect, years of neural pathway realignment, before it (apparently) took hold. Something in this shocking event brought my emotions of toxic shame, pain, and fear out into the open so that my thinking could have effect. That was what was healed—the underlying emotions of shame, pain, and fear. Then and only then could the rational thinking take hold to be cardinal. When I say the underlying emotions were healed, I mean my pain and fear of being abandoned, as if I were a little boy and would not survive if alone, were healed. Since I had done the work over years to emotionally mature to where I knew unequivocally that I could not be abandoned—I still had me and my faith—then the rational thought was effective.

In those years, I had risen out of the ashes from being a chronic and inveterate codependent, an addicted relationship addict, and a terribly low-self-esteem person full of toxic shame who compensated with arrogance and rage and was spiritually bereft. I had nearly recovered from the loss of the love of my life three or four years before, and now I had recovered to a happy and nearly healthy person who was whole and liked and useful to my large circle of friends. I had made myself ripe for the perfect right-thinking talk to make sense to me, to resonate within me and affect the healing. But it came only after working through all that other stuff.

But the anger was still there, because it was still comforting to me, for it was yet my power.

18

ESCALATION

The previous chapter shows that I was making progress in my recovery in nearly every area of my life except my rage. I told myself that my anger was not that bad, because I never really got into trouble. Oh, sure, there were a lot of broken relationships and divorces and heartaches, but I was improving in all other areas, so I was able to believe that a solution to my anger would come. And to top it off I felt capable and adequate even though some of those good feelings occasionally were from anger.

I have mentioned only the collateral damage that anger caused me, and I could always rationalize it as bad relationships with the wrong person, thinking that if I got better at relationships and at picking partners, I would have a good relationship. But there were at least six incidents when my anger put me in danger, danger which frightened me temporarily, but soon passed as the danger passed. I list them here as a reminder that denial is more than just a river in Egypt.

1. When I was about twenty-five years old, long before I was an alcoholic, in a city league basketball game an opposing player jumped on me and knocked me down. I jumped up and hit him, and I was kicked out of the league.
2. When my two boys were about six and ten, a neighbor boy did something to the older one, and I slapped the kid. His parent confronted me and threatened to call the police. I denied it until I saw that was not going to work. Then I admitted hitting the child and

talked my way out of the situation. It was the late '60s or early '70s, and such abuse issues were not prominent.

3. While my second wife and I were still drinking, I slapped her, the love of my life, so hard I gave her a black eye, and she called the police. They came to the door the next day and warned me, and I guess I talked myself out of that. It was the late '70s or early '80s, and again, things were different then.

4. I had a very irritating and troublesome foreign-born tenant who had continually caused costly damage to his apartment, probably because he had no mechanical sense. He always treated me and my workers like servants and generally acted entitled. One day in an altercation with him over a busted doorjamb that he had broken because he had locked himself out, we argued. He had tried to smash the locked door open instead of calling me or finding the resident manager to unlock it for him. In the argument I pushed or grabbed him, and he called the police. Again I talked myself out of the situation. This was in the late '80s or the early '90s.

5. A few years later, I evicted a tenant for nonpayment of several months' rent. When the marshal came to enforce the court order and return possession of the apartment to me, the tenant was not even packed. The officer gave him a couple of hours to move and left. At the end of that time, he still had not made any moving progress, so I started to carry out his things. We got into a scuffle, and he called the police. When they came, I denied touching him and talked myself out of that.

6. And of course, there was the physical altercation with my third wife in 2007, by which time things had changed. I could not talk myself out of the situation and was arrested.

But I skated free in the first five of these cases and perhaps others. They were scary for a few minutes or overnight, but I was never in any terrifying danger. If I had made a written list of such cases, perhaps I would have been able to overcome the denial and avoid the last situation. I did not, so I remained an angry man.

19

THIRD MARRIAGE AND ARREST

I was about fifty-one years old, was a happy bachelor, was dating occasionally, and had many male and female friends. I went to events with them just to be with them, not to fall in love. I was still needy but no longer looked needy, and I was indeed whole and complete, but I was not in a relationship.

After about a year of planning and throwing parties with the leader of the new singles' group, she started showing interest in me. Eventually, we did start a romantic relationship. After a respectable engagement of one and a half years we were married in a very big wedding, and we stayed married for just over eleven years. We had transformed our party-giving partnership into a romantic one with all the characteristics of the former transferred to the latter. I was radically codependent and just as angry as ever. We both suffered for it, but it is hard for a perpetrator (me) to claim damage when the victim (her) is considered.

After about seven years of marriage we were separated for about six months, and I should have gone through with the divorce that she filed. But my best trait, tenacity, worked against me. I did not want to fail in the marriage, and I was still a relationship addict, so I resisted divorce because of my other biggest failing, the old any-relationship-is-better-than-none mentality.

It was during this separation that I entered a thirty-day program at a well-known recovery center. (See chapter 15, "Recovery Junkie.") I was definitely angry, and it showed to the whole staff, although I would have described myself as codependent and believed I needed help with that problem. I still thought my anger was from shame and codependence. I checked myself in hoping to work on codependence and love addiction, and I was put in a sex-addict group. I thought I was misplaced, but I realized that relationship addiction was classified as a sex addiction, and that was not totally incorrect. I was not clear to myself or to the staff about my opinion about my problems. I did not unequivocally state that anger was a real problem for me—the old denial streak yet again. I really believed that love addiction was more a codependence issue than a sex issue, but I attended all the activities faithfully. I got little out of the program, though, other than a respect for the institution.

At the time I could associate the losses early in my life that seemed to repeat with my suddenly increased anger toward my wife, but my only solution to my anger was to control it. I had to keep my anger in check because, after all, I was first and foremost a relationship addict, and I knew I was risking my relationship with every raging incident. There was no doubt I had damaged my marriage by my anger. So I salvaged what I could of the relationship but in the process sacrificed a great deal of what was precious to me in the relationship. This gave me a tremendous reservoir of smoldering anger over that loss that often erupted in cascades of rage for the remainder of the marriage.

I had built a very large home for us to live in with her mother on the ground floor in a complete one-bedroom apartment and my parents on the third floor with room for two live-in caregivers. We eventually reconciled after my month of treatment at the center. Four years later we were stuck in a really strained relationship in the big house with all the other people living there with us. The marriage was marked by detachment and indifference on her part and resentment and anger on my part. Both of us were unhappy, angry, resentful, and stuck.

For my part, I tried to love her and to honor her, but I always ended up poking at her sarcastically, trying, I think, to get a response other than indifferent withdrawal. Codependents are often overly sensitive to being ignored or not listened to because of their childhood backgrounds of neglect and abandonment. I was extremely sensitive in this way. I was the classic love addict Pia Mellody describes in *Facing Love Addiction* (see Chapter 15, "Recovery Junkie," in the section "Relationships and Sometimes Anger" and chapter 20, "Back to the Recovery Center").

Her indifferent withdrawal was emotionally painful to me, since it was the result of a serious loss, the loss of love. It was a recreation or reenactment of childhood abandonment feelings. I reacted to the pain and loss by my old standby, anger. I felt rejection, which, as a not-so-recovered relationship addict, kept me constantly angry. This is not to blame my partner. The blame was entirely mine; it was my job to get over her lack of feeling for me and move on. That would have been true recovery. This is why I classify love addiction as extreme codependence. The path to recovery from either is in releasing the self-imposed shackles of dependence on another as a solution for one's own painful emotions. It was not her job to love me. She either did, or she did not. It was my job to accept that and to love (or, ideally, continue to love) myself. Emotional health is caring for one's own emotions. It is nice when someone also cares for you, but it should not be a condition of one's own happiness. And that is the condition I put on myself and, I suppose, on her also.

As a consequence, during this period my primary problems became not only codependence and relationship addiction but also anger. I resumed being sarcastic, and I knew it was anger. Years before I had called sarcasm chicken anger. If you do sarcasm right—and I was very good at it—the victim has no defense. I had given sarcasm up as unseemly when I'd seen that it was fighting dirty, but I resumed it in this marriage.

We lived, or existed, in this state for four years. One Sunday, I was baking a ham for a family dinner and had just glazed it and put it back in the oven. She took it out and started to glaze it again with another sauce. I allowed my feelings of rejection at what I took to be her condescension to take over, and in my hurt I argued with her about it. She ignored me, and finally I started to yell and scream. I grabbed her by the throat and pushed her up against the refrigerator in an attempt to get her to listen. I held her there and screamed at her. I was completely wrong in what I did.

I repeat, so it is not overlooked: I was wrong to grab her and push her and to try to intimidate her. According to the police report, she had no bruises or marks, but I am sure she was terribly scared by my violent actions and screaming. I used my rage to make me feel in control when I obviously was not, neither of her nor myself, and I was wrong. Anger again was my mood alterer; adrenaline was my drug of choice in this stressful situation. I used to think I was in control while raging, and I was eager to put up that out-of-control front to overwhelm and intimidate my victims. In a sense I was in control, because I usually could pull back before crossing the line. This time, and in at least those six others listed earlier, I did not, and so obviously I was not in control. But on a more basic emotional and chemical level, I had used my drug, adrenaline, and I was just as out of control as when I had used alcohol. Notwithstanding the highfalutin analysis, I was not in control, and I was wrong. She was a victim for sure, and in an effort to control her, I held her in an attempt to get her to listen. Anger was my power, my way to attempt to exert control, and it finally had gotten completely out of hand.

This acknowledged violence took place at midday as I was cooking dinner for all seven of us in the house—wife, adult stepdaughter (who had replaced my wife's now-deceased mother), my parents, two caregivers, and me. Two days later I was arrested and went to jail. According to the police report, she did not go to a doctor, and the arresting officers could see no marks. In jail, there was no provision for a phone call, so the officer in the holding area pulled a phone over to my small cell, and I tried to call an attorney. I guess the officer had broken the phone by stretching the cord, because it did not work. They made no other effort to let me make a call, and I did not get my one call until the next day. I was in jail about thirty-two hours and was finally released wearing only my T-shirt, shorts, and flip-flop sandals at eleven at night in October at an altitude of 4,200 feet in the Arizona desert. It had been hot during the day when I had been arrested, but at night in October, it was cold. The jail was out in the country about fifteen miles from any town, lights, other buildings, or phones. Before I was released out into the night air, I was allowed one call. I called one of my parents' caregivers at my home, and she drove twenty-five miles to pick me up. I waited outside in the cold until she arrived around midnight.

While in jail, I did not sleep at all the whole night. I was in a community cell with a plastic molded bed on the floor. All night I was alone with my thoughts about the details of the arrest. I was disturbed by the circumstances, but even more distressing was the knowledge that I had finally been arrested for violence, now had an arrest record, and I was facing trial and further jail or prison. I do not mean to minimize the trauma to my wife, but the mortifying knowledge that I had so attacked the one I loved was profound. I am sure it was even worse for her, and I am sorry for that.

I should have finally had a reason to give up the apparent power of anger and should have been motivated by fear to recover for myself. But denial in addictions is very powerful. I viewed my violence toward her not in terms of anger but in terms of lack of control over my anger. I was a long way from realizing my anger was an addiction. Being in denial and, I suppose, not wanting to give up the power of my anger—even though it had gotten me in great trouble and had not given me power or control—I did not look at my actions as the result of a progression of anger. I was like a drunk who had just wrecked his car and nearly killed himself and others but still did not want to give up drinking.

By the above I do not mean to trivialize in any way the effect my actions had on my wife. I am very sorry for what I did, and even though the charges were dropped, I still have my police record as a constant reminder of just how serious my attack on her was. But anger was that important to me, and as will be seen ahead in my story, this is a graphic illustration of the extreme effects of childhood issues. The impact of those hidden and deeply embedded emotions (pain, fear, losses from abandonment, and so on) from childhood abuse are so profound as to be super-resistant to rational attempts to overcome them—even when the need to do should be obvious. I never seriously considered switching my recovery efforts to anger. Anger was just too critical to my emotional self-protection for me to consider giving it up, even as I faced jail time! If asked back then why I clung to my rage so, I would have pleaded that I had been working on anger all along for twenty-five years. Like an alcoholic whose unattainable dream is to be able to drink moderately, as an anger addict my rosy world was to have my anger as a controllable tool to manage my life. As a practicing alkie, before I quit drinking, I had felt the same about my need for alcohol as a controllable tool to manage my life, even with all the problems it wrought.

In the thirty-two hours I was in jail my wife and her daughter had moved out of our home and gone back to the state we lived in before moving to the new house. The terms of my video arraignment were that I could not return to my home that I had built. The night I got out of jail I stayed outside the house while the caregiver went in to get me some clothes and toiletries and the key to my car, even though she said my wife and her daughter had packed and left the day before. Then I drove across town to another house I owned that was vacant and being used for storage while we settled into the new house with my parents and caregivers. I slept shivering there with no lights or heat the rest of that first night out of jail. The next day I went to the police station and explained that I was the primary caregiver for my elderly mother and father, who were eighty-eight and ninety years old respectively, and that my mother suffered from Alzheimer's and no longer recognized me. I explained that I had to cook and take care of them and especially take them to the doctor weekly and visit every day with them. The police said I would have to get my wife to agree to let me go to the house, even though she was in another state 475 miles away. Fortunately, the policeman at the desk said he would have someone call her and ask if she would give her permission for me to return to my home and parents. He told me to come back in a couple of hours, and that afternoon I got written permission to return home to live there and care for my parents. My wife had kindly faxed a letter to the police giving her permission.

A few days later she called me and asked my permission to stay in my parents' house in our former state. She had a key, and I agreed. I was now determined to get a divorce, but crazily I still hoped to salvage the marriage and get my desires met.

So my lifetime of anger had escalated, and now I had a police record and faced criminal charges, further jail or prison, and divorce. My anger had become clearly visible as a problem and not as a tool to get my way. Finally, thank goodness, my anger had become my paramount problem, though I did not yet recognize it as such—I was still lamenting my loss of relationship. All else should have paled in comparison to the anger that had gotten me arrested and thrown in jail.

But working on my anger was still not my primary agenda. That was to be put on hold for a few more months.

20

BACK TO THE RECOVERY CENTER

After I got back in my house with permission from my wife, I first visited my parents. Then I made an appointment to go to the recovery center again, this time to the one-week workshop "Love Addiction and Love Avoidance." This time I was determined to not only heal my relationship addiction but to also gain strength to go through with the divorce I knew I needed. I was not concerned about healing my anger.

I was still concerned about my legal troubles, but the immediate concern was getting through another divorce with my wife's extreme alimony and property demands. I was determined to go through with a divorce this time, unlike four years earlier during our separation when my relationship addiction had kept me in the bad marriage. The "Love Addiction and Love Avoidance" program seemed heaven-sent for me at this time. The workshop consisted of only three men and two women led by a male therapist.

While waiting for the workshop date in about four weeks, I got Pia Mellody's new book *Facing Love Addiction*[1] and studied it. This very fine book describes in theory what I had gone through in reality with my marriage and other relationships. My partners and I had played a sort of dance of avoidance and attraction with one partner dancing away from the other, distancing himself or herself in anger and silence to ignore the other while the poor other one chased the avoiding partner like a lovesick puppy. Then we would make up, and soon the former lovesick, chasing one would start the avoidance dance, causing the now-avoided one to chase the other in a fruitless display of neediness. In a way it was a power-and-control game with each side adopting the same sick method of manipulation to get his or her needs met. And of course, the key to health is that those needs should be met by the individual, not his or her partner. In this game I identified as the love addict desiring enmeshment. I saw my partners as the love avoidants fleeing enmeshment, and I could see this pattern was the same for most of my relationships

A great deal of the workshop was centered on Pia's first book, *Facing Codependence* (see chapter 11, "Pia Mellody"), so I reread most of my original copy and marked it up with a sixth color. The workshop was outstanding, and I got some new insights about my wife's and my relationship that I found helpful, but of course I got nothing about my anger, my new primary problem. I was still in denial. Even with my legal troubles, I still did not consider anger as a primary problem. I was unconsciously unwilling to give up anger, which habitually was the source of my power and control for helpless situations—I had not come to grips with these "helpless" situations that were only truly helpless to a child. Even with the threat of jail looming, the power my emotions left over from childhood abuse were enormous! I was still an adult child laboring under the various debilities of helplessness as if I were still a child. The workshop program did review Pia Mellody's theories of codependence, but I was still not conscious that my anger was a problem I had to solve immediately, for me and for others.

The workshop consisted of frequent short lectures to the five of us clients and long and intensive group therapy sessions or exercises together each morning and each afternoon. Every night there was reading and written homework on the day's topics and readings. Thursday we started having individual consultations face-to-face with the therapist leader. The rest of the group observed but did not participate. The leader pulled his chair up directly in front of the workshop attendee and faced him or her, keeping a respectful distance dictated by healthy boundaries. Nevertheless, it was somewhat intimidating to know that the whole workshop watched while one's whole life had come down to this. The therapist then shuffled through a sheaf of papers that I first thought were detailed notes on the patient. Each face-to-face lasted an hour or two and was emotional to me as an observer and even more emotional as a participant.

By accident my turn came last on Friday afternoon. As the therapist shuffled the sheaf of papers, I recognized my homework. Through the four others' ordeals I had not realized that he was working from notes on and about their homework. I had only marveled, *I wonder where all our homework has gone.* As he studied the many pages as if looking for a place to begin, I noticed the sheets of paper were covered with orange highlighter marks. The orange color had dried to a dark orange-brown-red color that looked like long-dried blood. It looked to me as if he had slashed his wrists and used my homework to stop the bleeding.

Finally, he looked up, and looking me directly in the eye, he said quietly to describe me, "A lifetime of loss and pain."

I lost it and broke out sobbing. No one had ever spoken any such simple words that had resonated so within me. It stirred me right down to my soul.

Finally I gathered myself, and he continued his work with me, but I do not remember any more. And then the workshop was over.

At first I thought the best part of the workshop for me was that I asked the staff members for a list of therapists who were versed in the subjects I was interested in, though I did not specify anger as a therapeutic subject. On the last day I finally got that list, and when I got home, I made a call to my last therapist. I cannot say that all that knowledge and understanding from the workshop was wasted, because of what was to shortly happen. It almost surely set the stage for the metamorphosis to occur. Thank goodness the new therapist and workshop leader talked on the phone about me and the workshop.

After the workshop and for some months, my anger still resided within me, waiting for any perceived need for it to flash out and give me power.

I did not realize until late into my new therapy that the workshop leader had seemed to open my heart by saying, "A lifetime of loss and pain," and that was truly the best moment of the workshop.

[1]   Pia Mellody, *Facing Love Addiction: Giving Yourself the Power to Change the Way You Love,* with Andrea Wills Miller and J. Keith Miller (San Francisco: Harper, 2003).

21

WAS MY THERAPIST A GENIUS, WAS I READY, OR WAS HE TIPPED OFF?

When the student is ready, the teacher will appear.
—Anonymous, often attributed to Buddha Siddhartha
Gautama Shakyamuni or to Mabel Collins, a theosophist,
in her treatise *Light on the Path* (1886)

When I got home, I called a therapist from the list from the recovery center. I started to see him within a couple of days after returning from the workshop. I was sure I could manage the legal and financial problems of the divorce, but I started therapy wanting to deal with the pain I was in over the separation, impending divorce, and loss of yet another marriage. I did not associate that pain with the pain the workshop leader had referred to with "A lifetime of loss and pain." Instead I thought of it as pain from loss of a love, as I had suffered in my second divorce nearly twenty years before, which is to say I was still thinking in terms of codependence and adult abandonment.

It is interesting to me that I believed I could handle the legal problems (the arrest and the divorce) as well as the financial problems posed by the divorce. My only worry was the emotional problems from the loss of a marriage and the associated loss of love and sex. I class such a need for sex as a form of acceptance from my partner. As such the former sets of problems, legal and financial, can be seen as adult problems, while the emotional problems can be seen as child problems, those issues left over from my childhood abuse. My adult child found those problems and losses extremely difficult to deal with. The adult me dreaded the financial and legal, but I knew I could handle it just fine.

I was determined not to reconcile this time, but not wanting to fail and still probably exhibiting relationship addiction symptoms, I tried my best to bring my wife back. There was no sense to my working for both the divorce and to save the marriage, except my relationship addiction. I was now sure there was no truth to the idea that any relationship, even a bad one, was better than none. Rationally, I knew that mantra was untrue, but unfortunately, I waffled for a couple of months because it was one of those childhood issue problems. Recovery is a process, not an event. So even knowing this idea for sure, I was still not able to cross the emotional moat separating me from a rational right-thinking action and my needy emotion-driven desires.

I came to my new therapist telling him I needed help with the pain of the breakup of the marriage and help to have the resolve to go through with the divorce. He led me from the start down the path I set. Eventually by design or intuition he took me where I most needed to go after the legal problems were being handled, the divorce waffling was resolved in favor of divorce, and the divorce property and alimony settlement were accomplished. I did the property settlement and alimony without his help except as a valuable sounding board. Any settlement is bound to appear unfair to someone. I wanted to make sure it seemed fair to a judge. There was a lot of fear and pain involved with the legal, divorce, and settlement issues, and my therapist, and I attended to those as we had to. I was able to deal with these as an adult.

Finally, I had a written settlement agreement and final decree, and the criminal charges were dropped. I was not thrilled, but I was satisfied and reasonably happy.

I would have probably stopped there if left to my own devices. But my new therapist sprung a new topic on me that was to revolutionize my recovery. He did it subtly and apparently on the spur of the moment. If so, I call him a genius. If he planned it, I still consider him a genius. If he acted in collusion with the workshop leader—at my therapist's suggestion I had set up a consulting telephone call between the two of them at the beginning of my work with the therapist—they both were geniuses.

In my introductory pitch to him about what I wanted from the therapy I had told him about myself. I'd told him that I was alcoholic, sober twenty-some years, now on my third divorce, and codependent and that, by the way, I was in court-mandated anger-management classes because I had been arrested for spousal abuse and had spent thirty-two hours in jail.

That anger-management class soon became the primary problem to be solved, because I saw it as ineffective. The instructor was a retired public school teacher with no psychology training and no resources other than downloads from the internet. Often as not those downloads bore little relation to anger and were about such diverse topics as how to be successful at work or get a good job. She seemed to take the position that being angry was normal (well and good) but that the way it was expressed, especially the intensity or violence of its expression, was the sole problem to be solved (also well and good, as far as it goes). But the problem for me was that attitude did not seem to have much promise to go very far at all. She had no concept of inner drives that may be caused by internal stresses left over from past events (think PTSD from war for an undeniable example of present behavior being based on past events or trauma). At one point I asked her what experts in the field she had studied or followed, and she gave me a blank look. When I asked about John Bradshaw, Pia Mellody, Claudia Black, Alice Miller, and others I had studied, she said she had never heard of them.

My new therapist was sympathetic to my complaints about the anger management program and, since he was familiar with it, he seemed to agree with my assessment of it. He wrote a letter to the court to allow me to substitute my sessions with him for the anger-management class. I was relieved because I did not want to manage my anger; I wanted it to be vastly ameliorated, downgraded as a problem to near zero—you know, normal, as in healthy. It was at about that time that curing my anger was starting to become an attractive goal.

Now that I was freed from the anger-management program, my therapist and I worked together to get me further along with the divorce, help that I insisted I needed at least in the beginning. I did not realize that he probably had my anger as an agenda or that he had a secret weapon, if indeed he had thought of it by that time.

I had one-hour sessions with him once a week. I could tell he had a particularly penetrating gift of insight because he regularly confounded me with simply stated questions, something that no other therapist had ever done or ventured to do. Despite my inability to answer them and my difficulty in following his eventual explanations of the questions, he showed great patience, and he led me more effectively than any other therapist ever had. He never left me to figure out one of those questions for myself, if I did not get it at first. He probably saw in me zeal to get well, so he explained the concepts he was stressing.

This may be a good thing to look for in a therapist. If a therapist asks you questions that stump you and embarrass you, maybe he or she is onto something that you should examine. If the therapist does not, maybe you have stumped him or her, or maybe the therapist is falling for your con, a con that you probably do not even know you are pulling. I stumped a therapist once by asking about why one emotion in me felt physically the same as another. He never did get back to me about that, but years later I figured out the answer for myself.

After several months with this new therapist I had made great progress on the fear and pain of my big three—legal, divorce, and settlement issues. Then he said, right out of the blue, "Well, maybe you should do what I did. I found myself at the edge of a deep, black, bottomless pit. I either had to jump in or kill myself. So, because I had no other choice, I jumped in. I fell and fell and fell, into a totally black and inky void, unable to see a thing. Suddenly, I saw a bright blue ribbon twisting down near me, so I reached for it, grabbed it, and held it to me to save myself. That blue ribbon was my *pain*. I held it and embraced it to me."

I remember that he said this right out of the blue. He may have well been leading up to the pain issue for some time. I may have been too dense to see it, or my denial or some other protective mechanism may have dulled my alertness. At any rate it seemed he broached the subject suddenly and spontaneously, and it came completely as a surprise to me.

Then he said something that made some sense, although I had a hard time grasping the complete concept. He suggested that pain may have been at the core of my being and that since there was fear associated with this pain—after all, pain hurts—and since anger is a natural protective response to show strength to conquer fear, maybe my pain had led to my anger.

For only the second time a therapist brought up the subject of my inner pain, the first being at the recovery workshop. My therapist saw I had a core of pain, and he brought it up as if we both knew the obvious: my anger was a problem, and pain caused anger. I do not remember any other therapist ever saying or even hinting at that or attributing those qualities to me.

We talked the rest of the hour not about anger but about pain. All I really remember was his leaving the room to get a book and returning to show it to me: *Unattended Sorrow: Recovering from Loss and Reviving the Heart* by Stephen Levine.[1] To this day when I utter the title words *unattended sorrow*, I have to stifle a sob, even though it is a bit embarrassing to me to suddenly start to sob in front of others.

Levine started this book as a thirty-two-page pamphlet for the Red Cross to distribute to the wives of the firemen killed in the fall of the Twin Towers on 9/11. Since I loved books and was willing to follow any suggestion he had, I ordered the book that afternoon from Amazon and started reading it as soon as it came. The only program that Levine recommends is to *grieve those losses to cure the pain*. He gives only a general outline of what to do and does not give a specific step-by-step method. Other than the book, the therapist also did not give me a specific program, but I am sure he had one in mind for following sessions. I just started on the general guidelines from the book he had recommended and went from there before our next session.

---

[1]   Stephen Levine, *Unattended Sorrow: Recovering from Loss and Reviving the Heart* (Rodale, 2005). Unfortunately, this book is no longer in print, but used copies are available.

22

A Simple Course of Treatment

Natural forces within us are the true healers of disease.
—Hippocrates

In AA it is often said, "This is a simple program. But it is not easy." And that is true. All an alcoholic has to do is follow a simple program of twelve steps and not drink. It is simple, but it's not easy, because the steps are contrary to all the habits of an addict or dysfunctional person.

With Levine's book I did not have twelve steps or anything like them to follow. I read the first thirty or forty pages and got what I thought was the nub of the matter to relieve pain. I kind of thought he was talking about grieving, but he did not emphasize that word. Instead he stressed losses due to pain and only peripherally mentioned further pain as one of many outcomes to losses and pain. But I followed what I thought was the idea. I meant to relieve my pain that had become obvious to me beginning when the workshop leader had observed me as a person with "a lifetime of loss and pain." I certainly had had a dramatic and sudden reaction to that simple observation, very much as profound and fundamental as body feelings, so it seemed fruitful to follow up on loss and pain. It seemed obvious that grieving might be indicated, and I guessed that grieving may have been what my therapist was pointing me to, for he had recommended the book. I guess he also saw me as being in a lifetime of pain.

Tired of reading and eager to start, I took the only action that I could think of, an impulsive and emotion-driven idea. I figured that if I was in pain and sad from losses, then I would look at photos of things I had lost that represented losses. I knew that doing that would make me cry. I welcomed the crying because it seemed like grieving to me, although the concept of grieving was mysterious to me, even though I had tried to grieve the traumatic loss of my marriage to the love of my life. I was nevertheless, without understanding it, attempting to grieve specific losses. I intentionally triggered sadness and grief in tears and induced body feelings and emotional catharsis as Levine suggested was necessary. I consciously grieved the losses I had never grieved before.

That was it. That was my program. It was a simple one, and I just let myself do it. I grieved the losses in my life by reexperiencing the things I had lost by revisiting them in photos and places that were synonymous or associated with those losses.

After reading just a bit of *Unattended Sorrow*, I got my soon-to-be ex-wife's and my large leather-bound album of eight-by-ten-inch photos of our wedding and formal dinner reception in 1996. I looked at each photo and cried. Being emotional, I did not have to struggle to cry; I just burst out bawling. The pain and the sadness overtook me, and I let them overwhelm me.

I cried at the loss. I felt the pain. I felt extreme sorrow. I held the pain of that sadness close to me. I refused to avoid it or to shift my attention away from it. I remembered my therapist and his blue ribbon he clasped and held close to him. I cried hard and as long as twenty minutes viewing each picture until I was done with it. Sometimes those pictures reminded me of past losses of love and relationship. Sometimes they did not. I shed real tears and lots of them over each photo. I let my attention wander around in the photo and even to other similar mental images in the more distant past of my life. I looked at my soon-to-be ex-wife's dress, her image, her smile, her figure, the church, the pews and furnishings, the decorations, the flowers, the guests, the minister, the singer, my parents, my other relatives, my children, and my friends. I played the music in my mind. I remembered the words and the vows and how happy I had been and how happy for me everyone else had been. My mind flashed back to my second wedding in 1974, and I remembered how we'd walked down the aisle in triumph and how in elation I had said, "We did it!" I looked at the 1996 photos of the grass around the country club reception hall and at the sky and clouds and remembered how beautiful the weather had been that day. I remembered the crushed velvet (!) tux I had worn in my wedding in 1974. I was merciful with myself and let myself feel and reexperience my 1996 wedding through the photos and how it felt to be losing that marriage. I was gentle with myself to let the pain and sorrow ease out of my system.

Then I went on to the next photo, remembering how I felt, how the guests must have had such patience waiting for us and the photographer. I remembered hearing Stanley Turrentine's jazz standard "Sugar" for the first time as my second wife changed for the honeymoon in 1974, and I remembered how the 1996 guests had chattered with excitement and happiness for my third wife and me.

I remembered how hot it had been that September day in 1996 and how hot I had been as my best man had driven me to the church and how I had sweat in the car. I remembered how green the grass on the grounds had been and how pretty the flowers had been. I remembered how happy we had been and how happy I had been and how much fun it had been. I felt what a huge and excruciating loss it was to me. I embraced the pain and felt it until I was out of tears, and on and on through each photo I went.

With each photo I felt slightly better all over, especially in my body. My chest and heart lost a small bit of tenseness and rigidity. My breathing came easier, and my lower body relaxed and loosened up. After each photo I felt a general loosening of the tension within me, of the tightness and stress relaxing. I felt the steel bands around my heart start to release that organ. As I repeated the whole process, I recalled every detail I could pull from each new photo. I felt and reexperienced how I had felt right then, looking and remembering until I was out of tears, until I felt better. And with each step I did feel better. I felt a loosening of tightness, a release of tension. The change was very slight with each succeeding photo, but the cumulative effect was large.

With each photo I was mindful of my childhood, consciously endeavoring to remember past losses and pain as they might pertain to my present loss of love. It was remarkably easy to associate this separation and pending divorce with past losses and pains—all those instances where I had felt abandonment, abuse, or neglect as a child. I sensed the connections emotionally, where before the association between the two eras had been rational. My books were right! There was a carrying forward in time in my wounded inner being, and they were repeated, reflected, and enhanced by my present emotions.

I looked at more and more album photos, repeating the entire procedure until I was out of tears for each photo. When I was done with the album, I felt better about myself and about my life. It was a strange result but very real—slight at each step but definite and the cumulative effect was a deep release, a lightening of some load, a freeing of pressure. I kept up my album surfing, because after so many years I had nothing to lose and everything to gain.

I cried all afternoon. Then I boxed up the album and sent it to my wife, for I was done with it. I had no photos from the 1974 wedding to grieve over, but the similarity in the joy of getting married both times rushed in together; the pain was a mixture of both events, and I grieved them together.

As a result I was beginning to feel compassion for others, more so than ever before. I felt gentler toward others in my thoughts. With everyone— friends, my aging parents, their caregivers, and strangers—I had a quieter, more lenient, and more compassionate outlook, and I liked it. It felt good, and in the process I felt more connected, like I fit in the world better. I seemed to belong more to the human race, not so shunned or weakened or unique in my pain.

By not grieving some of my losses and pain until that day I had allowed them to damage my life far beyond the original losses and pain. The cumulative effects of the original traumas added together with all the similar losses and pains had threatened to destroy me. They could have done so and nearly did because they had never left me. They had only expanded and intensified, their effects becoming more critical. I never got over the old pain. Without ever being grieved, my original pain had stayed within me for sixty years or more. And nongrieved, that pain had been added to all the instances of more-recent similar events that appeared in the normal run of life.

I went downstairs to the antique buffet I used as an entry table and looked at each small framed photograph on it. There were early photos of my mother, now laying upstairs emaciated by Alzheimer's disease, and I cried at losing her first when I was a child to her demons and now to her disease. I looked at the photos there of my father, and I cried knowing he must have felt a great loss from his frustrations over his humanistic, modern son and from the despair he must have felt over his inability to reach me even as he loved me greatly. I thought about how, despite the disappointment we both must have felt over the generation gap, and how he had been patient and loving to me in his own way. I looked at pictures of my son who died at twenty-five years old, and I cried. There were more pictures of my ex-wife and her dog, and I cried. I looked at photos of her daughter, my stepdaughter, the only daughter I had ever had, and I cried. I looked at photos of my parents together and their intense love and devotion to each other, and I cried. And I cried when I realized I had no photos of my second wife, except one in my album of astrophotographs that I had taken of her when we had been in the desert with our telescope at an astronomy star party. I allowed the memories of that eighteen-year marriage to come back, and I cried at that great loss.

There were two photos of me as a child on that table. In one I was around six months old and had a slightly puzzled or frightened look on my face as my mother, with a bit-too-smug look on her face, held me. In the other I was wearing black trousers, black shirt, and a black felt fedora like the perfect little man I was supposed to be even at about four years old. I cried, grieving my lost childhood, for it had not been permissible for me to have those five attributes of a child that Pia Mellody waxes poetic about. I grieved for having to grow up way too fast and be too perfect, for not being allowed to be unique, precious, spontaneous, imperfect, and immature and not being allowed to explore the world and my inner self in my own way.

Once a cousin of mine told me his father, my mother's brother, had said that my mother only wanted one child "because she wanted a perfect child." I laughed and said, "I wonder how that worked out for her?" The little boy in the photo was a "perfect child" or appeared to be trying to be. So I cried over him and his losses, primarily his loss of *self*, grieving them at last.

The next day I talked and talked to a friend about how I felt, especially about the sadness, the fear, the loneliness, and the losses. And, like always, he understood, and I cried. Even though he had never been able to cry, he understood my need to and supported it.

The immediate losses I felt were of my third marriage and love, the loss of a secure relationship, no matter how tumultuous, that was exciting and titillating in a sexy, sensuous way, and I grieved these losses. But the others came trickling back to me—losses from my childhood, my teen years, and my 1974 marriage, including the lost love of my second wife, the love of my life, and my stepsons from that marriage. So I wept.

I played a Kenny G jazz CD that had meant so much to both my third wife and me. Our first wedding dance had been to one of those songs. And I cried. I played Turrentine's "Don't Mess with Mr. T" and old Wes Montgomery tunes like "Bumping on Sunset" that my second wife and I had loved in the 1970s and '80s. And I cried. In the following days I played the professional video we had had made of my third wedding and reception, and I cried all through it. I felt a sense of further relief by reexperiencing the loss. I still have the tape but have never watched it since. Nearly all the pain is gone, so there seems to be no need.

I went to therapy for my next session, and we talked more about the losses in my life, and I cried. And my therapist tried to show me the connection between losses and pain and how they could cause anger. I struggled to understand this connection, although now it seems obvious. My difficulty with the concept is a measure of my denial—after all, it had taken me over twenty-four years of recovery work since I first walked into AA to reach this point.

A few days later the friend that I often talked to about such matters and I went to Phoenix to get my truck serviced, and we struck out on foot to find a cell phone store to fix his phone. "There's the Great Indoors," I said, pointing to the big box store. "That is where my ex-wife and I shopped for all the commercial appliances and fixtures for the house I had built for us. I've got to go in and cry."

I went into the appliance department, at least four thousand square feet of Viking, Wolfe, Bosch, Scotsman, and all the other top-end appliances, a stainless steel heaven. I walked through the department and cried recalling the time my ex-wife and spent there planning the construction of our house. I went to the bathroom fixtures and looked at all the fancy shower heads, faucets, and spa tubs, and I cried. Salesmen came up to me to make sure I was okay, and see if I needed help, and I said, "No, I just came in to cry." They walked away confused. There is no telling what they thought of me. (By the way, if you every want to ensure prompt service in a place like that, just walk in and start crying.)

When I was done in the bathroom-fixtures department, I moved to ceiling fans, then mirrors and wall coverings, and then fireplace equipment and BBQs. When I walked out of the store, I felt even softer, gentler, more compassionate, and more tender toward everyone and toward myself. My gut was looser and more relaxed. The steel bands around my heart were less constrained. My arms, shoulders, and legs were more flexible. The armor of self-imposed emotional self-protection against my dysfunctional view of society was falling away.

I also felt much less angry at others in general, strangers, other drivers, store clerks, friends. From the turn my therapy sessions had suddenly taken, I now knew that the pain had led to the anger. It was based on toxic shame, but only because toxic shame caused losses and pain, and I had somehow adopted the anger and raging behavior to salve the pain.

At the end of about three weeks of actively watching for opportunities to grieve old losses and allowing myself to cry over them, I was just about done. I went back to therapy only about three or four more times after that, just to see if there was any residual pain left, which there wasn't, since the pain was pretty well healed. The losses did not go away; they will always be there. But now that they have been properly and fully grieved, I don't have to carry them with me like a bag of red-hot stones strapped around my torso, burning in my gut, just waiting for someone to screw up so I can unload on them and temporarily feel relief, to hell with how they feel. There are few hot stones left, and if one shows up, I tend to it immediately and properly.

At this point many readers may be repelled by the prospect of crying to express old emotional pain again. Why not just let it be? After all, that seems painful to bring it up again. Why not just grow up, get over it, and move on? That approach would be all right, but it had not worked for nearly sixty years for me. I had tried to get over it, and even if I had been very emotionally mature, I probably would not have succeeded in doing so. I have doubts about whether this works for anyone. To me, bottling up emotions just to feel better is counterproductive. I do *not* feel better when I stuff my emotions inside of me. Those emotions stay with me, and in a sense they rot and get worse without dying away. That rotting makes them more harmful. They stink more and more and grow more powerful. They do not evaporate into thin air. They are reinforced and amplified by new similar events that pass through my mind. People may be able to fool themselves into thinking that they have put those feelings aside, but I do not believe that they can so ignore them. I believe from my experience in fact those feelings stay buried deep within the subconscious and as body feelings. The reason they appear to have dissipated is that they are most likely transformed into other effects, possibly other emotions but most likely destructive behaviors that are injurious to the perpetrator of those behaviors and others. One example is my pain coming out as anger. All I can say is that grieving worked for me. I think crying worked for me because as a child I was never allowed to cry unless my mother "gave me something to cry about," which she frequently did, and then I was further shamed by abandonment by being left in a closed room alone to cry as opposed to being soothed and comforted. Finally when I took the opportunity to cry, with "permission" from the workshop leader and my therapist, and the Levine book, I felt immediate relief and comfort. And I did so in the company of my adult self, who nurtured my wounded inner child, who was no longer alone in a closed room as a shamed and lonely child. And I cried with others watching, as in the workshop and store, or with my friend listening.

So in answer to the question asked by the previous chapter's title, "Was My Therapist a Genius, Was I Ready, or Was He Tipped Off?" I'm going to go with all three. I think my therapist recognized the pain in me just as the group leader at the workshop did. The comments he made about his near suicide to identify with me certainly are a strong indication that he had had tremendous pain in his life, and indeed he introduced the topic with a highly effective graphical description of a bright blue ribbon of pain as he fell through an inky-black void. His recognition of my pain, where so many others had failed, was genius, as was his poetic metaphor.

And I would be surprised if the group leader at the workshop and he had not discussed me having a pain core in their telephone consultation. It seems to me that the workshop leader had more intuition and perception about me than all the therapists that had gone before put together. And he did it in a one-week workshop of about forty hours while dividing his time between me and four others plus the administration of the workshop. And maybe my therapist also was intuitive and perceptive with me. I'll never know which one of them deserves credit or if it is both. At any rate, whoever had that insight, it was genius.

And I was ready. The workshop leader's comment about my lifetime of pain was a strong suggestion to my subconscious, and I paid immediate attention to the body feelings and flood of tears that rocked me when he said that. I was aware of the existence of body feelings due to my reading about them and having felt them many times in the previous years. Goodness knows I worked years to place myself in position to be so introspective, and even though I looked in the wrong places, I kept up the search. And by going to the therapist with pain (over my divorce) on my agenda for the first time, I showed awareness and willingness. I was ready to recognize not only my pain but also all my emotions. The workshop extended the study of pain from my present back to my distant past where it belonged. I was lucky to not have any reservations that emotions are bad, wrong, or undesirable or should be stuffed deep inside my psyche or otherwise avoided, but it was years of work and study in my recovery that had made me so open. It was both simple and easy once someone brought up my *pain* and said it as though it was obvious that the pain had resided within me for ages.

GRIEVING BY THE BOOK

I have read several times about the five stages of grieving in relation to losses suffered in adulthood. My losses so suffered were loss of marriages and love and the death of my younger son. Those five stages of grieving are *denial* (or numbness), *anger*, *bargaining* (with God, yourself, or fate or otherwise rehashing the loss), *depression or sadness*, and *acceptance*. I knew that there was no correct order to these stages; they can come once or often in any order and should be allowed to do so. As an adult I had managed to grieve my adult losses (divorces and son's death) properly, but when the losses were a reflection back to a childhood losses, I kept them inaccessibly stuffed away.

If I had considered the problem of my childhood losses being carried into adulthood, it would have seemed to me to be an issue of acceptance, how to not get stuck with unresolved grief and to go on with life intellectually to accept the losses and pain. This step seems the hardest of the five to me. I also knew that the memory of the loss would fade but never be gone. I could not expect to be "done" with it, but I wished its effects, intensity, and ability to control my life would radically decrease over time so that it would be only one of several other significant memories of my life. That had happened only partially to my childhood losses and pain; the effects remained far too intense. But given the frequency and intensity of my rages, perhaps there was not even any partial abatement of the pain. The abatement may have been in the form of transference of pain into anger.

What I had done by crying was to physically fully reexperience the painful childhood feelings, and to do so as an adult. In doing so, I recognized that the feelings were only intense and painful and *not bad or harmful. I accepted the feelings as they came* and found that they soon passed to remain as memories of lifetime experiences, which was healthy. I could not banish the memories, nor did I try. The losses had happened, and there was no denying them, but they did not have to rule my life. In *expressing the feelings of sadness and pain physically*, I cried, sobbed, and shook, feeling them all over my body and allowing myself to be conscious to them. To do this I followed my own advice about the nature of emotions and embraced them as friends who were helping me to heal. Finally, I shared my feelings unashamedly and in depth to a close friend and of course to my therapist. I also talked about my crying experiences looking at photos with others whom I could trust. At each of these steps I felt a tiny bit of relief, and I kept this program up intensely for many days and less so for a few weeks until I felt the painful effects fade to near zero.

Every one of the processing of those childhood experiences listed above were done as an adult, with adult powers and a mature outlook, something I never had before. My years of recovery work on each of my addictions finally came to fruition for treating my anger.

It seems to me that the five stages of grieving should be expanded to six stages, if the grieving concerns childhood issues. That sixth stage is *reexperiencing*. I got the most good out of emotionally processing my losses in real time as I reexperienced them. For me I did this by crying and allowing myself to feel sad. This was by far the biggest factor in my recovery, to feel those emotions as my inner child had felt them, and then additionally to feel them also as an adult with adult powers and resources to support and protect my inner child, so that no matter how sad or abandoned my inner child might feel, I was always there as an adult to take care of that inner child—after all, I am the only one who can!

After reexperiencing, I could move to the final step of acceptance, to be an adult caring for myself. As such, I can allow myself to always remember the things I was grieving, the losses and the pain, but they no longer need to weigh on me, for I can care for me as well as for my inner child, who still lives on as an inner child. Nowadays those painful memories are properly felt as being in the past, and they remain only as additional memories of my life along with all the rest, perhaps slightly more intense but not debilitating.

23

ANGER RECOVERY

Having properly grieved, or at least finally started to properly grieve, the pain from my losses, I was able to move on to the visible problem, my anger. With a much-diminished sense of loss, pain, and helplessness, I no longer held within me a profound consciousness of life having a basic hopelessness to it, and I could feel my anger leaving me. I was starting to lose the need to exert power and control through anger or rage. The effect when I first started crying over the wedding photos was immediate and encouraging. Over the next few days, as I continued to grieve at every opportunity by crying and being gentle and nurturing with myself, I made more progress, continually softening and lightening up very noticeably toward other people. This included the people I had regular contact with, strangers and even those I saw only at a distance, like other drivers or people in front of me in checkout lines (always good tests of my anger). I liked this new attitude that was suddenly coming so easily to me. I had tried to be this way for years and had never been able to fully succeed. Rational means could not overcome my deeply held emotions induced by childhood trauma. Those prior attempts were at "controlling" my anger. Now I felt less helpless and less fearful of loss, for the pain was vastly decreased, so now, at last, I had less use for anger. The experience was a confirmation of an emotional approach working better than a rational one. Anger now seemed nearly always to be groundless. Without those old tapes replaying pain and fear of an impending loss in my head, at least not so incessantly, anger was not a frequent and sudden knee-jerk reaction. And when, perhaps out of habit, I would start to get angry, a very strange thing started to occur: I was able to pause and think it through, and I could decide not to get angry just by thinking things like *It's no big deal*, *It's not worth it*, *He is doing the best he can*, and *Cut him some slack*. I considered that perhaps anger management really was effective for folks with smaller reservoirs of anger induced by pain and loss!

I liked my new attitude. I consciously continued to work not only on grieving my residual pain but also on not blowing up. Seven years later, my anger still comes up occasionally. In effect I had been working an informal set of steps like in a twelve-step program by pausing, analyzing, and reevaluating situations on the fly to avoid losing my cool. I can remember doing something similar in my early days and years of AA with drinking, drinking thoughts, and drinking opportunities (clubs, parties, and so on). It worked for booze, and it seemed to work for anger. One of AA's maxims to keep you from taking that first drink is "Think it through." That means think the drink through: from ordering and paying for it, or pouring it; to drinking it; to having a second, third, fourth, and more drinks; to getting drunk and blacking out; to losing your self-respect, job, family, and perhaps freedom and life. I did the same with my anger and was able to cool down immediately before too many steps in my mind.

This was absolutely *not* conventional anger management. This was anger management *after the extensive preconditioning and preparation of pain management and resolution*. It was like going through years of amateur and minor-league experience and expert coaching (who knew my pain and anger better than me?) and *then* stepping up to the plate and hitting a home run in the World Series. Conventional anger management seems to me like trying to go straight to the World Series right out of Little League. Chances are I'd strike out or get beaned.

Today, I continue my recovery from anger, just like I continue my recovery from alcohol addiction and codependence. Since they are all addictions, and since, as an addict, I am prone to slips, I take things one day at a time. I have to work at it, but it is worth it, and it gets easier and easier.

In my continuing work to recover from anger I am mindful to continue grieving my pain and losses. There is some residual hurt within me. As I get less and less sensitive to those past situations, the anger becomes easier to manage.

If you try this and find it works for you—grieving the pain of losses to heal anger—you may have slips in anger. I did, and I relate them in the afterword. To paraphrase AA's Big Book, "I claim progress, not perfection."[1]

How exactly, in detail, does this relationship of shame to losses to pain to anger work? To accomplish a full recovery, I think it needs to be understood. This chapter presents the simplified version, and the next few chapters will provide the details. You may prefer to skip to part 3, "What I Am Like Now," for the happy ending. The remainder of part 2 is my analysis in nontechnical terms of how the shame-to-anger chain is formed and, as such, contains information valuable in understanding that chain for recovery. The last three chapters of part 2 cover alternate and conventional treatments for anger, which I am not enamored of.

---

[1]   Bill W., chapter 5, "How It Works," *Alcoholics Anonymous*, 3rd ed. (New York: Alcoholics Anonymous World Services, 1976), 60.

24

OTHER EFFECTS OF LOSSES THAT ARE NOT PROPERLY GRIEVED

Let us examine the other ways I could have dealt with or managed the losses *that led to the pain that led to the anger.* You will recall that, for me, shame was a red herring as the cause for my anger. *The anger was caused by the pain of chronic or recurring loss in my life.* It is true that most of the pain and losses were caused by toxic shame, but healing the shame did not lead to anger recovery. Such healing had no effect on the underlying pain or memory of loss. Here are the other ways I could have dealt with or managed the pain of chronic or recurring loss without grieving. The following is not a mutually exclusive list or necessarily a complete one. I could have used (and did use) some or a combination of these methods, but I found them all inadequate:

+ Denial: "It did not happen" or "It's not that bad."
+ Rationalization: "It wasn't that bad," "Everyone has had something bad happen to him or her," and "Other people's losses were probably just as bad and maybe worse, and they are okay." In the recovery community this is called judging one's insides by the outsides of others (determining how one feels by how others look).
+ Blaming: "It is their fault, not mine." This method is obviously self-defeating. Here I mean blaming as a complete strategy, assigning blame to someone else with the sole purpose of avoiding dealing with it. I do not mean blaming in the sense of setting responsibility

to establish exactly what happened and who was involved and responsible so that you can determine a logical program of recovery to work on the problem realistically.

+ False reality: In this method you should act better than you feel or think you really are. You should be perfect or, even better, be so perfect you can be a caregiver for others, which is inappropriate. You should be so "good" you are needless—so needless that you are always available to help others. Or, as was a real favorite of mine at one time, you can be arrogant and boastful. And, as was another favorite of mine, you can overachieve in certain areas. I overachieved in school, at work, and in my career but sadly not in the functionality of my relationships, although I certainly overachieved in the number of them.

+ Vain attempts to control the pain of loss:
    + Being the victim: "Oh, poor me" or "Oh well ..." Playing the victim amplifies and justifies the pain, so that prolonging it has an attractive side.
    + Depression (any level from mild up to acute depression): Depression trades one pain for another, a worse one in the extreme.
    + Self-destructive hobbies and activities: This method includes things like participating in extreme sports, going into dangerous situations, brawling, driving fast and dangerously, mountain and rock climbing, right up to the extreme of committing suicide, which is a permanent solution to a temporary problem.
    + Substance abuse: Substance abuse includes drinking, drugs, gambling, sex, relationships, risky activities, religion, and other compulsive behaviors (as addictions in the extreme). The least harmful of these behaviors are merely financially or emotionally devastating; the worst are life threatening.
    + Chronic anger and rage: Say what?! You can salve the pain of chronic losses by raging? Yes, see below.

The trouble with any of these methods is that my losses did happen, they were that bad, and I was unable to outdistance the effects or ignore them. The effects of my losses were *independent of my failure to admit them*, and there were many destructive and injurious results down through the years, because I did hide them. Finally, when I was arrested and taken to jail, I could not deny, rationalize, or otherwise gloss over my anger as a nondestructive effect. I had hit my bottom for anger.

As to adopting anger as a method of dealing with pain, earlier I claimed that anger was one source of my power. Its gifts to me were strength, assertiveness, energy, courage, fortitude, and vigor. Why be depressed or live in a false reality when you can claim all the power anger can bestow? It does not even have to be justified anger. Any anger will do, although justified anger is best. The anger is not to be right or to accomplish anything. Such a goal is a self-justifying delusion. Anger is to feel better. It is to salve the pain—the pain of living and the pain of the losses that seem to have come just from living but in reality are as old as you are. That last is especially true if you are unreasonably loyal to your parents or to any other caregiving adult in your life who molested or abused you.

25

THE PATH OF MY ANGER

This chapter is not an abuse excuse for my behavior and for all the things I have done that are imperfect and bad in my life just because I was abused as a child. I am 100 percent responsible for my life, mistakes, errors, and sins of both omission and commission.

The chapters that follow explain the psychodynamics of my anger as I understand them in the language of recovery terms. They are in layman's terms because that is what I am. Taken together they are a simple-minded explanation that shows the origin of my anger in my losses and pain. The path was the trauma-producing childhood losses (an event or process), which caused pain (an emotion), which was amplified by similar-appearing later losses (more events; reoccurrences) up to and including adult losses (more events; all of which caused more reoccurrences), resulting in unresolved emotional pain. This series of processes created a huge reservoir of painful memories that showed as painful and harmful emotions. With nothing to dissipate the pain and with my inability to stifle or disassociate the childhood pain from the events of my adulthood (in

Why did my parents abuse me? The abuse was so natural to me that all through childhood and early adulthood I did not bother to ask myself this question. Likewise, I did not think about addressing this question until my seventh draft of this book. The why of the abuse is not a mystery to me, but it must be to the reader. Since the idea of addressing this occurred to me so late in my writing, I deferred it to the afterward so as to not further upset the flow of the theory.

which I was an adult child in some ways until recovery), every similar-appearing new event felt emotionally like a reenactment of the traumatizing event, sometimes resulting in sudden and accidental reexperiencing of that same pain or loss. The result was a burning rage within me from the constant fear of reexperiencing the traumas. I have called this rage an addiction to anger because by acting out with anger I could establish artificial control of the pain and fear through a false sense of power and control and thus feel temporarily better—like an alcoholic feels better with a few drinks. The result was a life of pain that came out as anger, raging, and violence, which were the life-damaging consequences of the addiction.

The trauma events caused loss events that hurt emotionally. When I was spanked, I learned that my body was of little value, at least compared to my mother's wishes. When my father was never available to protect me, my sense of low value was reinforced. When she left me in the bathroom after a spanking and told me I could come out only when I stopped crying, I learned that my emotions were valueless also. When I was humiliated by being yelled at, slapped (on the face—my persona), or otherwise condemned to remain seen and not heard, my self-esteem was damaged. When she yelled at me in anger, I wilted in self-condemnation and fear for the possible coming physical pain. On the other hand, sometimes she used me as evidence of how wonderful she was or how wonderful she and Dad were together. She would hold me up as a near genius and brag about how smart I was. I was confused—first I was a piece of junk, but then I was marvelous. So I picked marvelous and became grandiose, arrogant, and boastful. In short I lost my childhood and grew up overachieving and trying to be perfect. These losses of self and of childhood were the biggest losses of all. I never rebelled until I discovered at seventeen when I went away to college that other young people were of all types and that I was only one of those types. I grew up skewed in many ways, which caused losses of self—losses to my self-image and personality. I lost the chance to be any of the normal things that Pia Mellody says children naturally are—valuable, vulnerable, imperfect, dependent, and immature (see chapter 12, "Pia Mellody's Theory Summarized").

Those losses caused emotional pain, and I was left with a core of emotional pain. Being immature, both as a child and later as an adult child, I had nothing to compare my reality to or the means to change it. Furthermore, I was an only child with no siblings to compare my childhood experiences to or discuss them with; thus my childhood seemed normal to me, although in retrospect it sounds pretty awful in some ways. Since I had never been allowed to be imperfect, I had never learned how to adjust and fix the biggest mistake, which seemed to be *me*. I had not matured to have my own independent sense of value and worth; I was stuck with that implied very low value and low worthiness imparted to me by my abusive parents, and I was vulnerable to any action from them, my caregivers. My unalienable inherent worth as a child was lost, and it caused me sadness and pain, a near low-grade depression that the leader of the workshop detected in me.

Since pain hurts, I feared it. I feared the pain from the physical, emotional, judgmental, and high-expectation treatments. Most of all I feared the helpless feelings that were brought up when new events mirrored these old memories. And like most folks, one of my defenses against fear and against helplessness was anger, because anger seemed to replace the helplessness and pain with power, control, mastery, command, and presence.

As I grew up, I failed in some ways to mature emotionally and grew up to be an adult child. With my emotions frozen at the emotional age of the abuse, I never grew to be an emotionally mature adult able to recover from the childhood trauma. I remained stuck at an emotional age far behind my chronological age. In my adolescent years, I decided out of all the ways to react to my abuse in childhood, anger was a very good course of action. I also overcompensated by being arrogant and an overachiever. I do not mean any of these was a conscious decision. They were not events, but long processes of learning from my caregivers. Anger was modeled for me by my mother, and however negative a quality it was, it seemed to work well for her. At least, I was intimidated as a small child by it, and I imagined that her purpose was to intimidate others by it. She also modeled arrogance, and both my parents modeled overachieving. This last is a gift I gladly acknowledge with gratitude (one out of three ain't bad compared to where I came from).

So anger was an early strategy I used to try to manage my pain. Manipulation and whining only got me slaps or another spanking, and pouting was equally verboten. How could I develop out of being an emotionally immature, low-confidence, low-self-esteem teenager and start using a healthier strategy? I was emotionally stuck. I kept up the only behavior I knew, for even if it seldom worked, it made me feel better.

In chapter 24, "Other Effects of Losses That Are Not Properly Grieved," I listed several strategies for combatting losses. The one I chose that was devastating was anger. I was not invested in being angry early in life just because it felt so good or because it made me feel powerful. In the beginning I got angry probably for only two things: getting my way (natural selfishness, as children are) and surviving (natural helplessness, as children are). The strategy of anger helped me survive and helped me get my way, and eventually it came to feel good—that is, to feel not helpless.

So now the question is, survive what?

26

TRAUMA, THE CAUSE

I asked at the end of the previous chapter, "survive what?" What I needed to survive was the pain from the losses caused by all the trauma from my childhood abuse. Part of the abuse was fear that I would not survive the immediate event, but this was short lived; as the episodes ended, the fear faded. It is immaterial whether my life was in real danger or whether as a child some part of me just thought it was. Being not yet rational, the effect was the same. More sinister and damaging was the constant pain of rejection and of low self-esteem and belief in my lack of self-worth. All the cumulative effects of the lack of nurturing I received led to a failure to thrive. I was denied a full childhood with a sense of self-value, protection, and being nurtured; instead I was stuck in always being total dependent on others without hope of ever being self-sufficient or complete. As a child I reacted naturally enough as if I had one overarching problem: to survive the sense that I was inadequate. So many messages I got from my caregivers said I was inadequate, that I was defective in a way that could not be fixed. My interpretation of their reactions to my apparent inadequacies was that I was in danger of being discarded or abandoned. As such I felt in constant danger of perishing. It was real trauma.

To maintain that childhood trauma is a contributing cause of my anger may seem an outlandish claim, even if one grants my belief that I might not survive. Many children are abused, and certainly not all of them are wounded in ways that show up in later dysfunctional behavior, like anger and other less-than-perfect behaviors. But it is axiomatic in the study of childhood abuse that even a very little amount can do that type of harm in one child, while a great deal more done to another child may scar him or her far less or not at all. The amount, duration, and extended repetition of abuse do affect the extent of the wounding and later behavioral effects, but in many cases, even a little may be enough. It is exactly parallel to battle trauma. Some soldiers are affected to the point of PTSD where others, subjected to the same type and intensity of conditions, are not.

It is entirely possible that many of the people who apparently do not suffer in these ways have been harmed and just do not know it. Perhaps a few fortunate ones can consciously sense their damage and do something about it. Others may be unaware and suffer early onset of other symptoms like arthritis, heart problems, chronic fatigue, frozen joints, TMJ, asthma, lupus, cancers of all types, and a host of other "physical" diseases that are extremely resistant to drug, chemo, and radiation treatments and even to surgery, granting the questionable hypothesis that surgery is always a good cure. How else do we explain the mystery of deadly diseases at an early age in otherwise healthy people, coupled with the equally mysterious and puzzling number of spontaneous remissions? There are numerous studies that seem to correlate serious disease to known sufferers of childhood trauma. Alice Miller has written extensively about this. (See for example chapter 15, "Recovery Junkie," in the "Shame and Childhood Abuse" section.) Is it possible that the correlation is even higher than reported due to a serious underrating of childhood disease? This would not be as shocking as it seems at first glance if one grants that the poisonous pedagogy rules of childhood abuse are still with us. These rules protect the parents and society at all costs from exposure to shame for abusing their children or for allowing it. Such shame is at the children's expense and "for their own good." This situation almost certainly causes childhood abuse to be underreported.

My path from trauma to losses to pain to anger is simple, but I could not find it for twenty-five years, because I tried to jump directly from trauma causing shame to anger. Overlooking the losses and pain effects of the trauma made it seem like the cause of my anger was shame.

Any alternative explanation that pain did not cause my anger does not work. When I grieved the pain of my losses by crying with my impression of my childhood as a backdrop to viewing the photos, I could feel my pain hurting less and the tightness and tension in my body lessening. And my crying made me conscious in a dramatic way of the pain that was specific to the event or place that the photo commemorated and conscious of its similarity to events in my childhood. The anger started to go away with the tears of grieving.

My previous equation in chapter 7, "John Bradshaw, *Bradshaw on: the Family*," can now be modified but still not yet completed. It was

$$\text{Abuse} \rightarrow \underline{\quad\text{fill in blank}\quad} \rightarrow \text{anger.} \qquad (1)$$

and now becomes

$$\text{Abuse} \rightarrow \text{shame} \rightarrow \text{losses} \rightarrow \text{pain} \rightarrow \text{anger.} \qquad (2)$$

Note that this equation, while true, is still incomplete. It will be further modified in chapter 28, "Chronic Loss, the Antecedent of Pain." Furthermore, I do not claim that this is the only path leading to anger. It is mine, and I think it is a common one.

27

NECESSARY LOSS AND CHRONIC OR RECURRING LOSS

Not all losses are abnormal like losses from abuse. Life can be viewed as a succession of normal losses that lead to growing periods. These losses can be considered *necessary losses* if they happen normally during childhood and lead to normal stages of growth.

Birth is the normal and necessary loss of the warm, secure, oceanic existence where all physical and emotional needs are constantly met within the womb. The needs of sustenance, waste disposal, warmth, comfort, safety, and security are all met nearly perfectly in the womb. And then at birth it is all lost. It is not remarkable that our first expression is the normal one of crying out very loudly. But out of that loss is the opportunity to grow and develop, and we do so with a lot of help.

At every stage of infant development is a loss that is replaced by a growth and further development. As toddlers we lose the freedom to pee and poop our pants but gain freedom from not wearing urine and excrement. We go through the terrible twos and continue the separation from our mothers (a loss) at the apparent cost of rebellion, but that rebellion is really the beginning of individuation, of freedom, and of the development of self.

We lose the security of grade school and one class with only one teacher and with set recesses and rest periods for the growth and broadening of experiences of multiple classes in different rooms with different teachers with specialized skills and schedules not identical to any other student's. Ideally each schedule is fitted to individuals.

We choose a college, job, training program, military service, or other vocation and move away from home, and the move is marked by a loss and by a growth in the expansion of talents.

All these and others are normal or *necessary losses* because they are necessary for us to grow up and develop and to become all that we wish to be and are able to be. Judith Viorst discusses these at length in her excellent book *Necessary Losses*.[1]

There are also *chronic losses* in life, to borrow a term from Claudia Black's *Changing Course*.[2] Elsewhere I call these *recurring losses*. Acknowledging that there are normal losses as above, Black also describes these chronic losses, which are losses from events that continue over and over during a protracted length of time or recur frequently in slightly different forms. These losses can be normal or because of the action or lack of action of a caregiver. A caregiver is a person who cares for someone who is young, sick, or disabled, or a person who should give care and comfort to another of lesser capability or capacity, especially a child. Caregivers of children are supposed to, by the mores of our society, take care of us as children. Claudia Black uses the example of a child who suffers an accidental or natural loss, say a fall and bruise. If the child is loved, supported, and nurtured by his or her caregiver(s), the child feels sad and hurt but loved and secure. When a child suffers a loss because of the actions or no actions of a caregiver—for instance, say a caregiver laughs or belittles the child for being clumsy and causing the fall—the child feels sad, unloved, unwanted, or unimportant. A caregiver repeatedly failing to nurture an accidental loss by supplying care that is comforting and supportive is also a cause of chronic loss. Such children are emotionally abandoned, and if they feel so at a time when they are just beginning to develop feelings of self-esteem in the time of separation from their mothers, the effects can be particularly damaging. The effects of such feelings from chronic loss remain with the children until *resolved*.

Even if the abandonment is in late teens, if the child's self-esteem has not been allowed to grow normally because of ongoing or chronic abandonment events, there will be psychological damage to the child. He or she will not grow up fully happy and functional with a full set of tools to meet life's stresses and challenges. He or she will only be able to meet them as a child, by reacting with the tools normally available at the approximate psychological age of the arresting of his or her development.

In the extreme case of an adult child, even a series of normal losses can affect the adult child like a chronic loss, if the series of losses appear to be similar, especially similar to a childhood loss, all together they may look like one loss that has repeated over and over down through the years. As an example, say a particularly sensitive child has suffered emotional abandonment in childhood. This is real emotional abandonment where a parent was not there to support and reassure the child. Perhaps the parent had to leave the child all alone at home at an age far too young for the child to care for himself or herself. Perhaps it was late in the evening when things go bump in the night, and there was no one available for the child to turn to for

> *Resolution* is commonly given as the way to healthily get over harmful feelings, but it is rarely defined or described as a process. Generally resolution involves reexperiencing a harmful feeling in a safe and nurturing environment while analyzing and naming the feeling and considering its characteristics and meanings to the sufferer. Often this process puts the feeling into perspective, and the energy of the harmful feeling is dissipated. Grieving is just such a process, as is talking to a friend, therapist, or religious authority. With such conversations the implications of the feeling to one's reality are reframed into a more acceptable form. Resolution is *not* minimizing your feelings by ignoring them or toughing it out! It is facing your feelings, feeling them, and embracing them in a mature and nurturing manner.

relief. Now fast-forward in this child's life to an age of mid-twenties, and his or her significant other wants an innocent night out with friends—maybe to go to a baby shower or a ball game. None of these friends are known to drink, take drugs, or carry on in an unseemly manner, but the adult child who stays home alone experiences a very real feeling of abandonment, of being left behind and being all alone, because the one leaving is one who is special, analogous to the child's most significant other, the abandoning parent. When the partner returns, he or she finds a hurt, angry, or depressed lover. The adult child has experienced those lonely and fearful feelings, in fact *reexperienced the childhood feelings,* and it is real pain, the pain of a very real loss, at least to this adult child. As an adult child, this person does not have the emotional maturity to care for himself or herself—the adult child really needs to cling to his or her partner to feel good. There may be harsh words, and the relationship is damaged. The innocent person who just wanted to have his or her own life occasionally, which is entirely healthy, may think and feel, *What the heck! I leave one night and all this turmoil?* and he or she has a point. The event has triggered old experiences for the adult child—the sights, sounds, even the smells, and the feelings of being abandoned. The adult child reexperiences those feelings because he or she has never learned to deal with them in a healthy, adult manner.

All of the abuses I suffered in childhood from my parents were chronic (reoccurring) losses and could be characterized as either acts of frequent and direct abuse by my mother (beatings, aggrandizement of my intelligence, emoting at me, and so on) or acts of neglect or humiliation by my mother or father—things that my mother and father should have been done to protect me (my father should have put an end to the beatings and stopped my mother from raging at me, and they both should have presented a more balanced view of my intellectual capabilities). They were chronic because, except the spankings, the abuses continued until I was physically grown. Even as an adult I experienced further repetitions of my parents treating me abusively as if I were still their chattel child. The family pattern of an abusive top dog–underdog relationship replaced the abusive childhood as I became an adult, but the effects of the totality of the abuse remained until I slowly healed in recovery. This took until just a few years before my mother's dementia and my father's death. Between twelve and fifty years old I had similar repeated losses of nonphysical abusive treatments, because my parents' behavior changed only a little as I grew up. After that I conquered codependence enough to slough off their offenses and view each situation objectively and maturely and not as an adult child.

I would call their treatment of me in adulthood *repetition compulsion*. According to Judith Viorst this is a natural human desire that "impels us to do again and again what we have done before, to attempt to restore an earlier state of being. It impels us to transfer the past—our ancient longings, our defenses against those longing—onto the present."[3]

I was sure all my life that my parents wanted me to remain dependent on them so they could ensure their dependence and reliance on me. That would be an example of transferring their familiar matriarchal-patriarchal family system to the present so that I would be ever-present to be subservient to them. They could never fully shake that pioneer subsistence-existence outlook. They were happy to see me grow and mature and gain the skills of adulthood, but they wanted me and those skills available to them on demand.

Some of the repetition behavior was financial. Once in my restaurant, after I had written my own and my parents' paychecks and given them to my mom to record as always, my mom gave mine back to me in front of our bank manager. I was humiliated by Mommy paying me to run my own business. Another time I sold a small apartment house to them with the verbal understanding that they had to get new financing with the same lender I had used, so I would not have to pay a prepayment penalty. They used another lender whose terms for the new loan were exactly what my lender's terms were. It cost me $1,500 in 1970 dollars, and they had to get a new loan with more paperwork rather than an easier-to-obtain, identical refinance loan with the existing lender. Like with any other person, I should have made sure that agreement was in writing. When I sold my restaurant, I wrote the final checks to my vendors and kept them unsigned until escrow closed, intending to use the escrow funds to cover the checks. Upon closing escrow in a meeting together in the escrow office, I received a cashier check for sale funds to deposit in my restaurant checking account, which my parents could access in case I was not available, on vacation, for instance. I properly deposited the cashier check and attempted to check the account balance to make sure the funds were available for the checks I had written but not signed. Those checks were meant to close out the business. I made the deposit with the business teller, whom I had gone to every day of the week for six years to make my daily deposit of receipts, but she would not give me the account balance that day. Mom (and Dad?) had removed me from the account.* Humiliated, I left the bank and confronted them. When they refused to change the account back, I did the only thing possible: I gave them the checks to sign and mail, so all my vendors, if they cared, probably thought by the signatures that they had received payment from my parents for my failing restaurant. My parents also

---

* This is not possible under current post-9/11 banking laws; the account would have to be closed and reopened under new names today.

withheld my share of the sale of the restaurant proceeds from me. It was over a year until Dad came to me and gave me quite a large sum of money for the proceeds (in three payments three months apart), but it was still not the full amount. I guess it was to teach me never to fail; I never thought of a sensible reason. In fact, I never asked what their reasons were. Looking back now it seems like the patriarchal/matriarchal system was still functioning. What I learned from all these episodes was not to do business with them unless everything was in writing.

About five years later I rejoined their business, to allow Dad to retire. (Was I being loyal as an abused child tends to be?) I quit my aerospace research job and became the maintenance man for about 127 apartments. I did all the maintenance, relieving Dad of those duties. We all cleaned apartments with a cleaning woman the first few days of the month, but Mom and Dad were finally retired other than that. Then I took over all the bookwork, teaching myself accounting and computerizing the records and finances. Early in this stage of rejoining the business the third limited partner died, and my parents bought the shares that went to the heir for about one-quarter value. They "gave" me those shares, giving me a note for the shares payable to them to reimburse for their cost plus some money I owed them from our drinking days when my wife had borrowed from them to pay the house taxes. They had a written note. They knew better than to have anyone owe them money without a written note! I was very glad to have paid them back for that loan plus the interest, but I have always felt guilty about the bargain I got for the quarter-price share of the company.

In this property-management position, I was paid by them. Twice at the end of December they paid me my salary early the last day of the year, rather than the first few days of January. That way they could claim it on their income taxes for that year. I of course had to pay income taxes on it for that year. They got to take a thirteenth month of my salary as a deduction early, and I had to pay taxes on thirteen months' salary. It fit the pattern of doing whatever was best for my parents.

I relate these few instances of shenanigans as some of the more-egregious business and personal dealings I had with my parents in order to illustrate that the childhood abuse was not limited to my childhood. We still fought—these losses, similar to childhood abuse, caused me pain that was a recurring sort from my childhood, and then it turned into anger. I look back now at this treatment as a continuation of the childhood abuse well into my adulthood. My purpose in life was supposed to be me being completely subservient to my parents. These types of events continued until I was over sixty years old when I became their caregiver in their very old ages (eighty years old plus).

I grew up with the story of my dad, around ten to twelve years old, raising and fattening a 4-H calf, providing all the care for it. When it came time to take the calf to market, it was the family calf, and Dad got no money for it.

When I was about sixty and into model railroading, I mentioned to a close cousin who is six years younger than I that when I was a kid, I had a three-rail electric train set. I said that it had only been a Marx and not a Lionel but that it had been the best Marx made. He said he'd had a Marx when he was little too. He said that my mother had sold it to his mother, her sister. Then it hit us both! He had gotten my calf, I mean train, and my mom had gotten the money. Well, Santa had brought it to me years before, so she had paid for it.

Lately, I was discussing with my accountant cousin how children get a Social Security number and card when they are born now, and I got mine when Mom and Dad had a motel when I was about twelve years old. Mom got it for me so I could get a paycheck. Then it hit me—I never saw the money! I guess I had to pay for my raising.

But enough of fond childhood memories. Actually it is a sign of my recovery that I do not have anger or resentment over these things. I imagine that is the way it was when my folks were kids down on the homesteads. The parents probably owned everything, including the kids. I wrote about induced or carried emotions in chapter 13. Carried shame, otherwise known as induced shame, is shame from abuse passed down from generation to generation. Mom and Dad probably knew of no different way to treat their son.

I also relate the above childhood abuse not for sympathy but because I want to stress how long lasting the effects of such abuse can be—sixty-some years in my case! And it is obvious I did not just forget.

I have also told of relationship losses and divorces. Some of these losses may be normal, but when the circumstances are similar to childhood abusive events, the mind, especially the mind of an adult child, will link these losses to the childhood events. These losses then become part of the chronic losses.

Elsewhere I have used *recurring* to characterize such losses or pain. A lot of my relationship losses seemed like my childhood losses of abuse, abandonment, and neglect. All these chronic or recurring losses added up to more pain and more fear of the pain, which I was unequipped to deal with. This amplified my anger.

Strangely, the biggest loss of all, the death of my younger son when he was twenty-five, while terrible and a real shock, was relatively easy to mourn and get over—at least as much as one ever gets over the loss of a child. The loss of my son was such a normal loss (in the sense that tragic things like that do happen in a long life, and they can be expected occasionally). My loss of my son was not chronic, however, because it bore no relation to any child-hood abuse I had weathered. Therefore, the grieving period was relatively short—a year or so with occasional flashbacks of temporary sadness. The flashbacks of grief continue to this day twenty-three years later, but other people I meet tell of the same experience after the death of a child.

So there are two kinds of loss. There are normal or accidental losses, which are *necessary losses* because some losses are unavoidable in all lives. And there are repetitive losses, which are *chronic losses*. They are imposed on us by abuse and sometimes, but not often, by accidental occurrences if they appear to be a repetition of chronic losses.

I never did make the connection between losses to pain to anger until after I grieved, but I did know the inner dynamics as *separate pieces* of losses, pain, and anger. I had no idea how they fit together and were connected like a chain, so I did not know how to heal the results using the knowledge of the inner dynamics. So the anger remained unabated. Intellectually, I knew a lot about my anger. I just could not control it, meaning I did not know how to rationally manage my anger. It felt to me as if there were pieces missing. I will put it all together in the next two chapters.

---

[1]   Judith Viorst, *Necessary Losses: The Loves, Illusions, Dependencies, and Impossible Expectations That All of Us Have to Give Up in Order to Grow* (New York: Free Press, 1986).

[2]   Claudia Black, *Changing Course: Healing from Loss, Abandonment, and Fear* (Bainbridge Island, WA: MAC Publishing, 1999). I highly recommended this book for its insight, exercises, and advice about what works in recovery.

[3]   Viorst, *Necessary Losses*, 76.

28

CHRONIC OR RECURRING LOSS, THE ANTECEDENT OF PAIN

In this chapter and the next, I will complete my equation linking abuse to anger. I first introduced the equation with the middle links missing, such that

$$\text{Abuse} \rightarrow \underline{\quad \text{fill in blank} \quad} \rightarrow \text{anger.} \qquad (1)$$

Then I added to the equation, filling in the blank to get

$$\text{Abuse} \rightarrow \text{shame} \rightarrow \text{losses} \rightarrow \text{pain} \rightarrow \text{anger.} \qquad (2)$$

To put the equation in words, my childhood abuse led to shame, which led to chronic losses, which, because I was emotionally incapable of dealing with them, led to pain at each recurrence, which led to anger.

Differentiating the different types of loss, we have

$$\text{Necessary losses} \searrow$$
$$\text{Abuse} \rightarrow \text{shame} \rightarrow \text{chronic losses} \rightarrow \text{pain} \rightarrow \text{anger.} \qquad (3)$$

Because normal losses can lead to any severity of pain, mild to severe, the effect of the pure normal loss may be mild to severe. But if a normal loss is so similar to ongoing chronic losses, the emotional effect is like that of a chronic loss because of the similarity of the experience. However, compared to pain from chronic loss, the pain from necessary or normal losses is generally transitory because the grieving or other resolution is generally easier and quicker and not ongoing like that for repetitious chronic loss.

Like always, I do not claim that this is the only path leading to anger. It is mine, and I think it is a common one.

There is one more factor needed to complete my equation of anger.

29

FEAR, THE TRIGGER AND
INTENSIFIER OF ANGER

It is well known that fear will cause one to be angry, and I am no different. It is the *fight, flight, freeze, or fawn response* of *hyperarousal*, also known as *acute stress response*. It is a physiological reaction that occurs in response to a perceived attack or threat. This theory, first described by Walter Bradford Cannon, is that animals have an autonomous reaction to threats within the nervous system that readies them for fighting or fleeing. It is caused in part by the secretion of hormones that affect heart rate, respiratory rate, pupillary response, and other processes.

I was often cognizant of a cascade of emotions after I had gotten angry but never during the process. I never once found myself saying, "I am afraid; here comes the anger." Perhaps the fear happened too fast to notice except in retrospect.

I could only rarely moderate my behavior rationally, unless it was physically dangerous not to do so. This was my version of freezing or fawning. This is an indication perhaps that a rational approach to controlling anger might work, but usually I would flash into anger so quickly that a rational approach seemed unreliable as a solution.

Whether or not I was cognizant of fear being present, the feeling of power was present—I felt excited, alive, with a sense of well-being, assertive, and safe. Therefore, it is questionable whether a method of thinking through my anger and its likely results could have been expected to work. I would have had to give up the good feeling, and with a sense of helplessness as my constant habit, stopping my anger would have been exactly like trying to stop my drinking through rational thinking.

I needed anger to make me feel safe. I had no need to avoid the bad feelings that anger management presupposes, because getting angry did *not* make me feel bad. It made me feel good. Only rarely did I feel bad for getting angry, and if I did feel bad, it was only much later and was generally because I had hurt someone dear, in which case I feared a loss. In a way anger was a gamble, but it seemed that the odds were good that anger would work and that avoiding it would not.

The sole exception was the need for safety, in which case I could apparently evaluate my chances pretty well, because I never got physically attacked. If my anger endangered my physical safety, I was usually able to catch myself. Or if I did not stop in time, I was usually but not always able to talk myself out of it. In chapter 18, "Escalation," I relate the six incidents over a period of decades when my anger put me in danger. In five of these incidents, I never saw them as real reasons to get over my anger. Denial is not only a river in Egypt.

Now I complete the equation showing the path to my anger, which I think may be the path for many people. With the last iteration we had

$$\text{Abuse} \rightarrow \text{shame} \rightarrow \text{chronic losses} \xrightarrow{\text{Necessary losses}} \text{pain} \rightarrow \text{anger.} \qquad (3)$$

Now I add the factor of fear as an *occasional* causative agent.

$$\text{Abuse} \rightarrow \text{shame} \rightarrow \text{chronic losses} \xrightarrow{\text{Necessary losses}} \text{fear} \rightarrow \text{pain} \rightarrow \text{anger.} \qquad (4)$$

I add fear as a cause because occasionally I could look back and tell I got angry because of fear.

If fear is a factor in causing or triggering anger, equation (4) is the result. In other anger events, fear may enter the equation as an amplifying factor, and then equation (5) follows:

Necessary losses

Abuse → shame → chronic losses → pain → anger,   (5)

fear

I add fear as an amplifying factor because pain hurts, and that is something to be feared, so a larger anger response in the loss-to-anger path is required. Of course, this path portrays a series of autonomic responses. No conscious thought is involved in the simple case.

In a complex case with conscious thought involved, which I think is a special case (see below), such as when I could stop myself for my own safety, one could draw a vertical line at any point to block the flow of emotions to stop an angry response,

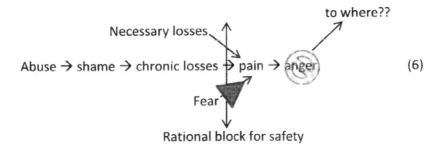

(6)

or a broken vertical line to filter the anger down to a milder episode,

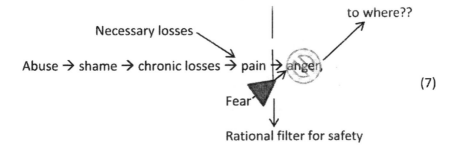

(7)

Equations (6) and (7) are certainly possible and occur often if the self-preservation instinct is activated by the circumstances. Like all instincts, self-preservation is not an intentional, rational act but an autonomic one.

The "to where?" in either diagram is not a trivial question. On either level, emotional or physical anger is a concrete thing. It cannot just disappear in a massless vapor. It has components of powerful chemical and physical hormones driving it. The effect of these hormones is a powerful energy, analogous to the energies in physics, potential or kinetic, and this energy has concrete characteristics. In recovery work, emotions are often described as *e-motions*: energy in motion. This is a reference to the hard-felt physical sensations from them. So the question "to where?" is important. My suspicion is that suppressing your pain, anger, or any other emotion merely drives it internally, where it resides waiting for a chance to break free.

Ignoring emotions by such means as denying, minimizing, suffering through them with a stiff upper lip, and so on are known to have adverse physical, emotional, and/or mental aftereffects that may show up soon after or a long time after the event or series of events. Emotions are not to be ignored. So even if anger could be blocked or filtered, which may be a good idea for safety, in the long run something must be done to dissipate the anger in a healthful way akin to what nature intended. *But the dissipation of anger itself is a tough job. The dissipation of the underlying emotion of pain and facing the losses is possible and not difficult.* One way is crying, which I discuss in chapter 31, "Is There a Link between Tears and Healing?" I present other methods in chapter 32, "Other Ways to Grieve."

There is no equivocation in the "to where?" arrow following *anger* and my proposed discussion of *grieving* to dissipate anger. Anger can be dissipated by several relaxation and distraction methods, and these, along with their efficacy, are discussed in Appendix II, "Anger Management: A Survey of the Professional Literature." The problematic nature of the efficacy of the methods shown in Appendix II mandates that for the highest state of emotional health, the dissipation must be at the core level (pain that must be grieved). The rational methods reported in Appendix II cannot totally dissipate anger. Besides, how often are we presented with a chance to get better results out of easier work?

Like always, I do not claim that the above equations are the only paths lead-ing to anger. These paths are mine, and I think they are very common ones.

To add rational behavior modification to this emotional diagram, one has to allow for three factors.

1. The mind must come up with an appropriate blocking rational truth argument nearly instantly. Considering that emotions are nearly instinctual in reaction time, I personally question the ability of my mind to do so reliably.

2. Such a rational control in general flies in the face of over fifty-five years of my personal experience of having anger. The exception of personal safety, which may be the freeze or fawn part of the hy-perarousal response, is because a survival instinct is the most basic instinct man and all other creatures have. I could not rationally control my anger to the degree I wished unless faced with such survival circumstances, and to count on being able to freeze or fawn successfully seems a big gamble to me.

3. The lack of efficacy of rational thought inhibiting emotions at all limits the method's usefulness. I add this due to my personal expe-rience. There is such a proliferation of books and therapy sessions featuring a copious number of rational methods—such as those to enable grieving, depression, zealotry, religiosity, antisocial sex behaviors, anxiety, and a host of others, to say nothing of anger— that it must be a fruitful field of both publishing and therapy. This proliferation raises the following questions for me:

    a. Why are there all those different books if a rational ap-proach works so easily?

    b. Why do advertisement websites push a particular program, therapist, group, or anger-management center if it is so easy to think yourself to emotional health? All these different programs, therapists, and so on claim to be best and/or unique.

    c. Why do all the court-mandated programs, which are based on a rational approach, not work (see chapter 35, "Anger Management: A Survey of the Web")?

    d.   Why are so many people still suffering if the answer is as simple as rational thinking?

Is the proliferation of books and programs based on rational thinking, because there is a hope for success? Or is rational thinking as a method of treating anger a simple, straightforward method with a goal only of managing anger that is, limiting the anger to a personally or socially acceptable level? My goal was the elimination of toxic anger as far as possible, and to do that I needed to look at the causes of my anger. By their very natures, those causes were hidden deep within my subconscious mind, and seeking, identifying, and eliminating them was a time-consuming and economically expensive proposition. This approach is contrasted with anger management, which does not seek causes, only ways to learn how to not act out the anger. If such ways work well enough for the individual or for society, well and good, but I did not believe they would work for me, at least not well enough to meet my goals. However, given the great expense and effort required for individual therapy, perhaps group therapy and anger-management classes are the only economically viable strategies.

This is such a critical question that I present some research on the efficacy of anger management programs in the last two chapters of this book and in Appendix II.

Special Case

I suspect that rational control of anger in a dangerous situation is a special case. In severe cases of anger (severe cases of perceived loss and pain), I wonder if rationally controlling anger is possible. Perhaps in dangerous situations rational control only *seems* to occur. Perhaps it is not rational thought that saves one's bacon in such a case (say, choosing not to go off on a biker gang in a bar late at night) but is instead the survival instinct, the old fight-flight-freeze-or-fawn instinct. It is probable that the instinctual survival response might trump the learned get-angry response. So in that bar, when faced with those sensitive, caring bikers, maybe I do not rationally choose not to get angry at them but instead instinctually opt to freeze or fawn. In either case, be it rational or instinctual, I choose to do nothing. Thus, it is difficult to distinguish the difference between a rational control of anger and an instinctual response.

This idea seems to me to be testable in a psychological experiment or study that could be controlled well.

30

GRIEVING LOSS, THE CURE

I tried anger management in two different programs and found them both useless for my goal of eliminating toxic anger (rage). They seemed designed only to get me to behave better, not to recover from harmful anger, and certainly not anger as an addiction. For me, recovering from anger meant I had to get down to the causes of my anger, which meant I had to heal the pain by grieving my childhood losses and subsequent losses that resembled those losses—that is, I had to reenact those losses in adulthood with adult powers to resolve them into nothing but bad memories. Better thinking alone would not eliminate my anger. I discussed why anger management failed and my need to heal the pain and to grieve losses in the last two chapters.

Furthermore, in twenty or more years of therapy over my thirty-two years of recovery, I got a tremendous amount of valuable and life-enriching information about my inner self, but rational emotive therapy (RET) and other rational-thinking-based therapies recommended by eight to ten therapists did not work on my codependence, relationship addiction, or anger, which were all addictions. Just like anger management, the application of RET or RET-like methods were designed to correct my behaviors, not to recover from addictions, which all my issues were. I required a healing of emotions. So it seems certain that for anger the only cure for me was grieving the losses that led to the pain.

My last therapist showed me the path to grieving my losses to ease the pain, which in turn eased my anger. This was functionally an emotion-healing approach to mend a related scarred emotion. I did not know at that time that my anger was an addiction in me.

It is perhaps no wonder that I needed an emotional cure for recovery from all my addictions. Bradshaw writes, "If you're shame-based, you're going to be an addict—no way around it. Addictions form the outer layer of our defenses against toxic shame."[1] Bradshaw is referring to any of the whole range of addicts who may be addicted to ingested substances, to people, to activities, or, like me, to a combination of them.

As to the converse, are all addicts shame-based? I can only say that every one of my addictions was due to shame and that I only found recovery through an emotional method. For my anger, recovery was definitely through grieving the losses through grieving the pain.

The reasonable question is, are there any other grieving methods other than crying to heal the shame-loss-pain-anger chain? Fortunately the answer is yes, and I list some of them in chapter 32, "Other Ways to Grieve."

But first let us look more closely at crying.

[1]   Bradshaw, *Healing The Shame*, 96.

31

IS THERE A LINK BETWEEN TEARS AND HEALING?

> There is a sacredness in tears. They are not the mark of
> weakness, but of power. They speak more eloquently than ten
> thousand tongues. They are the messengers of overwhelming
> grief, of deep contrition, and of unspeakable love.
> —Washington Irving

I pose the heading of this chapter as a question, inviting it to be taken as a hypothesis. Anecdotally, I think that there is evidence, but I cannot state any accepted scientific, medical, or physiological hard evidence that tears promote healing. But I did find 3.94 million hits on Google for "Crying healing effects of."

One of the first articles Google will point to is "7 Good Reasons to Cry: The Healing Property of Tears" by Therese J. Borchard, associate editor of PsychCentral.com. Borchard lists these seven reasons:[1]

1. Tears help us to see.
2. Tears kill bacteria.
3. Tears remove toxins (see discussion of Frey below).
4. Crying can elevate mood.
5. Crying lowers stress.
6. Tears build community.

7. Tears release feelings. As Bradshaw says in *Homecoming*, "All these feelings need to be felt. We need to stomp and storm; to sob and cry; to perspire and tremble."[2]

Another article returned by Google is adapted from *Emotional Freedom: Liberate Yourself from Negative Emotions and Transform Your Life* (Three Rivers Press, 2011) on the *Psychology Today website*[3]. This article is a book report by the books author, Judith Orloff M.D. that gives several health benefits of tears including a release valve for stress, sadness, grief, anxiety and frustration. She is a believer in the usefulness of crying from observing her patients, but does not give any scientific evidence.

At the bottom of the page is a link to "Crying is Not Always Beneficial" by Jonathan Rottenberg Ph.D.[4] in response to Orloff's article. This is a bit more scientific rather than anecdotal, similar to what would be expected as preliminary results to a study, but the overall sense is that the majority of people, articles, and practitioners felt that crying brings them psychological benefits. Then Rottenberg cites his group's analysis of over 3,000 detailed reports of recent crying episodes where respondents described the surrounding social context and the effects of crying on mood and his group found that social support increased the benefits as did the crier being able to resolve the issues of the crying episode. He ends his rebuttal with "We need to bring more science towards understanding this striking emotional behavior. What little science we have so far does not justify a one-size-fits-all approach."

That conclusion, that more scientific data is required, naturally leads to a book by William H. Frey II, a biochemist at the University of Minnesota. He claims in his book *The Mystery of Tears*[5] many of the same anecdotal benefits of crying listed in these three online articles. Orloff's article cites Frey's work, as an authority, but she is somewhat misguided. Frey's 1985 book gives several possible benefits of tears, but he admits it is far too soon to claim anything but tantalizing hypotheses from his research. This is implicit in the title. His book is interesting, but he admittedly was rushed into writing it as a series of only hypotheses. These hypotheses were evidently greeted with such professional skepticism that he had trouble getting funding to continue his research. He evidently switched to another related field without following up with a second publication on crying. His book is still available in paperback as a used book but requires some searching.

Noted health author Jane E. Brody provides a clear synopsis on Frey's book in the 1982 *New York Times* article "Biological Role of Emotional Tears Emerges through Recent Studies."[6] In Brody's thorough review of his book she points out that no one has ever proposed reasons for how often or why humans cry. Frey's theory is that tears help relieve stress. Frey attempted to analyze the biological content of tears but was limited in this by inadequate funding. Per Brody's article, Frey believes that research is needed to further the causes and effects of crying in stress-related illnesses and thinks that crying may release chemicals that the body produces in response to stress. Brody summarizes most of the rest of the book, which is about differences in crying by men and by women, frequency of crying, the emotions associated with crying, and some anecdotal evidence that crying is generally felt to help release stress and relieve emotional pain.[4]

There are numerous other Internet articles touting the benefits of tears, but I found no complete scientific study as Frey's started out to be, and perhaps the work of Rottenberg's group. Frey relates in his book that he was urged into writing his preliminary results before he wanted to by financial demands of his laboratory and its managers and that he sincerely hoped more funding would be found to continue his work. It evidently was not, for he has written numerous other papers in other somewhat-related fields.

There is at least one review of Frey's work by a medical doctor that dramatically disagrees with his hypothesis: Dr. Jeffrey P. Gilbard's "Crying: The Mystery of Tears."[7] In tone Dr. Gilbard appears to believe, or wish the reader to believe, that Frey is holding out his preliminary findings as a final theory, but Frey absolutely is not. In this article Dr. Gilbard lists *Reader's Digest, Psychology Today, Parade, USA Today,* the *New York Times, Good Morning America, Walter Cronkite's Universe, That's Incredible,* and *PM Magazine* as magazines, television shows, and newspapers that have had articles or segments on Frey's work as reported in his book. Gilbard quotes Frey's hypothesis: "the reason people feel better after crying is that they may be removing in their tears chemicals that build up as a result of emotional stress." This statement is true, but Frey clearly means it as a provisional hypothesis that needs much further and more-thorough testing. Again the title is *The* Mystery *of Tears*.

My own views are that I have found no definitive scientific answer but obviously do feel that emotional tears are beneficial, both for my benefits related in this book as well as from the numerous sages down through the ages who have commented on such benefits. I have sprinkled some of those quotes throughout this book.

[1] Therese J. Borchard, "7 Good Reasons to Cry: The Healing Property of Tears," Psych Central, May 29, 2011, http://psychcentral.com/blog/archives/2011/05/29/7-good-reasons-to-cry-the-healing-property-of-tears/.

[2] Bradshaw, *Homecoming*, 80.

[3] Judith Orloff M. D., "The Health Benefits of Tears," Psychology Today, accessed December 29, 2015,https://www.psychologytoday.com/blog/emotional-freedom/201007/the-health-benefits-tears.

[4] Jonathan Rottenberg Ph.D., "Crying is Not Always Beneficial," Psychology Today, accessed December29,2015,https://www.psychologytoday.com/blog/charting-the-depths/201007/crying-is-not-always-beneficial.

[5] William H. Frey II, *Crying: The Mystery of Tears*, with Muriel Langseth (Minneapolis: Winston Press, 1985).

[6] Jane E. Brody, "Biological Role of Emotional Tears Emerges through Recent Studies," *New York Times*, August 31, 1982, http://www.nytimes.com/1982/08/31/science/biological-role-of-emotional-tears-emerges-through-recent-studies.html.

[7] Jeffrey P. Gilbard, "Crying: The Mystery of Tears," *Archives of Ophthalmology* [now *JAMA Ophthalmology*] 104, no. 3 (1986):343–44, doi: 10.1001/archopht.1986.01050150037021.

32

OTHER WAYS TO GRIEVE

I certainly do not mean to say that crying is the end all and be all of grief work or the only way to alleviate pain in moving to recovery from anger. It is just what worked for me. Looking back, I can see that I had a deep and wide reservoir of sadness and pain from losses that I needed to grieve. I do believe that some sort of grief work to relieve the intensity and drive of sadness and pain from childhood losses will be beneficial to many people addicted to anger or rage.

I have already given a ringing endorsement of John Bradshaw's book *Homecoming: Reclaiming and Championing Your Inner Child*. I cover this recommendation thoroughly, as well as the theoretical basis of it, in chapter 30, "Grieving Loss, the Cure." His inner-child work is typically quite effective if you can get over the hang-up of not allowing yourself to assign responsibility to your upbringing and can overcome the invalid and abusive rules of child rearing in the United States and most of the rest of the world. To acknowledge that your childhood was painful and to assign proper responsibility to your abusive caregivers is the first step. It is not about blame; it is about clearly accepting the origins of your pain so that recovery is straightforward and possible.

In chapter 10 I also refer to Charles Whitfield's *Healing the Child Within: Discovery and Recovery for Adult Children of Dysfunctional Families*, his workbook *A Gift to Myself*, and Cathryn L. Taylor's *The Inner Child Workbook* as excellent ways to grieve. None of these books are specifically geared to anger or rage, but the principles are the same for all dysfunction from less-than-nurturing parenting. Anger is only one possible outcome to dysfunctional parenting, and these books do mention anger as a symptom.

The actual crying I did was based on Stephen Levine's book *Unattended Sorrow: Recovering from Loss and Reviving the Heart*, which is no longer in print but is available used. This is my synopsis of the book, or at least as far into it as I got before I took a break to look at my wedding pictures with the intention to cry. Levine actually does not suggest crying or any other specific acts or methods, but I knew before I started to go through the album of photos that I would cry.

In general terms my sorrow could have, as Stephen Levine points out, caused "a numbing of the spirit,"[1] "a diminishment of the life force,"[2] "depression and dysfunction,"[3] "the burden of disappointment and disillusionment,"[4] and the "loss of trust, confidence, and hope"[5] as well as "producing anxiety, fear, and anger,"[6] "addictions of all kinds,"[7] "guilt and shame,"[8] "a sense of psychological emptiness, or heaviness, a deadness of the spirit,"[9] "lingering disappointment and distress, doubt, [and] powerlessness."[10]

My sorrow certainly caused at least dysfunction, loss of hope, anxiety, fear, anger, addictions, emptiness, disappointment, powerlessness, and perhaps some of the others.

Levine says the cure for these general maladies lies in

> tapping the resources of the heart—the power to forgive, the strength to love, the trust to look deeper into what limits us ... we release the grief that's been held hard in the body: releasing, moment to moment the muscle shield that's tightened for self-protection across the abdomen, softening breath after breath to sorrow after sorrow. When we soften layer after layer of the armoring over the heart, we open to the possibility of a new life.[11]

He later moves quickly from the general to the specific:

> Sometimes we feel helpless to defend ourselves against the cramping of the heart, even years after a loss. Our shoulders

become heavy and our bellies sore, a dull ache defines our body, our necks stiffen, and our gait increasingly shortens.

Helplessness gives rise to our most noticeable griefs. It is the basis for a considerable amount of anger and aggression. In an attempt to overcome the feeling of having no control, the mind attempts to assert whatever power it hopes will hide the fear and sense of profound aloneness. Aggression toward others and ourselves is akin to the muscle fatigue of swimming as hard as we can and still being dragged farther out to sea. The less we investigate our state of helplessness, the greater the potential we have for self-destructive be-havior. But once we open our hearts to our pain and to our hopelessness, we find that we are never truly helpless.

When we turn toward our pain instead of away from it, self-mercy enters those parts of ourselves we had closed off, withdrawn from or abandoned to feelings of impotence. When it seems there is nowhere else to turn, when all our prayers and strategies seem to be of little avail, something deeper arises: a mercy that leads toward the heart.[12]

He continues,

Fear is our first unsuccessful attempt to protect ourselves from pain. The pretense of painlessness is the next. But it is the surrender of resistance that opens pain to healing ...

There comes a point where it is more important to just let our heart break and get on with it than to keep trying to figure out why we are so often in pain or who's at fault and what sort of punishment they deserve.[13]

Levine then describes the detailed practice of sitting quietly, closing your eyes, and just letting your attention come into the sensations of the body. Earlier in the book he emphasizes body sensations as feelings deeper than ordinary emotions; body sensations are the place where unresolved emotions go to hide. Then he recommends bringing attention to the abdomen feeling the belly rise and fall with each breath as a method to "soften the abdominal muscles, letting go of whatever holding tightens your belly and maintains your suffering, softening the tissue all the way into the belly."[14] we go as deeply as possible with this process attending to ourselves and let the mercy of self-healing occur.

In the next section Levine writes, "Softening the belly won't perfect us, but it can set us free. It initiates a letting go, which frees the mind to open the heart."[15] This is an explicit expression of intense emotional work aided by physical exercise concentrating on specific body parts that hold specific grief feelings. Such emotional work precedes and augments rational (the mind) processes to further heal the emotions. Note that the emotions come first, and the mind is a helper in the process.

Levine thus presents a general method for grieving pain and losses. At this point of reading the book, I decided to try looking at the wedding pictures, following Levine's general procedure with my specific method. I attest to this process in the strongest terms, swearing to its effectiveness in me to remove the pain that led to my anger. It worked for me. From my personal experience with this process, both in the methods and details of the effects on me, I think it is very valid. The maladies he notes as quoted above can be caused by loss, and the treatment is the same as my crying: deep body work with a merciful mind-set to ease the painful body memories trapped as depression, anger, emptiness, and perhaps more uncomfortable feelings.

I did subsequently read the whole book. Each later chapter covers a different topic, focusing on many great losses, including such chapters as "Loss of Trust," "The Meaning of Life," "In the Absence of God," and "Death of a Spouse." Many of these topics are wrapped around a hypothetical day of something, like a day of pain (allowing yourself to hurt), a day walking, or a day of silence. These suggestions seem excellent, subtle, and life affirming.

I have studied two other books that support this method of deep pain work, both by Peter A. Levine (no relation). In *Waking the Tiger: Healing Trauma—The Innate Capacity to Transform Overwhelming Experiences*, Peter Levine with Ann Frederick presents anecdotal evidence of animal trauma survival and recovery. Briefly, assume an antelope is downed by a big cat on the Serengeti Plain, but for some reason the cat leaves the antelope still alive and only lightly wounded but traumatized on the ground. Such downed antelope have been seen to rise and stand in place shaking violently for several minutes until they slowly recover. They then walk and then run off to join their herds. They have, Peter Levine claims, naturally recovered from the life-threatening trauma by attending to their fear and other effects of the trauma by "shaking" it off. In his theory, they have instinctually taken the time to be merciful with themselves and accepted and held the trauma close until it passes naturally.[16] He gives many more such examples of animals seeming to heal their own trauma, usually by shaking. He assumes they are healed because they return to the herd and continue as if nothing happened.

The program Peter Levin presents in the workbook *Healing Trauma: A Pioneering Program for Restoring the Wisdom of Your Body*, is based on more animal-world observations. He presents the program as a twelve-phase healing trauma program, and his book includes an audio CD disk. "Ultimately all the phases will help you get reacquainted with feelings and sensations in your own body," he says.[17] Such recognition of hidden body sensations and relearned ability to experience them to heal them and bring them out without internalizing them is, in his view, important to moving toward resolution of traumas.

I cannot vouch for this twelve-phase program, because crying worked for me before I read his book. Perhaps I was able to resolve my trauma on my own without a formal program because I had the advantage of years of practiced acceptance of my feelings as useful and natural, as opposed to rejecting them as bad. My conjecture is that there is something to his program. I believe it is twelve phases long to ready the patient for the deep emotional and body-feeling work required. I base this on my own experience of having years of emotional acceptance and study prior to my crying. When I cried, I first sat still and put myself in an open frame of mind that it was all right to cry *and, more importantly, that it was all right to feel the body feelings or sensations that might come over me.* In addition to crying, I also, per Steven Levin's recommendations in *Unintended Sorrow*, concentrated on my torso, especially my chest, heart area, and gut, where I always experience fear and anxiety. Naturally, I often sobbed so my body heaved and pitched, but those are not the feelings I tried to be aware of. Instead I felt for, as Steven Levine recommends, a tightness, constriction, or hardness in the heart area, and I did feel some. After crying, with or without sobbing, I felt a lessening of some tightness so that I felt slightly, only slightly, less hard and emotionally cold or distant to other people. At the end of a crying session, which typically lasted one to two hours, there was a definite effect. I felt lighter, less burdened, and more loving and compassionate toward others, although usually others were nowhere visible or present. It was an amazing set of experiences, over and over. As I showed mercy for myself and allowed myself to feel my own pain and sorrow from the losses, I lightened up and felt more gentle and caring toward myself and towards others. In this way the anger seemed to dissipate over a few weeks. So I would not at all be surprised that Dr. Peter Levine's program would produce the same salutary benefits for many if not all the deleterious effects of trauma.

In short, my crying method was ideal for me, as judged by the results and rapid recovery. But before I began, I had no doubts about what had happened to little Verryl Virgil as a child, how it had hurt, how wrong it had been, or who had been there at the time, even given their vastly different outlooks on child-rearing methods based on the time period. I had worked long and hard to know myself, and I undoubtedly knew myself better than most people know themselves. However, recall that all this self-knowledge was acquired over nearly twenty-five years. When I first saw my last therapist, I had all this knowledge but also still had my full measure of anger. So self-knowledge was not the answer. I believe crying was a good method for me because of the prior knowledge, though. I cried easily, I had no male-ego hang-ups about crying, and I did not buy into the common societal constraints over it. I cried easily, and I cried deeply. I just had never thought of crying about the losses in my life. For that matter I had never considered the losses in my life as potentially devastating. I thought only that I had to treat the shame and the effects of shame, thinking, correctly as it turned out, that my shame led to my low self-esteem and thinking wrongly that my shame led directly to my anger. As I at last found out, my pain and losses, not my shame, led to my anger. And finally, I had no hang-ups about emotions either, and a lot of that freedom was from my years of recovery that stressed that emotions are acceptable.

Finally, in one more pitch for inner-child work, I believe it is by far the most direct and easiest method, despite the fear of emotions a person may have. It is in essence what I did when I cried. I touched the pain of repeated losses from childhood up until the breakup of my third marriage. The loss of that marriage was the loss of the nurturing relationship I had (in fantasy) with my wife. As such, the loss of my third wife, like the loss of my second wife, was a replaying of the childhood memories of the loss of my primary caregiver, my mother, who was less than nurturing. You will remember that I feared death at the loss of my second wife, the love of my life. My crying in the appliance department of the Great Indoors was over the loss of the loving home that I had hoped to build to replace the missing nurturing and loving home I did not have as a child. Every tear I shed in that catharsis of crying was inner-child work, directly traceable to some loss in childhood, the childhood before I was rational, that is, earlier than six to eight years old.

It is scary to open these wounds again, but emotions will not kill you, *unless you refuse to feel them*. If you feel them, you will be healed by them, whichever approach you use.

My most important message is that anger was an addiction treatable by standard recovery methods in treating emotional wounds. Perhaps because I had such false high hopes about healing shame for so long, my second most important message is that, for me, shame did not cause my anger. The ungrieved losses of my childhood and childhood innocence, as well as many other losses through life that I had not grieved, were the painful cause of my anger. That stiff-upper-lip and sucking-it-up approach nearly killed me (heart disease) and nearly got me into prison.

[1]   Levine, *Unattended Sorrow*, 1.
[2]   Ibid., 2.
[3]   Ibid., 3.
[4]   Ibid., 2.
[5]   Ibid.
[6]   Ibid.
[7]   Ibid., 3
[8]   Ibid., 5
[9]   Ibid., 5
[10]   Ibid., 7.
[11]   Ibid., 7–8.
[12]   Ibid., 17–18.
[13]   Ibid., 19–20.

14   Ibid., 24.

15   Ibid., 25.

16   Peter Levine, *Waking the Tiger, Healing Trauma, The Innate Capacity to Transform Overwhelming Experiences*, with Ann Frederick (Berkeley, CA: North Atlantic Books, 1997), 15.

17   Peter Levine, *Healing Trauma: A Pioneering Program for Restoring the Wisdom of Your Body* (Boulder, CO: Sounds True, 2005), 36.

33

GUARDING AGAINST ANGER DUE TO NEW LOSSES

It is not as if I don't get angry anymore since my crying catharsis. I do in two general ways. I have normal, or usual, healthy anger, such as learning of an injustice, and goodness knows the nightly news provides many opportunities for that. That anger just makes me willing to do my part if the opportunity ever arises. That is the good and useful function of anger; anger is a source of power, ambition, and energy. At other times something may startle or frighten me or embarrass me, and I react by striking out at it or something or someone else. This does not happen too often, and it is probably another case of normal and healthy anger, something of a loss of face.

I have to analyze these occurrences of healthy anger carefully because as a recovering person I can easily be too hard on myself by trying to be perfect, especially about such common and usual events. I do not wish to be perfect, because I like having friends, and who would want to be around me if I were perfect?

The second kind of anger that I still have occasionally is not healthy anger. Occasionally my mind conjures up a perceived or predicted pain from the remnants of the demons still within, and my impulse is to rage, or at least be unreasonably vocal, but usually only for a short while. Such anger follows equation (6) or (7), the final equations that are developed fully in chapter 29, "Fear, the Trigger of Anger."

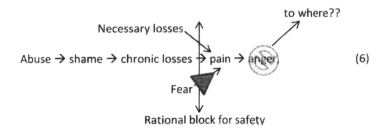

to where??

Necessary losses

Abuse → shame → chronic losses → pain → anger (6)

Fear

Rational block for safety

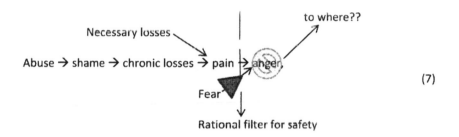

to where??

Necessary losses

Abuse → shame → chronic losses → pain → anger (7)

Fear

Rational filter for safety

This unhealthy anger or rage always follows a perceived loss or threat of a loss. A threat of a loss recalls the mental impression of one of my old childhood losses. It may seem like my experience starts with fear in equation (6), but with me, the whole equation comes into play, although the fear is the easiest to identify. The terms to the left of fear are present in the order presented.

These few instances of unhealthy anger have been both rare and relatively benign compared to those before my crying to grieve. That is not to excuse them, but to be accurate, that is the truth.

With my anger, I am like any addict. I am susceptible to slips. A slip in AA means I have slipped up and had a drink, or at least ordered one and taken or contemplated a taste. For a codependent it might mean being temporarily controlling or manipulative. The alcohol slip is serious because it is potentially so deadly for a real alcoholic, even one like me who has not had a drink for over thirty-two years. The codependence slip is more in the realm of normal (whatever that is). An anger slip is more like a codependence slip or when a food addict has an extra piece of chocolate cake. It may be bad, but it's not catastrophic, unless the anger, codependence, or food binge continues.

The point is, obviously I have to be alert and aware of slips in my behavior. "Normies," normal people, can afford to be lackadaisical. Recovering folks cannot. The stakes are too high.

34

ALTERNATE TREATMENTS FOR ANGER

There are at least three other common treatments for anger: anger-management classes, abreaction methods, and rumination/distraction.

The two methods of *rumination* and *distraction* are closely related in theory. Rumination about anger is defined as repetitively thinking about the angering event or person. Many studies have shown that this maintains or amplifies the emotional response. Furthermore, how one thinks about the event has an effect on both the type and the intensity of the experience. One corollary of this view is that modifying how an individual appraises an event should alter the emotional response to it. Rumination can be modified into *reappraisal* to find an alternate interpretation or possible outcome of an event. It is theorized that, by thinking about an event, one may reinterpret the event into one that has a better outcome, that is, an outcome with less anger. There are numerous specific strategies on how to do such reappraisal.

To counter anger with *distraction*, one thinks about something unrelated to move attention away from the upsetting event to something neutral or pleasant. It is generally recognized that this is not a solution to anger over the long run. Distraction is not cumulative in its effect of lowering an individual's level of anger over a specific event over time, so following encounters of the event have been found to be progressively more intense. The method has been found to work only on the one event, leaving future occurrences as potentially intense as ever. To me, distraction just seems like another way of "stuffing" my anger inside or otherwise ignoring it. Few therapists and successful recovering people would advocate this.

On close inspection, it appears that the rational-therapy maxim "Every emotion is preceded by a thought" (so right thinking is the curative answer) is plainly wrong. It is more likely that every emotion is followed by thoughts, and those thoughts may not help and may even increase anger in certain situations.

Another set of closely related methods is to make anger your friend by being competitive instead of confrontational, more patient, more understanding, or so on. All such strategies are somewhat laudable, but somehow I have a hard time seeing how they fit people with hard-core anger—the bar fighter, the spousal or child physical abuser, and the like—especially those who may view themselves as powerless unless they use anger or force. Often those strategies are just too mild, or at least they are perceived to be, to solve the problem, but for those with milder anger, it is easier to see that they might work.

This method sounds like the manner of pro basketball NBA great Jerry West, "the Logo" (because the NBA logo is designed from a photo of him). It was said that an opponent should never make West angry, because he just got better while empowered by his anger. I also went from a good to a very good handball player when I got angry. I never intentionally tried to get angry to play better or to do anything better; it just happened that way. Adrenaline was my drug of choice.

The most common treatment for anger is probably *anger-management classes*, because it is the generally prescribed method mandated by courts and employers. An anger-management program is usually given as a series of classes with students sitting in a circle like a discussion group led by a facilitator who acts as a teacher. The class can have a specific strategy, goals, and number of classes, or it can be open ended and ongoing with new clients starting at any time and leaving when they've attended their prescribed or sentenced number of classes. The programs with a set number of classes may, for example, be set up for employees, peace officers, or those who deal with the public in stressful jobs, to improve their job performance and help reach the goals of the employer. The set number of classes is also a parameter used in researching new methods because then the management parameters are fixed and comparable. Open-ended programs generally have no specific curriculum or progressing class plan and instead offer general principles whenever is appropriate in any given class. Open-ended programs lend themselves to court-mandated classes because of the ability to accept a steady flow of new attendees and because additional classes can be easily assigned for repeat offenders.

I have always found it odd that the studies I have read assume more classes mean more help. But the courts and sometimes employers designate the number of classes to attend, and there is little correlation between the sentence and the severity of the offense. Rather, a second offender probably will get a longer prescribed number of classes, which implies number of offenses, as opposed to severity of the offence, will get you more classes. This philosophy, if it is a philosophy, is not about healing but about punishment.

Anger-management classes teach how to manage or control anger. To control my anger was, as I have said, not an adequate goal for me; I wanted to be over and done with it. However, the rationale behind anger-management classes is rational emotive control therapy, or variations by other names, which holds that before each emotion a thought occurs that leads to the emotion. Therefore, a person can be taught rational methods and tricks to control his or her anger. These methods sometimes include distracting tricks like counting to ten, to give an overly simple example. The rational methods are generally of the think-it-through type. The idea is that as you think rationally, you can see how irrational, unjust, or inappropriate your anger is, so you can rechannel it or let it pass. I have found very few people who agree with this theory that thoughts precede all emotions or that such tricks can defuse their anger or otherwise modify their behaviors. In my case, my emotions seem to me to be much quicker than my conscious thinking, certainly quicker than any rational thinking I can marshal on the spur of the moment to counter my anger, which rises extremely fast. If I could graph the intensity of my anger and my rational thinking versus time, anger would have a sharp upward spike, reaching a high peak in a short amount of time, and rational thinking would be a smooth upward curve that takes much longer to reach an appreciable level—milliseconds compared to seconds. In me anger will win the race every time, and by then it is too late, no matter how much training I receive.

I have addressed the numerous instances in which I was able to control my anger easily because flying into a rage would have been potentially dangerous. At first glance this may look like a rational control of anger. More than likely it is a freeze or fawn response of hyperarousal. If so, it is another example of emotions trumping rationality, not the other way around. Simply put, not getting angry in these situations is part of my survival instinct, which is much stronger than my anger impulse.

John Bradshaw writes in the section "The Primacy of Emotions" in *Homecoming: Reclaiming and Championing Your Inner Child,*

> Silvan Tomkins, a research psychologist, made a major contribution to our understanding of human behavior by arguing for the primacy of emotions. Our emotions are forms of *immediate* experience. When we are experiencing our emotions, we are in direct contract with our physical reality. Because our emotions are forms of energy, they are physical; they are expressed in the body even before we are consciously aware of them.[1]

He continues five paragraphs later, "To put it very simply, our emotions are our most fundamental *powers*. We have them in order to guard our basic needs. When one of our needs is being threatened, our emotional energy signals us."[2]

As mentioned many times earlier in this book, another powerful reason a rational approach was unlikely to work for me was that anger was not my problem but my solution. Anger felt good because it gave me apparent power and control in fearful situations in which I otherwise felt helpless—it just felt good. There are numerous websites that promote their own anger programs or discuss anger. Particularly in the case of spousal abuse, such websites openly present the concept of an abuser using anger to get his or her way.

Nevertheless, there are a lot of anger-management classes or programs that are court mandated or required by employers to correct employees' uncivil behavior on the job. They are usually held weekly, and the clients pay a fee for each session. I suppose the collected fees go to the leader or the employing agency, which then pays the leader. Note that I did not call the leader a therapist, for in the court program I attended, the leader was not a therapist. She almost certainly had neither training in psychology nor any experience with therapy. She never mentioned emotions, and motives were not her focus. She was a public schoolteacher. I did not find out which grade she taught, but in that class I felt as if I were back in eighth grade, a year in which I found the boys to be particularly rowdy.

Both classes that I attended, one nominally for court-mandated clients that I attended voluntarily for about eight weeks and the one that I was sentenced to after my arrest, had only men in the classes. The voluntary one (for me) was taught by a man, and the schoolteacher other one was a woman. Both classes were pretty dismal affairs. In both, the fifteen or so clients sat in a circle with the moderator or teacher as part of the circle. The moderator led the hour-long session and tried to get each of us to participate by inquiring about everyone's week. Sooner or later a spirited discussion usually ensued about some bizarre experience that someone in the group had had the last week, and it was organized chaos from there on, with many suggesting and offering unsolicited opinions on how the occurrence should have been handled. There was often some amount of agreement that the class member was justified in his often-extreme reaction to the real or imagined slight that triggered the incident. There was no pattern to the anger episodes that I could see. I would have thought from my own experience that the others' anger would have been directed toward wives, other drivers, employers, or other authority figures, in that order, but it was more far ranging. It was hard for me to see why this one got angry in that situation and the next one in another. The anger was pervasive and frankly frightening. The classes were not a situation that someone like me, used to polite society, wanted any part of. In fact the others' anger made me continually appraise the distances and available paths to the doorways. Most were hooligans, with an occasional very quiet wallflower who almost never moved, spoke, or participated, the kind I could imagine going postal at any moment. The participation was mandatory, and the leader expected it, prompting all eventually during the hour. The leader had a lot of legally authorized clout from the court, employer, or whoever sent each client to compel participation.

The most striking aspect of the two groups I attended was that they were totally bereft of the notion of seeking deeper meanings and implications for each person's anger. There was no attempt to scratch the surface to see where the anger came from or what purpose it served. It was just accepted as an unacceptable behavior that must be controlled, that is, managed down to a socially acceptable level. Consequently, it would have been hard for the clients to adopt or even conceive of the notion that had been instilled in me by AA and the rest of the recovery movement that *we were not bad people trying to be better but ill people trying to get well.* This being bad instead of ill seemed to me a horrendous situation and a genuinely pitiful state to believe in. I still cannot see that it is a healthful or therapeutic situation for people to be placed in, particularly if they are predominantly shame- and pain-based men. I imagined that they were shame or pain based, but I have a very active imagination, so I do not know. However, if they were, it would make more sense of their behaviors they described in class, rather than the alternative— that there were that many bad people running around.

The downsides to anger were blatantly discussed in the programs I attended, as if all of us clients did not know it already! We were there as punishment as mandated by the court, an employer, or other authority. In a way it was as if maybe the staff could scare us into being not angry. I know I usually get angry when I am frightened, but maybe that is just me. The other side of the coin, to be cured of anger or to be in recovery from it, seemed completely foreign to everyone there, and it never came up. I certainly did not mention it. The sole goal was to control, moderate, ameliorate, or otherwise change a client's anger so it was not so destructive. Given that the clients undoubtedly had varying levels of anger in them and must have had varying degrees of skills to learn, to say nothing of vastly different backgrounds and psyches, it is hard to see the logic of a fixed sentence of once-a-week sessions for six months.

In all the programs I have read about, as was the case with my two programs, there is a set number of sessions that must be attended in a set amount of time, unless you are attending voluntarily. Then, no matter how much toxic anger remains in any particular person or how well he or she has learned to control it, that person has served his or her time. There is no testing or other scientific or quasi-scientific determination of wellness required to finish or even an opinion on such expressed. There were general hoorays and congratulations from other group members at the end of a member's last session because he had served his prescribed number of sessions, not because he had improved in behavior. The teachers initiated and encouraged the celebrations; it evidently was a reward to endure the set number of classes prescribed. Wellness had nothing to do with the "graduation." I do not remember anyone talking about how much better he felt or how empowered toward better behavior he now felt as a result of attending.

In twelve-step fellowship members get chips, coin-like medallions, struck with the length of time the member has attended meetings without a slip (for example, for AA, the amount of time sober). They are a reward and gift for a member's fellowship "birthday." The others enthusiastically urge the member to stand and tell how he did it. At that time the member does stand and gives a short speech or sharing of what it was like, what he did, and what it is like now—in other words, how bad it was, how he has recovered to date, and how much better it is today. This is de rigueur for the fellowship; it helps long-time members recall how bad it was or could get again, and it encourages newer members to persevere in their own personal growth. These birthday events in twelve-step groups are a real cause for celebration because of recovery progress, that is, improvement in feelings and deportment. The improvement in behavior and outlook and the personal growth attained is the message, and how the person did it are of interest, not merely the passing of a milepost.

In anger-management classes I saw quite a few completed sentences but heard no inspiring statements. There were celebrations, but not of progress, only of freedom earned by completing the sentence.

But I stress that this is my opinion based on my personal experience. You will remember that anger was my friend and close ally, supporting me with comfort, power, and control in times of fear and stress. It was not attractive to me to lose it as a tool to cope. But then, when I got arrested and faced criminal charges, that changed. It surely was just a matter of time, but I had a very long run with anger working for me. I started my recovery at forty-one years old. So conservatively calculated, I had anger working for me for at least forty-five years, or even fifty-five years if I go back to about age ten. Sure, my excesses of anger were awkward at times, but I always wiggled out of the trouble. Even the divorces were not enough for me to really want to give it up. Facing prison did.

My personal experience and observations of the others in my anger-management groups caused me to wonder if anger-management programs work. If so, how well do they work, and for what portion of the clients do they work? Or was I just a hard core case? It did not seem that I was, because it seemed that what got me sentenced to the class (or could have gotten me sentenced to the first voluntary class), was pretty mild compared to the offenses of almost every other class member.

I wrote in detail about the two times I attended the last kind of anger-treatment program, abreaction. In those two weekend programs, the process was to receive emotional support from professional therapists in a group setting and to beat cushions with Wiffle bats. In those programs there was a tacit assumption that childhood trauma was the likely reason for the clients' anger, and the emotional support was meant to enable the clients to release that anger in the physical exertion of beating cushions—whatever "release" meant. See near the end of chapter 15, "Recovery Junkie," and the following chapter for a further discussion of such programs.

1   Bradshaw, *Homecoming*, 68.
2   Ibid.

35

ANGER MANAGEMENT:
A SURVEY OF THE WEB

I am not about to claim that anger-management programs do not work in general just because I was a stubborn case and tried hard for years and failed to learn to manage my anger using them. I am acutely aware that *trying* is the world's best excuse. I therefore searched the Internet for information about the efficacy of anger-management programs. I found surprisingly few articles in generally available publications. Perhaps it was egocentric of me, but I thought there would have been a great many articles about such programs, and I expected the information to support the use of anger-management programs. It seemed to me that anger was a major problem in the world, from spousal abuse and road rage right up to terrorist attacks. But I found very few articles written about modern living that focused on anger as a problem to be solved or treated, other than ads for commercial programs touting their methods of anger management and a lesser number of abreaction programs.

In generally available publications I found quite a few articles when I searched Google for "Does anger management work?" Generally the sense that I got was that anger management gives mixed results, with some improvement for many and none for others (one practitioner gave a 30 percent failure rate—see below). None of the articles I found claim miraculous results. I did not find much suggesting a direct assault on the underlying painful or resentful emotions in order to heal them and thus anger, although some articles occasionally and faintly advocate it in passing, as if an afterthought. The bad-behavior approach is generally the method I found articles on, as opposed to a method of healing the underlying emotions.

A BBC News Magazine article about UK footballer Luis Suarez is "Luis Suarez: Does anger management actually work?" http://www.bbc.com/news/magazine-22264123, by Tom de Castella, accessed Sept 25, 2015. This article says that in the UK anger management has been given up on as a method for rehabilitating criminals when used as a substitute for punishment. This UK article shows UK anger management is more forward thinking, in my opinion, than programs in the United States in that it does consider more seriously the effects of underlying emotions, and it states that angry people have to acknowledge that they have a problem. However, the article gives no indication that this is or ever will be the primary treatment method, and quotes the failure rate for the government anger management to be 30%.

Some articles outwardly criticize some anger-management techniques or attitude-adjustment approaches taught as not only useless but also dangerous in that they tend to increase anger.

I am not so self-centered to think that all anger has its roots in pain, but it does seem odd to me that the root of anger in general and pain as a particular root are rarely mentioned and never as a primary topic of conversation. As I tried to indicate above the emotional content of anger was generally overlooked in the articles I found. This mirrored the anger management approach of training sufferers to be better, not to get well.

These are a few of the web articles I found. They are all about rational-emotive programs or thinking through your anger to control or manage it. For each article I summarize the main points.

- "The Case against Anger Control for Batterers," Alabama Coalition Against Domestic Violence, http://www.acadv.org/angermngv.dvip.pdf (see the "Resources" tab.)
    - Spousal abusers use anger as a tool to get their ways.
    - Spousal abusers function under dysfunctional rules that make it okay to demand their way.

- If spousal abusers give up physical violence, they are adept at switching to other manipulative methods to get their way.
- Note that in essence all of the above points is a behavior-modification point of view and not a find-the-root-cause point of view, but not as obvious is the attractiveness of anger to an angry person—they are pictured as using anger or alternates to anger to reap rewards that are attractive to them.

- "Why Does 'Anger Management' Not Work?" When Love Hurts, September 29, 2012, http://whenlovehurts.ca/articles/why-does-anger-management-not-work/
  - Again, anger is a tool for power and control (does that mean it feels good?).
  - Time-outs and other strategies focus on the abuser's behavior when the problem is his or her belief system (needing control).
  - Again people adopt other controlling methods instead of physical abuse.
  - Again the solution is to modify the behavior rather than get at the cause of the behavior.

- "Class Time and Not Jail Time for Anger, but Does It Work?" New York Times, July 1, 2001 by Tamar Lewin.
  - Article addresses the stepping-back and thinking method (cognitive rational approach).
  - Clients want to be heard, not lectured to (sounds like anger is their friend).
  - Many clients said they did not learn anything.

- "Does Anger Management Really Work?", http://doesitreallywork.org/anger-management/, accessed September 24, 2015. Following some very informative sections describing anger management and how it is meant to work, the following sections appear:
  - Evaluation: "Anger management seems to follow a rather outdated approach to giving yourself a good temper. There should be an in-depth analysis as to why you feel the way

you do and start unraveling the emotions you have that you are using anger to cover them up with. Often times it's not what's in front of us that is making us angry, it is just triggering something deeper within us. Rather than dealing with these complex emotions we bury them with anger and other false emotions. It's a safety mechanism that saves us from feeling the pain we have inside." Refreshing!

+ Does Anger Management Really Work?: "Anger management works if you have the right therapist and if you've been properly diagnosed as having an anger problem." Amen!

+ Our Recommendation: "If you're overly angry the goal shouldn't be to manage your anger, but to dispel it entirely. You should get down to the bottom of what's making you angry and sort your feelings out about it. Coming up with coping techniques is a good way to make it through the day, or through stressful situations, but it's only treating the symptom of an underlying problem." Can I get another amen?

+ Bunmi O. Olatunji and Jeffery M. Lohr, "Nonspecific Factors and the Efficacy of Psychosocial Treatments for Anger," *Scientific Review of Mental Health Practice* 3, no. 2 (2004–5), http://www.srmhp. org/0302/anger.html, accessed September, 2015.

+ This paper was sponsored by the NIMH NRSA grant 1F31MH067519-1A1 awarded to Bunmi O. Olatunji.

+ The two authors are members of the Department of Psychology at the University of Arkansas.

+ This general survey paper parallels the results obtained in Appendix II by Desiree Harris, whom I had research the efficacy of anger-management programs for me before I came across this article. This article covers most of the same papers Ms. Harris found and reviews in Appendix II, and its conclusions parallel hers.

Most of the Google hits decry the efficacy of anger-management programs as a behavior-modification approach compared to a belief-system problem, meaning that these programs try to change behavior even though the problem is a belief in self-helplessness, a need for power, or a fear of loss. The above paper, which generally comes to the conclusion that anger-management programs yield positive results in general but not the kind of positive result I wished for myself in recovering from anger. All the positive results cited in Olatunji and Lohr's paper and in Ms. Harris's paper (Appendix II) must be qualified as a lowering of anger or moderation of it, not a dramatic improvement as I was seeking and as many other people seek. Furthermore, both papers indicate that the literature cannot point to a consistently good approach if you want a striking and powerful improvement in behavior.

There were also even more web hits claiming good results with particular anger-management programs. These were commercial sites selling certain programs, so I discounted them completely as advertising.

Abreaction methods are completely different, and I found fewer articles about them. These programs are supposedly led by professional therapists who have a lot of insight as to the inner psychological workings of people in general and are skilled at applying methods to genuinely change those workings. But at heart of abreaction programs is the belief that clients' anger is from repressed anger or hatred against their parents or other authority figures in their past. A basic exercise has patients beating on pillows and crying "Mommy, Mommy, Mommy" or "Daddy, Daddy, Daddy" repeatedly or otherwise expressing verbally their known anger toward the person. Doing so is apparently supposed to purge trainees of those repressed feelings of hurt or anger. It is venting.

I personally tried one of these abreaction-based programs two different times. I describe the experiences in chapter 15, "Recovery Junkie." The program did not lessen my anger. I am not saying that it might not be a great solution for some, but my problem was hurt and pain, not anger. The anger was a symptom of my pain, and the program made no effort to deal with my pain. Expressing more anger was bound to help about as much as expressing anger always had. I had been angry and acting out for years, and it had never helped before. It felt good at the time, but it always felt good to be angry because it gave me temporary power or the allusion of power over the helplessness I felt. But the next day, I was just as angry with my parents and everyone else. I have a lot of respect for the woman and her other therapist helpers who ran both of the two weekend sessions I went to. It just did not work for me.

Several criticize abreaction programs because they think that these programs tend to enable the angry person and to make the clients' anger seem more socially acceptable. Some studies that use standard anger or irritation tests to evaluate the level of anger before and after have verified this finding. (See Appendix II).

The idea that the abreaction program I went to twice may have slightly increased my anger seems logical to me. I cannot say that it worked to lower my anger as I hoped it would. Maybe I was slightly angrier after the program, since I could have internalized the experience as social acceptance of my anger and violence, at least taking my anger out on helpless things like pillows. It was my most public intentional display of anger. While I waited my turn at the pillows, I remember thinking how easy this would be for me, because I was really "good" at anger. That was not the case. I was strangely inhibited and had to force myself to act out my presumed anger toward my mother and father. I was puzzled by this fact for years until I found that my pain was the underlying emotion that needed treating, not anger. I did not feel pain at the thought or sight of the cushion, and I was unable to transform it into my mother in my mind. Furthermore, I think now that I was justifiably embarrassed at publically raging at my parents in the session, probably because there was no pain to spur me into real anger action—not that I had not raged at them face-to-face or raged about them in front of others lots of times, but in those instances there was very likely a pain trigger that set the anger off as a survival response to the helplessness over the ungrieved pain from my losses. One of those old losses, some recollection about a past hurt, or a similar occurrence that reminded me of a similar hurt probably caused my earlier reactions of rage.

For whatever reason, I am positive that the abreaction sessions did not lessen my anger, that is, did not "release" it in a dissipative vapor. I did get a lot out of the program each time in self-knowledge, but as I have said, self-knowledge never helped me not be angry, until in the "Love Addiction and Love Avoidance" workshop and with my final therapist I gained self-knowledge of the right inner dynamic, my pain that led to a sense of loss.

36

ANGER MANAGEMENT: A SURVEY OF THE PROFESSIONAL LITERATURE

My personal experience with cognitive anger-management programs was limited to the two programs I attended, and since my experience with them was so dismal both in trepidation at attendance and in results, I was curious to see if there was a consensus that these programs did work or if at least the better ones were valuable. First I searched the web as related above, but I wanted to explore the professional literature of reputable psychology journals as well.

I tried to search online for professionally written articles about anger-management programs, but I did not have access to all the journals that I wanted to look in. I also did not have bulk search tools that institutions and universities have to make searches more efficient. Accordingly, I hired a master's student at a nearby university to look for and obtain articles for me, and if she was allowed to copy them to send me copies. Specifically, I asked for articles on the efficacy of anger management.

I found a capable graduate student with the flyer shown in Appendix I. I sought out the appropriate e-mails of the psychology department heads and, after first calling their secretaries, e-mailed them the flyer. I ended up with several candidates to choose from and picked Ms. Desiree Harris.

Initially, at my direction, she concentrated on the rational cognitive type of programs that attempt to teach clients to think rationally about the situation when they get angry and to think not only of the consequences of the anger but also of other ways to look at the event, its real importance and meaning, and its true impact on the one getting angry. The goal with these programs is for the clients to lessen their anger by changing their thinking about situations that cause anger.

A major goal of this research was to ferret out an optimum program to treat anger. If one did not present itself, then I hoped that a selection of programs that were more likely to help people desiring to diminish their anger could be identified by type.

Ms. Harris was able to send me many of the articles legally, and I read all that I got. In many of the articles I read, I encountered new types of programs or refinements to programs of which I was only vaguely aware. Accordingly, I suggested Ms. Harris expand her search to include them. I cover my thoughts about rumination, distraction, and abreaction programs in chapter 34, "Alternate Treatments"; chapter 35, "Anger Management: A Survey of the Web"; and chapter 15, "Recovery Junkie."

Ms. Harris did very well and found so many articles that I asked her to summarize her results, and that follows in Appendix II. My general comments on the articles follow hers.

PART III:
WHAT I AM LIKE NOW

All I ever wanted was to step out lightly.

—Anonymous, from an AA speakers' tape

37

WHAT I AM LIKE NOW

When one door closes, another opens.
—Anonymous

The epigraph of this chapter is a philosophical affirmation common in twelve-step recovery meetings. It means if there is a loss in your life, another opportunity will present itself. Usually the loss referred to is tragic or sad in nature, like a divorce or the loss of a relationship or a job, but something better will soon replace it. It always has seemed to work that way for me. If there is a sudden new void in my life, something better comes along to fill it. I suppose it is human nature to believe this, at least for most folks who have a generally optimistic outlook, even if not at the moment. It is logical to think that this attitude would tend to motivate people to work hard to replace their losses. In my case, following my third separation and divorce, I told myself this very same affirmation and dedicated myself to getting over the loss of the marriage; the love, such as it was; the companionship; and so on, and to get on with my life. Although I wanted another relationship, I knew I should not get enmeshed in another codependent relationship.

I am convinced that I have truly lived these seventy-three years of my life to the fullest, and I continue to do so. I have never just existed. It has been a tumultuous life, but I did not come here to be bored. There have been a lot of "real moments,"[1] those moments that make life matter.

---

[1] Barbara De Angelis, *Real Moments* (New York: Delacorte Press, 1994).

38

TOGETHER AGAIN

A few days before Christmas 2008 I received a DVD in the mail from James, the oldest of the four boys my second wife, the love of my life, and I raised in the 1970s and '80s. My second wife and I had separated in 1988 and again in 1990 for good, and that had been the beginning of the twenty-month trauma-filled separation that I suffered through, as I wrote about earlier. We had been divorced nearly eighteen years when the DVD came.

The DVD from James was the Frank Capra movie *Pocketful of Miracles*, starring Glenn Ford, Bette Davis, and Peter Faulk. It is adapted from Damon Runyon's short story "Madame La Gimp." The movie is about Dave the Dude, a New York mobster who is superstitious and needs to buy lucky apples from Apple Annie, a beggar woman on the streets of New York. It is a feel-good movie, like *It's a Wonderful Life*, and both are often shown on TV around Christmas, although neither of them is strictly a Christmas movie. Attached to the DVD was a note that said, "Merry Christmas. You got me out of bed when I was a kid and made me watch this, and now it is one of my favorite movies." After his signature, James had provided a phone number.

I called him immediately. "James, this is Verryl," I said. "How are you? How is your mother? Answer the second question first."

After that we talked daily, sometimes for an hour or more, catching up with each other. He lived near the East Coat and had recently quit his job because he'd gotten tired of being sent to manage a troubled new store every six months. He wanted to stay in one place after getting a store going well. In early March, he left home and moved across the country to help me manage my business. I wanted to retire but had no one capable of running my business. I had hired professional management and had been trying to manage the management company for three years, but at sixty-six, I needed to slow down completely and retire. James looked like the solution to that problem, and he has been. Within six months I was able to turn it all over to him.

Naturally, I pestered him to put me in touch with his mother. She was still my dream girl. After about three months, she agreed to me taking the phone from James after their calls, and we talked. After about three or four more months, James and I drove to her state to take her to lunch. Then she allowed James to give me her phone number, and I could call her. In another month or two, I made a date to take her alone to see Jay Leno at an Indian casino. Then she came to visit James and me at our home. Finally, she moved to live with me in July 2009. After eighteen years of divorce following eighteen years of marriage, we were back together. We have now been together over six years, and this is the way I always wanted a relationship to be.

I still don't have a good definition of *healthy interdependence* like I do for *dysfunctional codependence*. But like pornography was to Justice Potter Stewart, I know it when I see it.

In the eighteen years of our separation my second wife worked on her own issues, owned and operated a home for women at risk, wrote and published a book, and toured the country promoting the book on radio and television. She was such a good guest to interview about all things recovery that she frequently appeared on several local shows. To this date she practices her helping ways in public institutions.

Her having her own life is one of the ways I know we are interdependent. I am not dependent on her to manage my emotions, and I am not peeved when she gets a call from a friend, as she does several times a day. Sometimes these calls are not at a convenient time for me, but she is independent of me, as well as dependent on me, as I am on her! If I don't want to be overly dependent on her, I have to know when to let go. The same is true for independence; I have to know when to exercise my independence.

Our life together is a fabric woven of threads of mutual dependence and independence. We both have our own lives as well as a life together, as described in Kahlil Gibran's interdependence-defining poem "On Marriage." I guess I do know what *interdependence* is.

A circle of creosote bushes or a grove of aspen trees are both examples of a single organism made up of many individual bushes or trees connected through a shared root system. As healthy people we are similarly connected and separate. Like a community of people dependent on each other for community services, utilities, police, government, and food from grocery stores, we depend on each other for some things but do other things for ourselves. The important things I used to depend on a woman for—like my feelings, self-esteem, and inner happiness—I now do for myself. After all, who else can I always depend on—who is the one who will never desert me?

Codependent people are also mutually dependent on each other, but they additionally exhibit patterns of obsession, self-sacrifice, dysfunctional communication, manipulation, and control. These patterns are self-destructive and hurtful to themselves as well as to their partners and to others. Codependent people are often abusive and/or allow themselves to be abused. Interdependent or functional people are functional exactly because they have boundaries and limits to behavior to protect themselves and others.

Not only are my wife and I interdependent, but my anger also keeps lessening and lessening. Like all my other addictions, it is a process, not an event. Actually, it is a process started by an event. Sobriety from alcohol is similarly a process started by an event—my first AA meeting.

It took me eighteen years to grow to the point where this functional relationship feels good and right. Eighteen years before we got back together again, or even five years before then, I would have thought you were crazy if you had recommended to me a relationship with such characteristics, even if you assured me they were healthy characteristics. To me, growing up codependent seemed normal. Now it sounds abhorrent.

When my wife and I meet new people, after I finish telling my story about the DVD and how we got back together, I tell everyone around, "She has always been the love of my life." Then I turn to her and ask, "Why'd we get divorced?"

She answers, "We had to grow up."

Maybe letting the love of your life have the punch line is functional. I only know I never would have done so before. I was too insecure and needed the attention too much.

This is the chapter I get to end with.

And the anger? It is all but gone away.

39

HOW IT WORKS

People familiar with *Alcoholics Anonymous* will recognize that the title of this chapter shares a title with chapter 5 of the Big Book.[1] In that chapter Bill W. writes the twelve steps, which are the core of the AA program of recovery. The following are the original twelve steps as published by Alcoholics Anonymous:[2]

1. We admitted we were powerless over alcohol—that our lives had become unmanageable.
2. Came to believe that a Power greater than ourselves could restore us to sanity.
3. Made a decision to turn our will and our lives over to the care of God *as we understood Him*.
4. Made a searching and fearless moral inventory of ourselves.
5. Admitted to God, to ourselves, and to another human being the exact nature of our wrongs.
6. Were entirely ready to have God remove all these defects of character.
7. Humbly asked Him to remove our shortcomings.
8. Made a list of all persons we had harmed, and became willing to make amends to them all.
9. Made direct amends to such people wherever possible, except when to do so would injure them or others.

10. Continued to take personal inventory, and when we were wrong, promptly admitted it.

11. Sought through prayer and meditation to improve our conscious contact with God *as we understood Him*, praying only for knowledge of His will for us and the power to carry that out.

12. Having had a spiritual awakening as the result of these steps, we tried to carry this message to alcoholics, and to practice these principles in all our affairs.*

In detailed fact, these steps have been the path of my recovery from alcoholism, codependence, love addiction, and anger addiction. This book is written record of my working all the twelve steps again, this time for anger.

1   Bill W., chapter 5, "How It Works," *Alcoholics Anonymous*, 3rd ed. (New York: Alcoholics Anonymous World Services, 1976), 58.

2   Ibid., 59.

---

* Non-AA programs that use the twelve steps change the word *alcohol* and *alcoholics* to words that identify the particular substance, activity, thing, or person from which to be recovered. Some programs remove gender-biased language, changing instances of *Him* to *God*.

40

THE PROMISES

I have many favorite sections from the beloved Big Book, but this one seems appropriate here:

> If we are painstaking about this phase of our development, we will be amazed before we are half way through. We are going to know a new freedom and a new happiness. We will not regret the past nor wish to shut the door on it. We will comprehend the word serenity and we will know peace. No matter how far down the scale we have gone, we will see how our experience can benefit others. That feeling of uselessness and selfpity will disappear. We will lose interest in selfish things and gain interest in our fellows. Self-seeking will slip away. Our whole attitude and outlook upon life will change. Fear of people and of economic insecurity will leave us. We will intuitively know how to handle situations which used to baffle us. We will suddenly realize that God is doing for us what we could not do for ourselves.
>
> Are these extravagant promises? We think not. They are being fulfilled among us—sometimes quickly, sometimes slowly. They will always materialize if we work for them.[1]

My recovery started for me in Alcoholics Anonymous, and it continued with Codependents Anonymous and numerous other resources. In my experience all these promises have come true. You will notice that the above passage does not specifically mention alcoholism, codependence, sex addiction, or even the term or idea of addiction. Part of the enduring genius of twelve-step programs is the universality of the twelve steps and the principles of treatment for all addictions.

As for "stepping out lightly," I do that all the time now. I now fit in, and I like people, and they do not irritate me.

My losses have been grieved; the pain is gone—not forgotten, but gone as an irritant that needs the salve of anger to cover it up and make me feel better. I am no longer an angry person who needs anger for power, because I no longer feel helpless and helplessly in pain. I had many losses, but I now see them rationally and emotionally as well within the limits of normal human experience. I occasionally feel a small loss, as we all experience in daily living, and occasionally these losses are over my unreasonable expectation that my wife, a friend, or an employee should be there for me—exclusively or at least at that moment. Sometimes that old mantra of "Nobody loves me; nobody cares," returns, but it is very mild, and I always laugh to myself and at myself, smile inwardly, and think, *Well, maybe it seems that way now, but I love me, and I care, and God loves me, and God cares. And that is enough, at least for now.* And I laugh at what a character I am, and I am grateful at how far I have come.

I love recovery.

¹ Bill W., *Alcoholics Anonymous*, 83–84.

AFTERWORD

There are three kinds of men. The one that learns by
reading. The few who learn by observation. The rest of
them have to pee on the electric fence for themselves.
—Will Rogers

I was nearly done writing this book when I came upon a realization that I
probably should have seen quite a while ago. Although the book had not
been completed, I decided to relate this realization in an afterword.

My realization was that I had missed the few clear signs about the path
of recovery from anger that were buried in my books about shame and codependence recovery. I had decided *not* to make changes and had left the text
largely as it came to me to show the true path of my recovery just as it happened. I think my path was pretty typical. My path was both like a pinball
bouncing around the bumpers of reality and like a single-minded compulsive
forging and slashing ahead to cure a preconceived idea of what the problem
was. I hope that I serve as a valuable example for why people should be open
to all ideas and not follow a personal preconceived theory.

With my realization, I decided to add to my book that the references to
anger in my recovery books were indeed there but that I just missed them
for years until I did the final writing of this book. This is an example of how
powerful and pervasive denial is to protect an addiction. That denial continued even after the catharsis of crying and the immediate relief and lowering
of my anger level so low that I was able to convince myself that I was over it!
I was not, of course. I had a few serious raging episodes at a very good friend

whom I had been collaborating with on a very big project. I apologized the next day after first writing these words.

Additionally, I have to apologize to those good and true intimate friends whom I know and who know me very, very well, even though we have never met—John Bradshaw, Pia Mellody, Janet Woititz, Claudia Black, Louise Hay, Tian Dayton, Stephen Levine, Bob Earll, and others. I apologize to them for overlooking their cautions and wisdom about both anger as an addiction and pain as anger's source. My oversights were not intentional.

As a final afterword, I may well owe an apology to some or all of my therapists if they did indeed try to steer me in the way of grief work as a cure of my anger or if they recognized my anger as an addiction. If that happened, I am sorry for any frustration I caused you.

In a text box in chapter 25 I ask the disconcerting and disjointing question, "Why did my parents abuse me?" This is the answer to that question.

My parents were not bad people. They were ill people *filled with their own shame and pain generated and foisted upon them by their parents in the patriarchal and matriarchal systems in which they grew up. They were raised, just as I was, "for their own good."* They had the same choices I had, and through ignorance of modern humanistic child-rearing methods, they adopted the *generational abusive methods* that they had been raised with. *They did it to cover and salve their own pain and losses.* They passed their pain on to me, as their parents' pain had been undoubtedly passed on to them and as I am sure I passed my pain on to my children for years and years until I got into recovery. Actually, what they did was quite proper for their time and environment—in my time and environment it was sadly, and thankfully, necessary for me to grow beyond that antiquated system and into a new enlightened system, one that is sadly not at all universal as we would wish. Such changes in paradigms are nearly always painful and fraught with conflict and usually take one or more generations to effect.

There were many hints about the old dysfunctional ways, and they indicate that they caused pain in that past generation.

My maternal grandfather would never speak about his riding up from Texas at fourteen with two grown men. Had he run away from home? Why?

Once, my paternal grandfather told in an ordinary conversation of seeming to prejudge a stranger who came to the door of the homestead—he was afraid the man might be dangerous, which seemed to me at about twelve years old to be a fairly reasonable caution given the isolation of the house. But my usually mild-mannered father soundly and loudly rebuked him, judging his own father for prejudging the man. My dad was angry! I was shocked. Grandpa stiffened and stared straight ahead in seething but helpless resentment. I was doubly shocked at his acquiescence and stoic passivity. My grandfather was suddenly the child, being berated by his son who had not been within five hundred miles of the event! It was a definite case of carried feelings between two generations.

My maternal grandmother was a formidable person. She ran the huge family that had spread out over 1,500 miles in all directions (which in itself may be indicative of pain and escapism). She ruled with an iron fist until she died, and all got in step. She seemed to receive universal respect and loyalty, except from me. I thought that she was deserving of such praise but was also an overbearing and autocratic person. I was always the black sheep of the family. When she died, my mother stepped in and took over with the same force and unwavering determination. All her generation obeyed, and her nephews and nieces seemed to worship her—everyone except me. I respected her for her many good points but refused to kowtow to her domineering manner.

There were other examples of dysfunction. I am sure that they were an intergenerational legacy. I just wanted no part of that legacy, and I have done all I can to reject and heal it. I prefer the unvarnished truth, and I believe that if you know the truth, it will set you free.

I have written that perhaps the reason I was so affected by my parents' abuse was because I was so sensitive, even supersensitive. Maybe that is true and not just in a hypersensitive sense but also in an introspective sense. As I have said, I vowed to end this stuff with my generation.

My parents were quite a pair, a pair I admired tremendously, but the truth be known, they had severe parenting flaws by current and post–World War II standards. They were charismatic characters in a grand life-long play of heroic proportions. Displaying bigger-than-life accomplishments and contributions, they also were flawed by present standards. I had the good sense to see and follow a better way and to recover from the effects of those flaws, and I have the bad manners to relate the whole story in the hopes that it may help someone else.

Verryl Fosnight, July 2015

Appendix I

"Research Associate Needed" Flyer

Research Associate Needed

To do Literature Search for Articles pertaining to
- Efficacy/non-efficacy of Anger Management Programs
- Or Usefullness of other Anger Recovery Therapies

In Support of a Book the Author is Writing on Recovery from Anger

Contact Verryl Fosmight 5██████ or verrylf@███om

Terms: $20/hour. 10 hours maximum
              Output to be email to above address providing:
- List of articles,
- Including publication with issue and date and
- with Abstracts attached.
- Article listing to be sufficient to buy articles from publications on line

Appendix II

Anger Management:
A Survey of the Literature

I tried to search online for professionally written articles about anger-management programs, but I did not have access to all the psychology journals that I wanted to search. Accordingly, I hired a master's student at Arizona State University, Desiree Harris, to look for and obtain articles for me. Specifically, I asked for articles on the efficacy of anger management. She did very well and found so many that I asked her to summarize her results; her essay is below. I also read the articles, and my general comments on them follow Desiree's.

An Empirical View of Theoretically Based Anger Management Programs
By
Desiree Harris, M. C.

The studies that were examined of the various theoretical orientations of anger management interventions for the purpose of this book show that these programs produced very similar results, as discussed below individually. Two pieces of information that are the most important to take away from the information provided here are: 1. With a few exceptions, any treatment to help with anger management is more effective than receiving no treatment (the exception being the misconceptions of our society which have been disproven through scientifically designed studies); and 2. Because no one theoretical based program has been shown to have statistically significant improvements above others, the most important consideration in choosing a program is to find one that resonates with you.

Many studies use university students as subjects, including most that were looked at for this book, because it is easy to gain access to those individuals and easy to get them to participate by having their instructors agree to give extra credit for the student's participation. The use of this population can impact the ability to generalize the results to the "normal" population. The participants and their relevance to the population as a whole is an important factor to think about along with the results of any study.

Before the studies are reviewed, I think it is important to address one common misconception of venting anger and to discuss one major dilemma of treating anger issues that can be confusing to many individuals. The misconception I am referring to is the belief that finding a way to vent anger physically can reduce anger. This idea is perpetuated in culture through sentiments of using a punching bag and has had treatments based on it that involved beating the padding on a chair, breaking things, punching things, etc., while thinking about the events that incurred the anger. Numerous studies have been done on this very topic and nearly all of them produce the result of the venting of physically anger actually increases anger rather than depleting it (Hornberger, 1959; Geen & Quanty, 1977; Bushman, Baumeister, & Stack, 1999). Other studies have shown that rumination, the tendency to constantly repeat negative thoughts to oneself, increases anger as well (Rusting & Nolen-Hoeksema, 1998).

One compelling study conducted by Bushman (2002) analyzed levels of anger of 600 undergraduate students after having an essay criticized by another individual they believed was an actual participant, though was not. These individuals were then randomly assigned to one of three groups: a control that consisted of sitting quietly for two minutes, a distraction group consisting of hitting a punching bag while thinking of getting in shape, and a rumination and distraction group that was left alone to hit a punching bag. Individuals were allowed to hit the punching bag as much and as long as they wanted. After the sessions, a form was completed that measured anger and positive feelings (Bushman, 2002, p. 727). The individuals who were in the rumination group scored higher than individuals in the other two groups by a statistically significant amount. The individuals who were in the distraction while thinking about exercise and those who were in the control group did not have a statistically significant difference in scores. However, in measurements of aggression the levels of each group were statistically significant in their difference from each other. Individuals in the control group were less aggressive than the distraction group, which was less aggressive than the rumination group. Other data was gleaned from the study that is not mentioned here because they do not pertain to the subject of the book. I felt this study was important to mention to help the reader find a program that will produce the most benefit. While most programs have leaned towards an empirically based treatment, some may still exist that operate on antiquated theoretical perspectives. Bushman has published several articles on this concept that can be found through using Google.

The major dilemma I referred to above is in the diagnosis and treatment of anger issues. Currently insurances follow codes found in the Diagnostic and Statistical Manual of Mental Disorders, Fifth Edition (DSM-5), and the DSM-5 does a poor job of addressing anger. Even intermittent explosive disorder focuses more on aggressive outbursts rather than the underlying emotion of anger. There are many disorders where anger can be seen as part of the description or a symptom of the disorder, but treatments generally focus on the underlying problem to reduce the symptoms. In fact, for the most part the DSM-5 uses the word "irritable" in most cases, rather than using the word "angry". This can be confusing for an individual because irritability can seem minimizing for an individual who is feeling quite angry. The DSM-5 helps with diagnosis, but the treatment is what impacts the experience of the individual.

RATIONAL EMOTIVE THERAPY VS. GESTALT

In 1983, Conoley, McConnell, and Kimzey conducted a study comparing Rational Emotive Therapy (RET) and the Empty-Chair technique of Gestalt therapy. During that time these types of therapy were very popular. These two techniques continue to be used to some degree, or an evolved version of them; however, the effective parts have been parceled out and are typically used in conjunction with other techniques. RET is focused on discussing the process of anger, from the initial event and the interpretation of that event, to the corresponding actions as a result of that event. The focus of RET is similar to the cognitive behavioral technique cognitive restructuring. This involved identifying an automatic thought, identifying distortions that correspond to the thought, creating alternative perspectives that challenge that thought, and finally using those challenges to create an undistorted thought. Gestalt therapy focuses on experiencing the event by creating an environment where the client acts out different and often opposing parts of his or her personality with the goal of experiencing the emotions (Conoley, et. al, 1983).

The study had sixty-one participants, all being female undergraduate students. As mentioned above, this is problematic because it limits the ability to generalize findings to the normal population. Three treatment groups were used, one for each technique and a third for a control group, and the participants were randomly assigned to one of the three. The participants were asked to write down five recent events that made them angry in order to induce anger. After anger was induced, the experimenters checked blood pressure to assess the anger level. The experimenters built rapport by talking with the participants for 5 minutes. The results showed a statistically significant difference between the control group and the techniques; however neither technique was shown to be statistically better at treating anger over the other.

Cognitive Behavioral Therapy

Fuller, DiGiuseppe, O'Leary, Fountain, and Lang conducted a pilot study that was published in 2010 to test the effectiveness of cognitive behavioral therapy (CBT). As mentioned above, rational emotive therapy has progressed into CBT and those techniques along with other CBT techniques were used in this study. The sample consisted of 5 men and 7 women. This is a rather small group of people for an ideal study, and that should be kept in mind. Small samples often mean that the study does not have enough power to discover small, but meaningful, differences between groups. Each participant was given a diagnostic interview and all had a diagnosis from the DSM. However, the authors did not provide the names of the diagnoses. The treatment consisted of 2-hour sessions, with a total of 16 sessions conducted, with a focus on building adaptive coping skills. No control group was included, which means that the study tests for levels of anger, provides a treatment, and tests again. The groups before and after tests are compared to determine if a statistically significant change occurred in the levels of anger.

To determine the levels of anger, four scales (similar to questionnaires) were used. The experimenters also measured depression symptoms, symptom distress, interpersonal relations, and social role congruence. They also tested to see how the client viewed the relationship with their therapist. The researchers found statistically significant improvements between the before treatment and after treatment tests. The participants stated they had a consistent number of circumstances that provoked anger, but experienced less physiological symptoms of anger.

The beneficial components of this study include the length and number of sessions. This is considered inoculation, similar to receiving a series of vaccine inoculations. The researchers looked into the optimal time of treatment for appropriate inoculation. The second impressive feature mentioned in the article was that after the participants learned the coping skills, they were encouraged to practice them rather than avoiding situations that made them angry. The authors acknowledge the limitations of this study and encourage a follow up study with a larger sample size and the inclusion of a control group along with other design features.

ANGER PSYCHOEDUCATIONAL TRAINING

A study was conducted with 92 police officers from the Rochester Police Department (RPD) by Abernethy and Cox (1994. The focus of the study was to determine an effective way to decrease police brutality. The researchers linked anger to aggression through the use of Megargee's (1985) theory of the motivations for aggression being anger and instigation. The researchers also looked at Bandura's theories on the development of characteristics in response to aversive environmental conditions. This was followed up by Toch's two-dimensional view of anger, consisting of ways to dehumanize others and methods of self-preservation.

The treatment consisted of 48 offers, divided into five groups with each consisting of nine to twelve officers. The officers were asked to complete psychological questionnaires, attend a six-hour psychoeducational course right after, and then to complete more questionnaires. Four to six months after the completion of the initial treatment, the officers were asked to return to complete additional psychological questionnaires that were used to measure anger and performance. The psychoeducational course was an Anger Management Training Module developed by members of the Professional Development section of the RPD along with Abernethy. The curriculum included information on psychological theory, psychopathology, and instructions working with mentally ill citizens. No information was provided on anger management. The 44 officers in the control group were divided into five groups as well, with each consisting of eight to twelve participants. The difference between the control and treatment groups was the six-hour course. The control group participated in a mental health course. The concern with this study is that no information on the control mental health course was provided which causes concern with using the control group as a comparison for improvement of anger symptoms from the treatment.

The results showed that the control group provided a biggest change in angry mood than those officers in the treatment group, with the treatment group showing little change in angry mood. The gender of the participants was correlated with angry mood in a very interesting way. Female officers experienced a statistically significant increase in anger and male officers had a statistically significant decrease in anger. While this is an interesting finding, it should also be looked at with some skepticism because of the potential confounds. For example, there was only one trainer and he was male. The fact that the trainer was a male with an unknown demeanor could have had an impact on the females' angry moods. The design of this study has some concerning flaws. However, the benefit is in showing that education is not enough to impact anger.

A META-ANALYSIS OF ANGER TREATMENTS

A meta-analysis involves data mining many previous studies to try to gain a larger picture of a specific topic. This meta-analysis focused on a variety of anger treatments. The researchers, Del Vecchio and O'Leary (2003), determined the need for the analysis due to the previously mentioned studies that showed the venting of anger actually increases anger and the concerning link of anger to physical aggression. The physical damage caused by anger, such as an increased rate of cardiovascular disease, was also mentioned. The authors also touch on what was mentioned above regarding the DSM's lack of diagnoses that address anger issues.

The analysis only included studies with participants who had clinically significant levels of anger as determined by standardized anger measurements. The researchers used online databases of articles from *PsychINFO* and *Dissertation Abstracts International* and covered a span of 60 years, from 1980 to 2002. The researchers had six requirements in order for the study to be included in the analysis. The requirements are summarized as follows: the use of a standardized anger measure, participants with clinically significant levels of anger, random assignment of participants to treatment and control groups, the inclusion of specific data analysis or information that allows for specific data analytical computation, a sample size of at least five individuals, the exclusion of batterers and inmates due to special considerations. Five therapeutic interventions were identified: cognitive-behavioral, relaxation, cognitive, and other. A total of 23 studies were analyzed, with 73% of them having a sample of college students. The study looked at different types of anger.

While no one type of treatment was shown to be significantly better than others at treating all aspects of anger, different treatments were shown to be more effective than the others in treating specific types of anger. However, the authors note that most studies had limitations the reader should consider when looking at the results. Cognitive therapy had the largest impact on driving anger, as determined by only one of the studies. Cognitive therapy also was shown to be slightly better than relaxation for individuals that tend to suppress anger.

Cognitive behavioral therapy was shown to be most effective with anger expression issues and cognitive therapy was least effect. Cognitive therapy is a specific intervention developed by Dr. Beck and cognitive behavioral therapy is a term used to describe many different interventions. A better explanation of the difference can be found in the website by the Beck Institute found in the reference section, written by Cognitive Behavior Therapy News.

Therapies that fell into the designation of other, which were any that could not fit into the other groups, were shown to be the best at treating individuals who had difficulty in controlling anger. The researchers were unable to parcel out the different types of therapies for further analysis and a breakdown of which of the other types of therapies were most effective. It is possible that one therapy in this group was extremely effective while the others were not, and that would skew the results.

The benefit of this meta analysis is that it shows all therapies looked at had a statistically significant impact. This supports the idea that no one therapy is the right answer, but that the most important part of treatment is finding the best therapy for the individual. Looking at types of anger to determine which therapy is best is a bit tricky because of the limitations of the studies that were looked at. However, it is an interesting concept to keep in mind as further research is developed.

CONCLUSION

As mentioned initially, no one theoretical approach has come out as a hands down cure all for anger issues. If anything, the studies above highlight things that do not work. These results are not very different from other studies on different ailments that have shown the most important aspect of counseling is the therapeutic relationship, or alliance, between the counselor and the client. Having a relationship where a client can experience unconditional positive regards may be the basis of all the improvements shown above. I reiterate that the most important things, while considering the information above, is to pursue treatment in the program that feels right to you. The techniques above can be used by a counselor who is focused on the patient no matter what his or her theoretical orientation happens to be, and can be changed based upon what is or is not working for you.

REFERENCES

Abernethy, A., Cox, C. (1994). Anger management training for law enforcement personnel. *Journal of Criminal Justice, 22*(5), 459–466.

American Psychiatric Association. (2013). *Diagnostic and Statistical Manual of Mental Disorders* (5th ed.). Washington, DC: Author.

Bushman B. J. (June, 2002). Does venting anger feed or extinguish the flame? Catharsis, rumination, distraction, anger, and aggressive responding. *Personality and Social Psychology Bulletin, 28,* 724–731. Retrieved from: http://psp.sagepub.com/content/28/6/724

Bushman, B. J., Baumeister, R. F., & Stack, A. D. (1999). Catharsis, aggression, and persuasive influence: Self-fulfilling or self-defeating prophecies?. *Journal of Personality and Social Psychology, 76*(3), 367. Retrieved from: http://dx.doi.org/10.1037/0022-3514.76.3.367

Cognitive Behavior Therapy News. (February, 2007). Does cognitive therapy = cognitive behavioral therapy? *Beck Institute Blog.* Retrieved from: http://www.beckinstituteblog.org/2007/02/does-cognitive-therapy-cognitive-behavior-therapy/

Conoley, C. W., Conoley, J. C., McConnell, J. A., & Kimzey, C. E. (1983). The effect of the ABCs of rational emotive therapy and the empty-chair technique of gestalt therapy on anger reduction. *Psychotherapy: Theory, Research & Practice, 20*(1), 112–117. doi: http://dx.doi.org/10.1037/h0088470

Del Vecchio, T., O'Leary, K. D. (March, 2004). Effectiveness of anger treatments for specific anger problems: a meta-analytic review. *Clinical Psychology Review, 24*(1), 15–34.

Fuller, J. R., DiGiuseppe, R., O'Leary, S., Fountain, T., Lang, C. (April, 2010). An open trial of a comprehensive anger treatment program on an outpatient sample. *Behavioral and Cognitive Psychotherapy, 28*(4).

Geen, R. G., & Quanty, M. B. (1977). The catharsis of aggression: An evaluation of a hypothesis. In Bushman, Does venting anger feed or extinguish the flame? Catharsis, rumination, distraction, anger, and aggressive responding. *Personality and Social Psychology Bulletin, 28,* 724–731.

Hornberger, R. H. (January, 1959). The differential reduction of aggressive responses as a function of interpolated activities. *American Psychologist, 14*(7), 354.

Rusting, C. L., & Nolen-Hoeksema, S. (1998). Regulating responses to anger: effects of rumination and distraction on angry mood. *Journal of Personality and Social Psychology, 74*(3), 790. Retrieved from: http://dx.doi.org/10.1037/0022-3514.74.3.790

COMMENT ON RESEARCH BY VERRYL FOSNIGHT

Desiree Harris received a bachelor's of science in psychology in 2008 from the University of Phoenix. Six months after completing this research, she graduated with a Master of Arts degree in counseling from Arizona State University. She spent approximately thirty-two hours compiling the information and writing this presentation. She skimmed or read seventy-five to one hundred abstracts of papers in psychology and related journals. She sent me a brief synopsis of twenty-five of them, and I commented on ten of them. In her submission to me she added the following:

> This is not including the additional resources I used that I researched and gathered from the other articles to support my writing. Of those 10 I believe I used half. One I did not choose because of the focus of the study being on a population—having borderline personality disorder or bipolar disorder—and anger was just mentioned as a factor. One was a write up of an approach to anger, though good, was not empirically validated; one did not really refer to anger issues; one only focused on an adolescent population and was based of theories that pertain to youth. The last was just an explanation of what Gestalt therapy was. I weeded out studies or told you initially if I thought the data was so skewed it should not be included. Of the articles you selected, if I included them, I just made a point to explain flaws in the experiment.

Ms. Harris did exactly what I wanted: she produced a short article that might be used for a person who was battling anger but was not a psychologist with any expertise to evaluate the different programs available. As an untrained person, while I read all the information she sent me, I was struck by both how inadequate, *by my standards of wanting complete recovery,* the available programs seemed to be and how the authors claimed these programs to be more effective than I judged them to be by their reported results. *Again, this judgment was by my standards of wanting completely to be free of toxic anger.* Perhaps, due to my personal experience in healing my own anger, which was very successful and complete, I was overly optimistic about the potentials of conventional anger-management treatment, but I expected a fair percentage of the subjects would experience dramatic improvement. If this were the case, I could not tell it by the meta-analysis numbers quoted.

Meta-analysis gives a relative score between programs—in this case, where they otherwise would not be comparable due to wide differences in techniques, sample size, judgment criteria, and many other details. The score is created by normalizing the differences in the individual programs to make them as comparable theoretically as possible. If a program does not meet certain critical technique levels, it is not included in the analysis. Grading the programs and ranking them with an absolute intuitively meaningful score was not done, and perhaps it is impossible to do so given the divergent factors of the many programs.

The meta-analysis results showed an average reported improvement for all the studies; that is, on average programs were ranked as to how much they helped their clients with their anger *to make it less of a problem for them and presumably for others.* No spectacular reduction of anger, either immediately or long term was reported. I naively expected the results to be more than fair to moderate and to even be good, although such qualifiers were never stated. No programs was presented as providing a revolutionary or radical lowering of anger in even a few subjects, let alone for all subjects in the aggregate, and many subjects were not helped at all. However, if the goal was only improvement and not great improvement—not outstanding but moderately helpful—then perhaps the positive comments are justified, *at least in the average of all subjects.* I was most disappointed with the reporting of the results in that not only were dramatic improvements in behavior not found or reported, or reported as such, but the metrics reported (meta-analysis) were of little help to a layman in evaluating the programs. I am confident that the values reported have standardized definitions, but those values are only relative values between programs. To a physicist like me, this is maddening.

This dissatisfaction is most likely unfounded because of my

physical-science bias. As a physicist I look for measures of change that are intuitively meaningful, like percentage of improvement, and I grant that with the hazy definition of *anger* available (even in the *DSM-5*), it is very hard to quantize such improvement. But physics is easy compared to psychology. A free electron, for example, has a precise and certain mass, charge, and spin—three properties—and they all are given in specific and rigorously defined units of measure. Humans have hundreds of properties or thousands or … by the way, how do we define a human "property" and how precise can we be in that definition? You can see the problem. So to expect an evaluation to read 50 percent or 75 percent improvement may be unrealistic. At this point I suggest you research meta-analysis for yourself, say at http://en.wikipedia.org/wiki/Meta-analysis.

It is certainly true that the stated meta-analysis results are useful in comparing different treatments and treatment types, and this is the point of meta-analysis. So if these programs or similar ones are the only choices available, or the only ones that are practical for time and economic reasons, then there is a good guide here. But I believe there is another choice, and that is anger *resolution*, not anger *management*. I discuss the difference of these two terms in the glossary, where I show that I hold a higher standard of reduction of anger by *resolution* rather than by *management*. And I found that, for me, grieving the underlying pain of losses from childhood abuse was the path to resolution of my anger.

My personal program with an individual therapist was vastly different from the group-class setting. I worked intensely one on one with each qualified therapist over a significant amount of time, usually one hour per week for at least months. All my therapists were qualified, and some were naturally better than others, but they all guided me and helped me see healthier ways to view my problems and behaviors. Since this approach is time consuming and expensive, it requires a hefty devotion of effort and resources. I found that beyond the time of the sessions and the monetary cost, I spent a lot of time thinking and contemplating the issues each session revealed. All this taken as a process, in my opinion, should be balanced against the extreme cost in money, effort, and life-damaging consequences that unresolved anger can bring—again I use *unresolved* as in the concept of *resolution* as explained in the glossary.

Resolving anger in the sense I mean the term is not one of the goals of anger management, at least not to the extent of healing I found in my method. It seemed to me that anger management's goal was a lower standard of reforming the behavior of an angry person and lessening the effects of his or her anger to make the person's behavior socially or personally acceptable. Reaching and healing the root causes of the anger was not a goal or even considered. Fundamentally, self-discovery with a goal of healing was the point of my recovery, as it is of this book. I do not believe very great progress in recovering from anger may be claimed without it.

Groups are less expensive to the client and therefore more efficient at reaching numbers of clients, if efficiency is calculated without taking efficacy into account. In my experience, class or group settings greatly limited the amount and quality of interaction and feedback between therapist and client—or perhaps it was just due to the raucous and aggressive clientele in the classes I was in. This is not to deny that such group settings are less expensive than individual work with a therapist and thus attractive. Because of the point I had come to in my life (facing a criminal record), I was interested in "Does it work?" meaning, "Can I get past constant life-damaging behavior *without an undue strain at* controlling *it?*" If I were just now approaching the crossroads and had those criteria, I would be discouraged if these programs were all that were available. I might even start to believe the fallacious summation of myself as a person who was inherently bad and could never be better. My fervent wish is that readers of this book who suffer from anger or rage, or who suffer from the anger or rage of another, *not* adopt or continue such an assumption, for that is all it is, an assumption. That assumption can probably be disproved if one looks deeper into the real causes and uses of anger.

APPENDIX III

MIND

I have referred to extra-positive thinking, which I call *positive knowing*, as a way of life that will lead to abundance in all phases of your life, relationships, finances, health, serenity, and anything at all that you desire, and I recommend it, as long as it does not involve harming someone else. I have collected some of my favorite quotes about this way of thinking that I have come across in the past twenty-five years. I hope you will get the idea that this is not a new idea and not unique to me, to anyone else currently or recently alive, or to any particular time in history. The earliest records of such thinking go back to the followers of Epicurus (341–270 BC). This thinking is so pervasive to successful, creative, and notable people that those qualities seem to be the way we are or can be if we adopt a certain positive attitude. Call it consciousness, call it the power of the mind, call it connectedness at an unimaginable level, or call it praying to God. My point is a lot of distinguished people have believed in it. I believe that in a sense all illustrious people have had such an attitude. These quotes are presented in no particular order, except the order that I came across them as I collected them.

I honestly believe and have demonstrated that this power works in my life. There is a discrepancy, however. I was unable to use rational thinking to change my emotions, which are part of my health. Why? Perhaps it is because emotions, which came before rational thought in evolution, still tend to rule us. That rational, meaningful mindfulness works for actions and purposeful conscious behaviors but not for unconscious feelings that may direct behaviors (see quote 19). This is maybe borne out by my failures to change my behavior by right thinking, as with RET-like regimens. Positive knowing's failure to always change behavior may imply that something controls behavior prior to the right thinking even if right thinking is being practiced. If it is "wrong" thinking, it is easy to see that changing your thinking can change your life (see quote 77). But if emotions are the prior controlling thing about which some of our thinking is based, as the time line of evolution would imply, it may be a different matter.

As far as "wrong" thinking, see quotes 2, 3, 4, and many others. Wrong thinking has the same determining power over our actions to produce deleterious results as positive thinking does to produce wonderful results. Think about despicable characters like Adolf Hitler. They can be understood as acting on their hard-held beliefs to produce the results they wanted, despite true right or wrong; to them it was "right." On a less dramatic scale, I have found myself pursuing a harmful goal in the mistaken (or selfish) belief that it was right and proper. My only cure was to change my thinking. In my most serious case, anger, before I could change my thinking, I had to change my beliefs, that is, my unconscious bound-in emotions.

Here is my list.

FAVORITE QUOTES OF MIND

1. There is nothing either good or bad,
   But thinking makes it so.
   —Shakespeare, *Hamlet*, act 2, scene 2, line 251

2. The most necessary part of learning is to unlearn our errors.
   —Zeno the Stoic (ca. 340–265 BC)

3. Man is not what he thinks he is, but what he thinks, he is.
   —Elbert Hubbard (June 19, 1856–May 7, 1915)

4. A man's life is what his thoughts maketh it.

    —Markus Aurelius (AD 121–180)

5. We are what we think about all day long.

    —Ralph Waldo Emerson

6. As thou hast believed, so be it done unto thee.

    —Matthew 8:13, King James Version (KJV) (Jesus to the centurion)

7. Verily, verily I say unto you, Whatsoever ye shall ask the Father in my
    name, he will give it you. Hitherto have you asked nothing in my name:
    ask, and ye shall receive, that your joy may be full.

    —John 16:23–24, KJV
    (I do not mean to start a religious war, but many modern translations of
    name in ancient Aramaic is "nature," that is, "in my nature.")

8. How would you like your immediate future to be determined by your
    present thought? It is, you know.

    —Louise Hay

9. Verily I say unto you, if you have faith and doubt not, ye shall not only
    do this which is done to the fig tree, but also if you shall say unto this
    mountain, Be thou removed, and be thou cast into the sea, it shall be
    done. And all things, whatsoever ye shall ask in prayer, believing, ye shall
    receive.

    —Matthew 21:21–22, KJV

10. Be not afraid, only believe.

    —Mark 5:36, KJV

11. Ask, and it shall be given you; seek, and ye shall find; knock, and it shall
    be opened unto you: For every one that asketh receiveth; and he that
    seeketh findeth; and to him that knocketh, it shall be opened.

    —Matthew 7:7–8, KJV

12. For as he thinkest in his heart, so is he.

—Proverbs 23:7, KJV

13. And be not conformed to this world, but be ye transformed by the renewing of your mind, that ye may prove what is that good, and acceptable and perfect, will of God.

—Romans 12:2, KJV

(I believe that the renewing of my mind starts with the renewing of my heart, that is, my unconscious beliefs bound in those old emotions.)

14. We build our future, thought by thought, for good or ill, yet know it not.

—Henry Van Dyke (Presbyterian theologian, died 1933)

15. We need only in cold blood act as if the thing in question were real, and it will infallibly end by growing into such a connection with our life that it will become real. It will become so knit with habit and emotion that our interests in it will be those which characterize belief.

—William James, *The Principles of Psychology, Vol. II,*(New York: Henry Holt and Company, 1905), 321 .

16. It is indispensable that in all existing things there must be an active cause, and a passive subject, and that the active cause is the intellect of the universe.

—Philo

17. So shall my word be that goeth forth out of my mouth: it shall not return unto me void, but it shall accomplish that which I please, and it shall prosper in the thing whereto I sent it.

—Isaiah 55:11, KJV

18. All we are is the result of what we have thought.

—Beginning of the Buddhist text Dhammapada

A different translation has this as

All that is comes from the mind; it is based on the mind, it is fashioned by the mind.

—Dhammapada, chapter 1, verse 1

19. All things can be mastered by mindfulness.

—Dhammapada

20. Thou shalt also decree a thing, and it shall be established unto thee: and the light shall shine upon thy ways.

—Job 22:28, KJV

21. If you can do,
    or dream you can, begin it.
    Boldness has genius, power,
    And magic within it.

—Johann Wolfgang von Goethe

22. "I am not at all remarkable," Georgette Mosbacher says, perched on the sofa in the pale yellow drawing room of her Upper East Side townhouse office. "I grew up in a one parent family, I worked my way through college, I had very average grades and I was very average looking, but I've lived a remarkable life only because I *believed* I could."

—*Los Angeles Times* (September 22, 1993)

23. The mind is its own place, and in itself can make a heaven of hell, a hell of heaven.

—John Milton, *Paradise Lost*

24. He that soweth sparingly shall reap also sparingly; and he which soweth bountifully shall reap also bountifully.

—2 Corinthians 9:6, KJV

25. Imagination, which in truth, is but another name for absolute power and clearest insight,

amplitude of mind and reason in her most exalted mood.

—William Wordsworth (1770–1850)

26. Ere man's corruptions made him wretched, he
    was born most noble that was born most free;
    Each of himself was lord; and unconfin'd
    Obey's the dictates of his godlike mind.
    —Thomas Otway (1562–1685), *Don Carlos*, act 2, scene 1, line 3 (1676)

27. On earth there is nothing great but man; in man there is nothing great
    but mind.

—Sir William Hamilton (1788–1856), *Lectures on Metaphysics*
(1859–1860)

28. Let this mind be in you, which was also in Christ Jesus: who, being in
    the form of God, thought it not robbery to be equal with God: But made
    himself of no reputation, and took upon him the form of a servant and
    was made in the likeness of men.

—Philippians 2:5-7, KJV

29. One man who has a mind and knows it, can always beat ten men who
    haven't and don't.

—George Bernard Shaw, *The Apple Cart*, act 1

30. Our remedies oft in ourselves do lie
    Which we ascribe to heaven
    —William Shakespeare, *All's Well That Ends Well*, act 1, scene 1, line
212-3.

31. Everything you see is a result of your thoughts.

—*A Course In Miracles: Workbook for Students*, p. 26

32. Everything is possible to him who dares.

—A. G. Spaulding, second National League president

33. Nevertheless, every failure to cope with a life situation must be laid, in the end, to a restriction of consciousness.
> —Joseph Campbell, *The Hero with a Thousand Faces*, p. 121

34. It's not what you don't know that hurts you. It's what you do know that ain't so.
> —Mark Twain

35. Yield not thy neck
    To fortune's yoke, but let thy dauntless mind
    Still ride in triumph over all mischance.
> —William Shakespeare, *3 Henry VI*, act 3, scene 3, line 16-18

36. Our doubts are traitors,
    and make us lose the good we oft might win,
    by fearing to attempt.
> —William Shakespeare, *Measure for Measure*, act I, scene 4, line 77-79

37. For nimble thought can jump both sea and land
> —William Shakespeare, sonnet 44, line 7

38. We, ignorant of ourselves, beg often our own harms,
    Which the wise powers
    Deny us for our good; so find we profit
    By losing of our prayers.
> —William Shakespeare, *Antony and Cleopatra*, act 2, scene 1, line 5-8

39. One of the greatest discoveries a man makes, one of his great surprises, is to find he can do what he was afraid he couldn't do.
> —Henry Ford

40 Mind is cause and your experience is effect. If you do not like the experience or effect that you are getting, the obvious remedy is to alter the cause and then the effect will naturally alter too.
> —Emmet Fox, *Around the Year with Emmet Fox*, fifty-third day

41. You think, and your thoughts materialize as experience and thus it is, all unknown to yourself as a rule that you are actually weaving the pattern of your own destiny, here and now, by the way in which you allow yourself to think day by day and all day long. Your fate is largely in your own hands. Nobody but yourself can keep you down.

    —Emmet Fox, *Around the Year with Emmet Fox*, fifty-fifth day

42. God favors the brave, victory is to the audacious.

    —General George S. Patton Jr.

43. Nothing can stop the man with the right mental attitude from achieving his goal; nothing on earth can help the man with the wrong mental attitude.

    —Thomas Jefferson

44. People who say it cannot be done should not interrupt those who are doing it.

    —George Bernard Shaw

45. Truly, it is in darkness that one finds the light, so when we are in sorrow, then this light is nearest of all to us.

    —Meister Eckhart (ca. 1260–1328)

46. You cannot tailor-make the situations in life but you can tailor-make the attitudes to fit those situations.

    —Zig Ziglar

47. We can complain because rose bushes have thorns, or rejoice because thorn bushes have roses.

    —Abraham Lincoln

48. Once you replace negative thoughts with positive ones, you'll start having positive results.

    —Willie Nelson

49. Positive thinking will let you do everything better than negative thinking will.

—Zig Ziglar

50. I'm a success today because I had a friend who believed in me and I didn't have the heart to let him down.

—Abraham Lincoln

51. We are what our thoughts have made us; so take care about what you think. Words are secondary. Thoughts live; they travel far.

—Swami Vivekananda

52. Your living is determined not so much by what life brings to you as by the attitude you bring to life; not so much by what happens to you as by the way your mind looks at what happens.

—Khalil Gibran

53. It had long since come to my attention that people of accomplishment rarely sat back and let things happen to them. They went out and happened to things.

—Leonardo da Vinci

54. A negative outlook is more of a handicap than any physical injury.

—Christopher Paolini

55. Every great dream begins with a dreamer. Always remember, you have within you the strength, the patience, and the passion to reach for the stars to change the world.

—Harriet Tubman

56. You gain strength, courage, and confidence by every experience in which you really stop to look fear in the face. You are able to say to yourself, "I lived through this horror. I can take the next thing that comes along."

—Eleanor Roosevelt

57. If you think about disaster, you will get it. Brood about death and you hasten your demise. Think positively and masterfully, with confidence and faith, and life becomes more secure, more fraught with action, richer in achievement and experience.

—Swami Sivananda

58. Optimism is the faith that leads to achievement. Nothing can be done without hope and confidence.

—Helen Keller

59. Willpower is the key to success. Successful people strive no matter what they feel by applying their will to overcome apathy, doubt or fear.

—Dan Millman

60. Keep away from people who try to belittle your ambitions. Small people always do that, but the really great make you feel that you, too, can become great.

—Mark Twain

61. Success is a state of mind. If you want success, start thinking of yourself as a success.

—Joyce Brothers

62. And be renewed in the spirit of your mind.

—Ephesians 4:23

63. Have you learned the lessons only of those who admired you, and were tender with you, and stood aside for you? Have you not learned great lessons from those who braced themselves against you, and disputed passage with you?

—Walt Whitman

64. God helps them that help themselves.

—Benjamin Franklin (1706–1790)

65. He who lives upon hope, will die fasting.

        —Benjamin Franklin (1706–1790)

66. Adversity is sometimes hard upon a man; but for one man who can stand prosperity, there are a hundred that will stand adversity.

        —Thomas Carlyle (1795–1881)

67. Follow your bliss

        —Joseph Campbell (1904–1987)

68. People say that what we're all seeking is a meaning for life. I don't think that's what we're really seeking. I think that what we're seeking is an experience of being alive, so that our life experiences on the purely physical plane will have resonances within our own innermost being and reality, so that we actually feel the rapture of being alive.

        —Joseph Campbell (1904–1987)

69. We are what we repeatedly do. Excellence, then, is not an act but a habit.

        —Aristotle

70. Few things in the world are more powerful than a positive push. A smile. A world of optimism and hope. A "you can do it" when things are tough.

        —Richard M. DeVos

71. In the long run, we shape our lives, and we shape ourselves. The process never ends until we die. And the choices we make are ultimately our own responsibility

        —Eleanor Roosevelt

72. The greatest discovery of any generation is that human beings can alter their lives by altering the attitudes of their minds.

        —Albert Schweitzer

73. Man often becomes what he believes himself to be. If I keep on saying to myself that I cannot do a certain thing, it is possible that I may end

by really becoming incapable of doing it. On the contrary, if I have the belief that I can do it, I shall surely acquire the capacity to do it even if I may not have it at the beginning.

—Mahatma Gandhi

74. I learned this, at least, by my experiment: that if one advances confidently in the direction of his dreams, and endeavors to live the life which he has imagined, he will meet with a success unexpected in common hours.

—Henry David Thoreau

75. Most folks are as happy as they make up their minds to be.

—Abraham Lincoln

76. Change your thinking, change your life.

—Louise Hay

77. The voyage of discovery is not in seeking new landscapes but in having new eyes.

—Marcel Proust

78. All life demands struggle. Those who have everything given to them become lazy, selfish, and insensitive to the real values of life. The very striving and hard work that we so constantly try to avoid is the major building block in the person we are today.

—Pope Paul VI

79. Yet he who reigns within himself, and rules
Passions, desires, and fears, is more a king.

—John Milton, *Paradise Regained*

80. I hope that in this year to come, you make mistakes. Because if you are making mistakes, then you are making new things, trying new things, learning, living, pushing yourself, changing yourself, changing your

world. You're doing things you've never done before, and more importantly, you're doing something.

—Neil Gaiman

81. The greater part of our happiness or misery depends on our dispositions
and not our circumstances.

—Martha Washington

82. If you would be a real seeker after truth, it is necessary that at least once
in your life you doubt, as far as possible, all things.

—René Descartes

GLOSSARY

acute stress response

The fight, flight, freeze, or fawn response of hyperarousal; a psychological and physiological response to stress, particularly danger or fear.

addiction

Following John Bradshaw's working definition (see chapter 4, "Recovery versus Cured"), an addiction has three characteristics:

1. The behavior is pathological.
2. It is mood altering (changes your feelings for the better).
3. It has life-damaging consequences.

adult child

A person who is an adult in age but is emotionally immature in some ways, usually ways that have resulted from childhood abuse, which stunts and tends to freeze emotional growth at an age near where the abuse happened or began to happen. This phenomenon often explains why grown adults habitually act and react to adult situations in an immature way—to them the situation is a reenactment of the old abuse.

Alcoholics Anonymous (AA)

A self-help twelve-step program as outlined in the book *Alcoholics Anonymous*. There are no dues or fees, and local meeting groups and service offices are entirely volunteer run, except for a few special paid workers in a few cases. People wishing to stop drinking alcohol may join just by attending meetings where other members share their experiences of alcoholism and recovery. AA is the original twelve-step program; the twelve steps to stop drinking are recited and talked about at every meeting. It is easy to find the national website and local meetings on the Internet.

anger management

A therapeutic method of managing one's anger by circumventing it and drawing attention from it on a case-by-case basis, usually by mental exercises to lessen the intensity of the reaction to the triggering event. Note that in anger management there is generally no attempt to lessen the intensity of any given triggering event by seeking out special personal meanings of that event to the client or by training the client to do such self-seeking. The efforts are to rechannel the energy of the angry outburst or otherwise manage it or push it aside with self-imposed controlling thoughts. This method is generally taught in anger-management classes, usually on a weekly schedule of a prescribed number of classes.

anger resolution

This is my term to designate recovery from anger in the sense of a great reduction of anger as a result of *resolving* (see Textbox chapter 27) and healing the underlying causes carried as emotional subconscious memories that dictate how one lives one's life today. The idea is that toxic anger will dissipate in direct relation to how much the painful carried unconscious stuff and other emotional burdens are eased by some form of grieving or equivalent therapeutic process. This is opposed to anger-management methods.

boundaries   Limits we assume for ourselves so as not to infringe on others' rights and space or limits we prefer others have in their behavior so as not to infringe on our rights and space.

carried emotions   Emotions passed down from one generation to another mostly unintentionally; emotions from attitudes assumed through habit and through watching an older generation habitually demonstrate such attitudes. The result of carried emotions is the members of the younger generation feel those emotions of the older generation rather than their own. One's own emotions are much more authentic than another person's. Often such carried emotions are harmful, such as anger or shame; the older generation unintentionally but grievously passes its emotions to members of subsequent generations, expressing and modeling through subtle actions, attitudes, and beliefs emotions like blame, pain, hate (prejudices), fears, and low self-esteem. The older generation is relieved of the burden of those emotions as they are passed on. Also termed *induced emotions*.

child abuse   Less-than-nurturing child upbringing. See chapter 12, "Pia Mellody's Theory Summarized," for specific types. See *trauma*.

child trauma	Child abuse. See *trauma*.
chronic losses	Losses in life that occur often enough to be considered chronic. Subsequent losses may not be an exact repeat of the former loss or losses, but do feel similar to the victim of the loss; that similarity is enough to have an additive adverse effect on him or her. Also termed *recurring losses*.
dysfunctional	Behavior, actions, beliefs, and attitudes of a person or group (family) that are far from optimum for a happy, peaceful, and productive life. That type of life should *not* to be contrasted with *normal*, because normal behavior, actions, beliefs, and attitudes are largely dysfunctional. The opposite of dysfunctional is *functional*, a fancy word for healthy and well adjusted.
fight, flight, freeze, or fawn	See *acute stress response*.
functional	See *dysfunctional*.
hyperarousal	See *acute stress response*.
induced emotions	See *carried emotions*.
inner child	A construct that within all adults an "inner child" resides that remembers the great or small trials and tribulations of childhood. Inner-child memories are largely nonrational and nonverbal representations and recollections of what happened to the person as a child. As such these recollections, while open to question on many grounds of accuracy, meaning, and intensity, still play a powerful role in the actions, fears, beliefs, and present emotions of the adult, particularly if those recollections are intense, such as would be expected of a badly abused child. Many in the helping professions and

recovery world firmly believe that the best way to heal the adult is to heal the inner child through feeling work, or work on the emotions. The healing results in a more emotionally mature and stable adult.

love addiction
An extreme form of codependence wherein the sufferer is addicted to and dependent upon a primary love in his or her life. As a love addict, my self-esteem depended on what *other* people thought (or what I imagined they thought about me because I was married, going with, or dating a certain woman whom I considered attractive). It is like being overly proud and dependent on what car you drive or how rich you are for your good feelings about yourself. Love addiction may also be known as *relationship addiction* if the relationship features love.

mood altering
The characteristic of the substance or activity of an addiction, which the addict uses to alter his mood, that is to change his mental or emotional state usually by making him or her happier or more comfortable. For example, alcohol does this because it is a depressant. It could be said that anger is an upper.

other-esteem
A semitechnical term that is derived from slang. A person with other-esteem formulates his or her self-image based on what others think and how they act toward him or her or on things that he possesses or does—his self-esteem is driven by *other* things. In the extreme it is the complete absence of healthy self-esteem in which a person depends on things or station in life

or others and his or her association with all or many of these things for his or her self-image as opposed to having a healthy awareness of his innate self-worth which should lead to a natural sense of self-esteem.

pain

In this book, pain nearly always refers to emotional pain, that is, extreme emotional distress.

perfectly imperfect

A slang expression that implies that a person is perfect, healthy, and functional even while having normal human imperfections like all people have. Those imperfections are acceptable as long as they are under control and do not adversely impact the person's life. *Perfectly Imperfect* is also a book by Lee Woodruff about being a wife, mother, and person who accepts what modern life brings with grace and charm. It is also the title of American singer-songwriter Elle Varner's debut studio album, which was released on August 7, 2012, under RCA and MBK Entertainment.

poisonous pedagogy

A term popularized by Alice Miller in many of her books to describe less than nurturing child rearing methods (child abuse) and mores that both damage the child perhaps physically, but certainly emotionally, while absolving the parents or caregivers of all blame and responsibility for their actions. Such absolution is not done consciously by caregivers, and in the collective, by society, but habitually, and a primary unconscious benefit to the abusing caregiver is to find relief from his own destructive emotions, primarily toxic shame, and to pass them on

	to the child as *carried emotions*. A simple example is telling a child *This is for your own good* as he is spanked or beaten.
recovery	The act of being returned to functional condition, restored. As used in this book it is always recovery from some addiction. Thus, to recover is not to be cured but to be restored—one is always an addict of the addiction, but in recovery the addiction is no longer active in the addict. However, being dormant, the addiction can always return in a relapse or slip.
recurring losses	See *chronic losses*.
relationship addiction	See *love addiction*.
resolution of feelings	See Textbox, chapter 27
trauma	*Trauma*, as used in this book, is any terrifying event that is or *seems to the sufferer* to be life threatening. Thus, the hard spanking of a child, though ordinarily thought of as "normal," may be traumatic, depending on the child and the circumstances. In other words, it is not for the perpetrator or any bystander to decide; the victim gets to decide how serious trauma feels to him or her.
toxic	An adjective indicating dysfunctional or causing dysfunction or harm, as applied to emotions, behaviors, and activities.
toxic anger	Anger that is harmful to both the angry person and to whomever it is directed; rage, fury, or violent anger, as differentiated from healthy anger, which is usual and normal (in the sense that it is acceptable) as a source of ambition and motivation and even power to accomplish a worthy goal. Acting out in anger in self-protection is also acceptable.

	Taking umbrage to a slight but not retaliating to get even, while also usual and normal, is different from healthy anger and toxic anger, falling somewhere in the middle.
toxic shame	Shame that is learned usually in childhood as a result of childhood abuse. To fit in or please his or her parents, the child (or person) assumes an opinion of himself or herself that is other than what he or she inherently is as a valuable human being (self-worth). Toxic shame's effects are debilitating. The term was first coined by Sylvan Tomkins in the early 1960s and is now used by many authors in the recovery field.
twelve-step program	Any program or fellowship of people with the common goal of recovery from some malady, usually an addiction. Twelve-step programs are modeled after Alcoholics Anonymous's twelve steps to recovery. Such programs use with permission those same steps modified to fit the particular addiction.

INDEX

CPSIA information can be obtained at www.ICGtesting.com
Printed in the USA
LVOW07*1550130916

504433LV00007B/56/P